READING and RESEARCHING

Writing a Research Paper for College Students

Virginia Heringer

Pasadena City College

Ann Arbor
University of Michigan Press

Acknowledgments

Thank you to Kelly Sippell, my editor at the University of Michigan Press, for her constant understanding and support of my vision of this book; to my colleagues at Pasadena City College, especially Krista Goguen, Mike Riherd, and Connie Taus, who read and commented on parts of the book; to my children, who inspire me, and my husband, who kept the computer going; and most of all to my students, from whom I have learned so much!

Grateful acknowledgment is made to the following authors, publishers, and organizations for permission to reprint previously published materials.

Collier & Son Company for material reprinted from *The Autobiography of Benjamin Franklin*, with Introduction and Notes Edited by Charles W. Eliot LLD, P. F. Collier & Son Company, New York, 1909.

Colorado Springs Pioneers Museum for photograph of unidentified woman (Accession No. S2001.0032.0336), from *The Cragin Collection*, circa 1905, at http://www.springsgov.com/cspm.

Harvard University Press for material from *The Gospel of Wealth* by Andrew Carnegie, © copyright 1962 by the President and Fellows of Harvard College. Pages 14–24, 26–29: "The Gospel of Wealth" published originally in the *North American Review* CXLVIII June 1889 and CXLIX December 1889. Pages 3–13: "Introduction" written for "Youth's Companion."

The Henry Ford for photograph of "Overhead View, Assembly Line Final Chassis Assembly, 1914," from the Collection of The Henry Ford.

Library of Congress Prints and Photographs Division, for 1793 Boston Residences, LC-USZ62-99618; Andrew Carnegie, LC-USZ62-15566; Frederick Douglass, LC-USZ62-94490; Former slave quarters near Bardstown, Kentucky, LC-USF34-055114-D; Ben Franklin, LC-USZ62-28235; and Utah Indians in Utah Valley, LC-USZ62-111112.

Macmillan Company for material reprinted from *Twenty Years at Hull-House* by Jane Addams, copyright © 1910, by the Phillips Publishing Company, copyright © 1910 by the Macmillan Company.

Marquette University, Special Collections/University Archives, for photograph of Black Elk from "Honoring Youth through Native Heritage: Indian Givers" by Mark Thiel from website: *America's First Nations Collection: American Indian Social Studies Curricula* at http://www.marquette.edu/library/neh/general/index.htm.

Material reprinted from *Narrative of the Life of Frederick Douglass, an American Slave*, first published in the United States of America by The Anti-Slavery Office 1845.

University of Nebraska Press for material reprinted from *A Bride Goes West* by Nannie T. Alderson and Helena Huntington Smith by permission of the University of Nebraska Press. Copyright © 1942 by Farrar & Rinehart, Inc. Material reprinted from *Black Elk Speaks: Being the Life Story of a Holy Man of the Oglala Sioux* by John G. Niehardt by permission of the University of Nebraska Press. Copyright © 1932, 1959, 1972 by John G. Neihardt. © 1961 by the John G. Neihardt Trust. © 2000 by the University of Nebraska Press.

Every effort has been made to contact the copyright holders for permission to reprint borrowed material. We regret any oversights that may have occurred and will rectify them in future printings of this book.

Copyright © by the University of Michigan 2005
All rights reserved
ISBN 0-472-03045-0
Published in the United States of America by
The University of Michigan Press
Manufactured in the United States of America
2008   2007   2006   2005   4   3   2   1
No part of this publication may be reproduced, stored in a retrieval system, or transmitted in any form or by any means, electronic, mechanical, or otherwise, without the written permission of the publisher.

Contents

To the Teacher: How to Use This Book   v

The Autobiographical Reading Passages   1

    1   The Founding Fathers: Benjamin Franklin
        (from *The Autobiography and Other Writings*)   1

    2   Slaves: Frederick Douglass
        (from *Narrative of the Life of Frederick Douglass, an American Slave*)   29

    3   Native Americans: Black Elk
        (from *Black Elk Speaks*)   67

    4   Homesteaders: Nannie T. Alderson
        (from *A Bride Goes West*)   103

    5   Great Industrialists: Andrew Carnegie
        (from *The Gospel of Wealth and Other Timely Essays*)   148

    6   Reformers: Jane Addams
        (from *Twenty Years at Hull-House*)   185

The Yellow Pages   216

    The Basics of Research and Writing   216
        The Research Process   217
        Using the Generalization to Organize Your Writing   220
        More Requirements for the Topic Sentence and the
            Thesis Statement   224
        Final Remarks   225

CONTENTS

1. Research Sources: Difference Sources for Different Purposes   228
    - A. Reference Materials: Only the Facts   229
    - B. Books: For Details   231
    - C. Periodicals: Magazines, Journals, and Newspapers   235
    - D. The Internet: Users Beware!   237
    - Summary Chart for Research Sources: Different Sources for Different Purposes   241

2. Research Writing Skills: Documentation, Quotations, Paraphrases, Summaries, and the Research Paper   243
    - A. Documentation   243
    - B. Quotations, Paraphrases, and Summaries   245
        - B.1. Quotations   246
        - B.2. Paraphrases   250
        - B.3. Summaries   253
    - C. The Research Paper   255
        - C.1. Choosing a Topic   256
        - C.2. Doing the Research and Writing a Working Thesis Statement   256
        - C.3. Writing the Paper   257
        - C.4. Documenting the Sources   259
        - C.5. Typing the Paper   259
    - Time Line/Checklist for a Research Paper   260
    - A Comparison of the MLA and APA Documentation Systems   262

3. Sample Student Research Paper   266
    - MLA Format   266
    - APA Format   275

Answer Key for Scanning for Specific Information   284

Answer Key for Yellow Pages   289

Additional Writing Assignments: Connections   291

TO THE TEACHER:
How to Use This Book

At first glance, this textbook appears to be a reader for a history class because it includes reading passages by well-known figures in American history such as Benjamin Franklin and Frederick Douglass. However, the real goal of this book is to develop the academic reading, writing, and research skills of students who are about to attend or are already attending American colleges and universities. The book is intended for students who have studied English grammar and basic essay form and who are ready to extend these skills into more authentic contexts in order to work comfortably and effectively in American college classes. The autobiographical reading passages by historical figures provide the context for practicing these skills. As students use this book, they'll develop the writing and research skills to work independently in American college classes, and they'll learn about some of the important people and events of American history at the same time. The book could also be used in an academic reading or reading-writing course.

The book has two parts: the first part of the book consists of **six authentic reading passages** taken from autobiographies by real-life figures in American history—Benjamin Franklin, Frederick Douglass, Black Elk, Nannie T. Alderson, Andrew Carnegie, and Jane Addams. These passages provide stories of human interest and topics for personal writing as well as actual names, places, and events for the research activities and writing. The passages are presented as originally written.

The second part of the book is the skills-building **Yellow Pages,** which include a review of paragraph and essay form and an introduction to research resources and writing skills.

The two parts of the book are meant to be used together: Students should begin by reading one of the autobiographical passages and completing some of the beginning exercises in the Yellow Pages, such as the review of paragraph and essay form and the use of reference sources to do the scanning exercise. References to these exercises are provided in each chapter. With the next reading passage, the students can continue on to the

TO THE TEACHER

use of quotations, paraphrases, and summaries and of other sources such as books, periodicals, and the Internet. It's not necessary to do all the exercises that accompany a reading passage: Classes can review when necessary and then progress step-by-step through the skills. A (short) research paper (three to five pages) should be assigned as a final project after the students have completed the skills exercises and had a chance to explore the various library and Internet sources. More on the research paper can be found in the Yellow Pages.

PART I: THE AUTOBIOGRAPHICAL READING PASSAGES

The reading passages are presented with few of the supporting materials that are usually found in ESL textbooks, and teachers should avoid providing additional historical background to the students. The goal of this textbook is to *engage the students in discovering this information for themselves through their reading and research* so that they will develop and gain confidence in their own skills to move from the sheltered environment of ESL classes into the less supportive mainstream classes.

The purposes of the individual exercises are as follows.

Introduction

The introduction provides background information about the time period and the author's life. The amount of introductory material is minimal to give the students a more authentic experience and to stimulate them to ask questions for the research activities.

Pre-Reading Questions

These questions ask students to relate what they already know and have experienced to the content of the reading passage. These questions can be used as prompts for journal writing or for personal essays.

Autobiographical Reading Passage

The passages are authentic pieces of writing, not simplified in any way, so students will find many words and expressions that are not familiar. Although only excerpts are provided, teachers are encouraged, when and where possible, to introduce students to the full-length book, particularly Franklin's and Douglass's, as they are readily available and often required in college courses. *Only the archaic and unusual vocabulary is glossed on each page;* teachers should reinforce the warning that students should not study or use these words in their own writing. (The glossed meanings refer to the way the words were used in the original and are not always current definitions.) You may want to point out some of the British or unusual spellings. Other new vocabulary in the passages may be useful to the students for their reading and writing, and students should be encouraged to keep a personal vocabulary log of words that they would like to learn to use. A selection of *useful words* for academic study has been chosen for inclusion in the Vocabulary Development section of each chapter.

The passages also include some explanatory notes for necessary background information. Each passage is divided into two parts for the convenience of making assignments.

Exercises

Comprehension Questions

These questions have two purposes—first to check that students understand the main ideas of the reading passage, and second to give students a chance to practice writing the basic paragraph form described in the Yellow Pages.

Vocabulary Development

This section provides a list of words taken from the reading passage, chosen for their value for students' passive or active vocabulary. The words are grouped according to topic to provide a context for learning and using the words.

Students should be encouraged also to keep a vocabulary log for any other words they find useful from the passages, being careful not to choose the archaic or unusual words that are glossed on the pages.

Quotations and Paraphrases

The purpose of these activities is to introduce the use of quotations and paraphrases in academic writing and give students practice using them. Sentences to use for the quotation and paraphrase exercises can be taken from the reading passages and from library and Internet source materials.

Writing Summaries

This activity introduces and provides practice in writing summaries—an important academic writing skill—based on a set of paragraphs from the reading passage, with appropriate introductory sentences and documentation. Again, students can also apply this activity to passages from other source materials.

Questions for Discussion and Writing

These topics can be used for various kinds of essay writing, including personal essays and essays using sources. A few of these questions refer to other reading passages in the book.

Scanning Exercises

Scanning for specific information is a necessary skill for research and other academic work. It can be a difficult skill to develop in a second language. These exercises provide an opportunity for students to practice their scanning skills and at the same time learn more about the time period and become aware of the kinds of information available in reference books. Suitable sources for this exercise include any standard encyclopedia as well as high school or college American history textbooks. Answers will vary slightly depending on the source used, but answers are provided.

Suggested Topics for Research and Writing

These topics are intended for use in the library and Internet search exercises in the Yellow Pages and can be used as research paper topics.

Expansion Activities

Expansion activities are provided to offer students opportunities for further exploration of the content of the passage and include music, art, maps, movies, websites, and additional readings.

PART II: THE YELLOW PAGES

The Yellow Pages include the academic writing and research skills that are the primary focus of this book. The pages begin with a review of paragraph and essay form based on the use of a generalization followed by supporting details. The Yellow Pages then introduce the sources most often used in college writing assignments—reference materials, books, periodicals, and the Internet—and the writing skills necessary to present researched information, such as documentation, quotations, paraphrases, summaries, and the research paper.

    The Yellow Pages should not be assigned all at once. A class should work with one or two sections of the Yellow Pages at a time, reviewing and progressing according to the abilities and needs of the class. The exercises and examples in the Yellow Pages are based on the Benjamin Franklin reading passage in Chapter 1, so students should begin with this chapter. After that, a class can progress through each of the remaining five reading passages, completing a section or two of the Yellow Pages with each one.

    The last section of the Yellow Pages introduces the **research paper.** Teachers may choose to assign the paper as a cooperative class project, with all the students writing on a single topic and using the same sources. For a more advanced class, the teacher may assign individual topics or have students choose their own topics related to the readings. Students

TO THE TEACHER

should be encouraged to see the research paper not as a formidable task but as a chance to explore their own interests and to become experts in some area of American history, learning more about a topic than the other students in the class and possibly more than the teacher.

Because this may be the first research paper assignment for many students, the teacher might want to put a limit on the number of sources and pages (two to three sources and three to five pages is a good start) and ask students to hand in working bibliographies, drafts in progress, and all source materials as they work on their papers. The teacher can plan several class "workshop" days for activities such as checking sources, working on paraphrases, and writing documentation to make sure that the papers turn out well.

USING THE BOOK

A 16-week syllabus using all six Autobiographical Reading Passages would include:
- **Chapter 1: The Founding Fathers: Benjamin Franklin** (2 weeks)
  - **Yellow Pages**—Paragraphs and Essays (pages 218–27)
  - **Writing Assignment**—a personal essay related to Franklin's autobiography
- **Chapter 2: Slaves: Frederick Douglass** (2 weeks)
  - **Yellow Pages**—Documentation, Quotations, and Paraphrases (pages 243–52)
  - **Writing Assignment**—an essay based on a quotation from Douglass's *Narrative*
- **Chapter 3: Native Americans: Black Elk** (2 weeks)
  - **Yellow Pages**—Reference Materials (pages 229–31); Summaries (pages 253–55)
  - **Writing Assignment**—a summary of an article from a reference source related to the Sioux Indians
- **Chapter 4: Homesteaders: Nannie T. Alderson** (2 weeks)
  - **Yellow Pages**—Books (pages 231–35)
  - **Writing Assignment**—an essay using information from a book source
- **Chapter 5: Great Industrialists: Andrew Carnegie** (2 weeks)
  - **Yellow Pages**—Periodicals (pages 235–37)
  - **Writing Assignment**—an essay using information from a periodical source
- **Chapter 6: Reformers: Jane Addams** (2 weeks)
  - **Yellow Pages**—the Internet (pages 237–40)
  - **Writing Assignment**—an essay using information from an Internet source, incorporating quotations, paraphrases, and summaries
- **Research Paper**—combine all skills to write a 3- to 5-page research paper on a topic related to the reading passages, using at least one of each kind of source (4 weeks)

To the Teacher

Two possible 16-week syllabi using four Autobiographical Reading Passages would include:

(1) **Chapter 1: Benjamin Franklin** (3 weeks)
   Yellow Pages—Paragraphs and Essays (pages 218–27)
   Writing Assignment—a personal essay related to Franklin's autobiography
Chapter 2: Frederick Douglass (3 weeks)
   Yellow Pages—Reference materials (pages 229–31); Summaries (pages 253–55)
   Writing Assignment—a summary of an article from a reference source related to Douglass's narrative.
A Western Theme
Chapter 3: Black Elk (3 weeks)
   Yellow Pages—Reference Materials and Books (pages 229–35); Documentation, Quotations, and Paraphrases (pages 243–52)
   Writing Assignment—an essay using information from a book source about the Sioux or Plains Indians, incorporating a quotation
Chapter 4: Nannie T. Alderson (3 weeks)
   Yellow Pages—Periodical and Internet sources (pages 235–40); Summaries (pages 253–55)
   Writing Assignment—a summary of an article from a periodical or Internet source about Western settlement
Research Paper—combine all skills to write a 3- to 5-page research paper on a topic related to the Native Americans or Western settlement (4 weeks)

Or

(2) **Chapters 1 and 2** (as shown above)
An Industrialization and Reform Theme
Chapter 5: Andrew Carnegie (3 weeks)
   Yellow Pages—Books (pages 231–35); Documentation, Quotations, Paraphrases (pages 243–52)
   Writing Assignment—an essay using information from a book source about Industrialization or Immigration, incorporating quotations
Chapter 6: Jane Addams (4 weeks)
   Yellow Pages—Periodical and Internet sources (pages 235–40); Summaries (pages 254–56)
   Writing Assignment—a summary of an article from a periodical or Internet source about reform

TO THE TEACHER

Research Paper—combine all skills to write a 3- to 5-page research paper on a topic related to Industrialization, Immigration, or reform (4 weeks)

Teachers may also want to take advantage of the rich opportunities to have students make connections between and among these historical figures. See page 291 for more ideas.

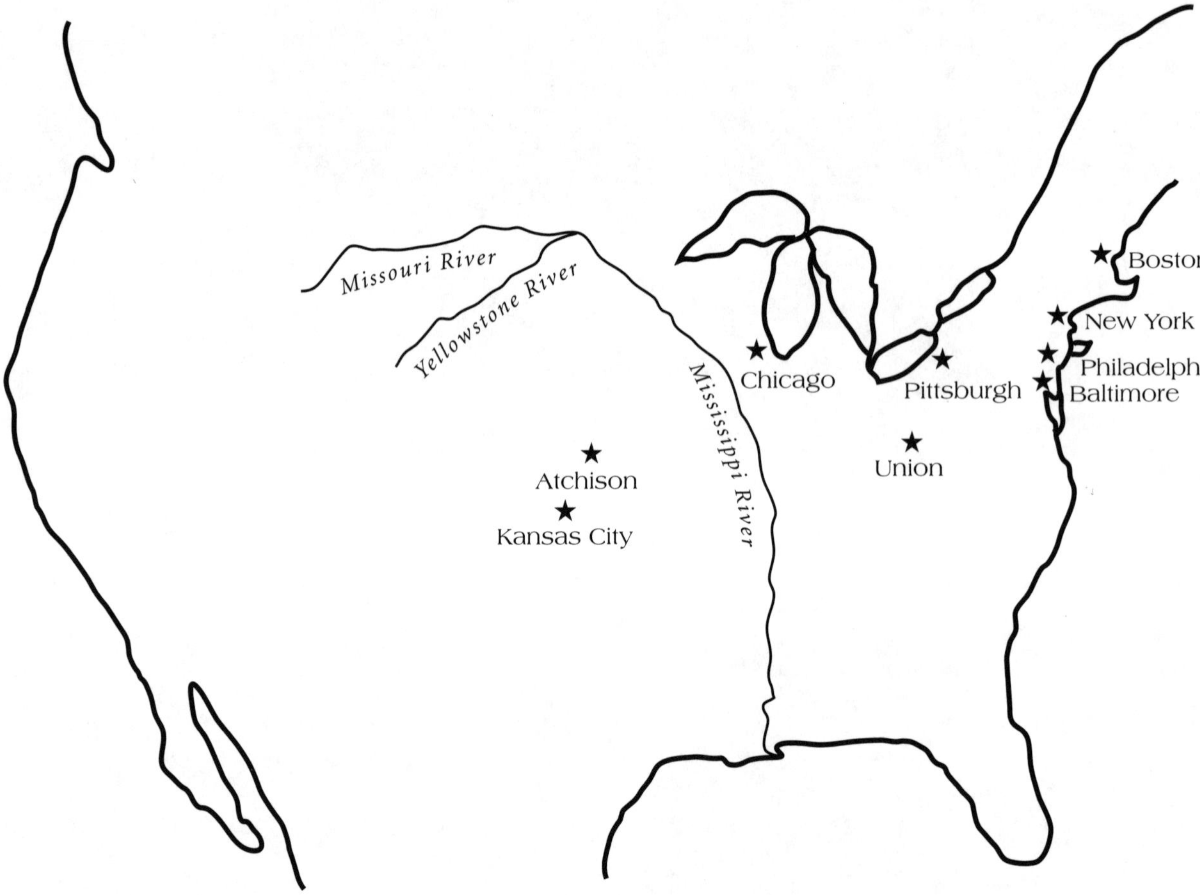

READING AND RESEARCHING AMERICA

1

THE FOUNDING FATHERS
Benjamin Franklin

(1706–1790)

★ ★ ★

INTRODUCTION

The names of the Founding Fathers of the United States, the men who wrote and signed the Declaration of Independence in 1776 and the Constitution in 1789, are still well known today—George Washington, Thomas Jefferson, John Adams, Alexander Hamilton, James Madison, Benjamin Franklin, and others. Although these men often disagreed about the exact form the new government would take, they agreed that each individual has natural rights to life and liberty and that all people are equal under the law. They thought that governments should protect these rights, and that if a government failed to do so, then the people are justified in changing the government. This new political theory had been developed during the late eighteenth century by the great philosophers of the Enlightenment, John Locke of England and Jean Jacques Rousseau of France. The new philosophy resulted in revolutions in France and England, as well as the revolution in the American colonies (Revolutionary War).

Benjamin Franklin is famous as the personification of Enlightenment philosophy. Intelligent, independent, and practical, he believed in the ability of individuals to think for themselves, to make their own decisions, and to create their version of success in the pursuit of happiness. A man of wide interests and great energy, Franklin was successful as a printer, writer, scientist, and diplomat, and he became the model of an American hero.

Born in Boston into a family of Puritans, Franklin had only a few years of formal education before he went to work to help support his family. As an apprentice in his brother's printshop, he continued his education through extensive reading and soon set up his own shop in Philadelphia. In addition to printing and selling books and newspapers, he wrote *Poor Richard's Almanac*, a popular yearly book of advice and information for farmers and tradesmen. An example of the type of advice offered in the Almanac was, "Early to bed and early to rise, makes a man healthy, wealthy, and wise." His business was so successful that he was able to retire in his forties and devote himself to civic affairs, science, and inventions. He is responsible for the first library, the first hospital, the first volunteer fire department, the first paved city streets, and the first university on American soil, all in Philadelphia.

When the American colonists demanded independence from Great Britain, Franklin was one of the representatives of the colonies who met to write the Declaration of Independence. During the Revolution, Franklin was sent to Paris to gain the support of the French government in the fight against the British. In 1787, when he was in his eighties, Franklin helped write the Constitution of the United States, using his good humor and intelligence to suggest compromises that enabled all the participants to sign the document. He died in 1790, just as the new nation was beginning its life.

In his old age, Franklin wrote his autobiography in the form of a letter to his son, giving him useful advice for a successful life. In the first part, "Early Years," he tells about his early interests in reading and writing and his job as an apprentice at his brother's printing shop. In the second part, "Moral Perfection," Franklin describes his attempts as a young man to improve his character.

Pre-Reading Questions

Americans consider Benjamin Franklin to be one of the heroes of our country. Before you read, think about some heroes of your country. What makes them heroes? What did they do, and what are their personal characteristics?

THE FOUNDING FATHERS: BENJAMIN FRANKLIN

→ READING PASSAGE ←

BENJAMIN FRANKLIN:
From *The Autobiography and Other Writings*

Franklin wrote his autobiography in an informal style, but many features are old-fashioned, and he used British spelling. The words defined on each page are *archaic,* no longer used in Modern English. When you write about Franklin and his experiences, avoid these old-fashioned features by simplifying the style and using modern vocabulary. If you are studying in the United States, you will want to use American spelling.

PART 1: EARLY YEARS (Paragraphs 1–9)

(1) From my infancy I was passionately fond of reading, and all the little money that came into my hands was laid out in the purchasing of books . . . . My first acquisition was Bunyan's works in separate little volumes. I afterwards sold them to enable me to buy R. Burton's historical collections; they were small chapmen's books and cheap, forty or fifty in all. My father's little library consisted chiefly of books in polemic divinity, most of which I read. I have since often regretted that at a time when I had such a thirst for knowledge, more proper books had not fallen in my way, since it was now resolved I should not be bred to divinity. There was among them Plutarch's *Lives,* in which I read abundantly, and I still think that time spent to great advantage. There was also a book of Defoe's called an *Essay on Projects* and another of Dr. Mather's called *Essays to do Good,* which perhaps gave me a turn of thinking that had an influence on some of the principal future events of my life.

was laid out—was spent

Bunyan's works—books by John Bunyan, an Englishman who wrote about religion

R. Burton's historical collections—books about British history

chapmen's books—inexpensive books

books in polemic divinity—books about religious disputes

now resolved—now decided

be bred to divinity—become a clergyman or minister

Plutarch's Lives—a book about the lives of the Greeks and Romans

Essay on Projects by Daniel Defoe (1697)—a book about economics

Essays to do Good by Dr. Cotton Mather (1710)—a book about religion

a turn of thinking—a way of thinking

READING AND RESEARCHING AMERICA

(2) This bookish inclination at length determined my father to make me a printer, though he had already one son (James) of that profession. In 1717 my brother, James, returned from England with a press and letters to set up his business in Boston. I liked it much better than that of my father, but still had a hankering for the sea. To prevent the apprehended effect of such an inclination, my father was impatient to have me bound to my brother. I stood out some time, but at last was persuaded and signed the indenture, when I was yet but twelve years old. I was to serve as apprentice till I was twenty-one years of age, only I was to be allowed journeyman's wages during the last year. In a little time I made a great progress in the business and became a useful hand to my brother. I now had access to better books. An acquaintance with the apprentices of booksellers enabled me sometimes to borrow a small one, which I was careful to return soon and clean. Often I sat up in my room reading the greatest part of the night, when the book was borrowed in the evening and to be returned early in the morning, lest it should be found missing or wanted.

(3) After some time a merchant, an ingenious, sensible man, Mr. Matthew Adams, who had a pretty collection of books and who frequented our printing house, took notice of me, invited me to see his library, and very kindly proposed to lend me such books as I chose to read. I now took a fancy to poetry and made some little pieces. My brother, supposing it might turn to account, encouraged me and induced me to compose two occasional ballads. One was called the "Lighthouse Tragedy," and contained an account of the shipwreck of Capt. Worthilake with his two daughters; the other was "Sailor's Song on the Taking of the Famous *Teach*, or Blackbeard, the Pirate." They

---

bookish inclination—a love of reading

letters—type for printing

that of my father—Benjamin's father's trade was making candles and soap.

a hankering—a wish, a love

have me bound—entered into a legal contract as an apprentice in order to learn a trade

stood out—refused

the indenture—the contract to be an apprentice

journeyman's wages—increased wages for someone who has finished an apprenticeship

lest it should be found—so that it should not be found

took a fancy to—took a liking to

little pieces—short poems

turn to account—be advantageous for business

"Lighthouse Tragedy"—based on a true story about the death of a Boston lighthousekeeper and his family

Capt.—Captain

"Sailor's Song"—also a true story about the death of a famous pirate called Blackbeard

were wretched stuff, in street ballad style; and when they were printed, he sent me about the town to sell them. The first sold prodigiously, the event being recent and having made a great noise. This success flattered my vanity, but my father discouraged me by ridiculing my performances and telling me verse-makers were generally beggars. Thus I escaped being a poet and probably a very bad one. But as prose writing has been of great use to me in the course of my life and was a principal means of my advancement, I shall tell you how in such a situation I acquired what little ability I may be supposed to have in that way.

(4) There was another bookish lad in the town, John Collins by name, with whom I was intimately acquainted. We sometimes disputed, and very fond we were of argument, and very desirous of confuting one another—which . . . is apt to become a very bad habit, making people often extremely disagreeable in company, by the contradiction that is necessary to bring it into practice; and thence besides souring and spoiling the conversation, it is productive of disgusts and perhaps enmities where you may have occasion for friendship. I had caught it by reading my father's books of dispute on religion. Persons of good sense, I have since observed, seldom fall into it, except lawyers [and] university men . . . . A question was once somehow or other started between Collins and me on the propriety of educating the female sex in learning and their abilities for study. He was of opinion that it was improper and that they were naturally unequal to it. I took the contrary side, perhaps a little for dispute sake. He was naturally more eloquent, having a greater plenty of words, and sometimes, as I thought, I was vanquished more by his fluency than by the strength of his reasons. As we parted without settling the point and were not to

wretched stuff—badly written
street ballad style—the style of common street songs
prodigiously—extraordinarily well
made a great noise—been very popular

desirous of confuting one another—eager to prove each other wrong

thence—therefore

for dispute sake—for the sake of the argument

see one another again for some time, I sat down to put my arguments in writing, which I copied fair and sent to him. He answered and I replied. Three or four letters on a side had passed, when my father happened to find my papers and read them. Without entering into the subject in dispute, he took occasion to talk with me about my manner of writing, observed that though I had the advantage of my antagonist in correct spelling and pointing (which I owed to the printing house) I fell far short in elegance of expression, in method, and in perspicuity— of which he convinced me by several instances. I saw the justice of his remarks and thence grew more attentive to my manner of writing, and determined to endeavour to improve my style.

pointing—punctuation

perspicuity—clarity

(5) About this time I met with an odd volume of the *Spectator*. It was the third. I had never before seen any of them. I bought it, read it over and over, and was much delighted with it. I thought the writing excellent and wished if possible to imitate it. With that view, I took some of the papers, and making short hints of the sentiment in each sentence, laid them by a few days, and then without looking at the book, tried to complete the papers again by expressing each hinted sentiment at length and as fully as it had been expressed before, in any suitable words that should occur to me. Then I compared my *Spectator* with the original, discovered some of my faults, and corrected them. But I found I wanted a stock of words or a readiness in recollecting and using them, which I thought I should have acquired before that time if I had gone on making verses; since the continual search for words of the same import but of different length to suit to the measure, or of different sound for the rhyme would have laid me under a constant necessity of searching for variety, and also have tended to fix that

met with—came across, encountered

odd—left-over, remaining

the *Spectator*—an English magazine famous for its excellent style of writing

with that view—with that aim or hope

hints of the sentiment—notes about the ideas

laid them by—put them aside

faults—mistakes

stock—supply

of the same import—of the same meaning

measure—meter

laid me under—put me under

variety in my mind, and make me master of it. Therefore I took some of the tales in the *Spectator* and turned them into verse, and after a time, when I had pretty well forgotten the prose, turned them back again. I also sometimes jumbled my collections of hints into confusion, and after some weeks endeavoured to reduce them into the best order before I began to form full sentences and complete the paper. This was to teach me method in the arrangement of the thoughts. By comparing my work afterwards with the original, I discovered many faults and corrected them; but I sometimes had the pleasure of fancying that in certain particulars of small import I had been lucky enough to improve the method or the language, and this encouraged me to think that I might possibly in time come to be a tolerable English writer, of which I was extremely ambitious. . . .

fancying—thinking, believing

in certain particulars of small import—in some unimportant ways

(6) My brother had in 1720 or '21 begun to print a newspaper. It was the second that appeared in America and was called *The New England Courant*. The only one before it was *The Boston Newsletter*. I remember his being dissuaded by some of his friends from the undertaking. . . . I was employed to carry the papers to the customers, after having worked in composing the types and printing off the sheets. He had some ingenious men among his friends who amused themselves by writing little pieces for this paper, which gained it credit and made it more in demand; and these gentlemen often visited us. Hearing their conversations and their accounts of the approbation their papers were received with, I was excited to try my hand among them. But being still a boy and suspecting that my brother would object to printing anything of mine in his paper if he knew it to be mine, I contrived to disguise my hand; and writing an anonymous paper, I

approbation—praise, approval

to try my hand—to try to write pieces for the paper myself

contrived to disguise my hand—was able to disguise my hand-writing

put it at night under the door of the printing house. It was found in the morning and communicated to his writing friends when they called in as usual. They read it, commented on it in my hearing, and I had the exquisite pleasure of finding it met with their approbation, and that in their different guesses at the author, none were named but men of some character among us for learning and ingenuity. I suppose now that I was rather lucky in my judges and that perhaps they were not really so very good as I then believed them to be. Encouraged, however, by this attempt, I wrote and sent in the same way to press several other pieces, which were equally approved, and I kept my secret till my small fund of sense for such performances was pretty well exhausted, and then I discovered it, when I began to be considered a little more by my brother's acquaintance. However, that did not quite please him as he thought that it tended to make me too vain. . . .

(7) This might be one occasion of the differences we began to have about this time. Though a brother, he considered himself my master and me as his apprentice, and accordingly expected the same services from me as he would from another; while I thought he degraded me too much in some he required of me, who from a brother expected more indulgence. Our disputes were often brought before our father, and I fancy I was either generally in the right or else a better pleader, because the judgment was generally in my favour. But my brother was passionate and had often beaten me, which I took extremely amiss. I fancy his harsh and tyrannical treatment of me might be a means of impressing me with that aversion to arbitrary power that has stuck to me through my whole life. Thinking my apprenticeship

none were named but men of some character—only men of character were named

my small fund of sense—my small supply of ideas
discovered—revealed
considered a little more—considered more favorably, admired

apprentice—person legally bound to a master worker in order to learn a trade
degraded me—insulted me, didn't respect me
indulgence—tolerance, favor
I fancy—I think, imagine

took extremely amiss—resented very much

very tedious, I was continually wishing for some opportunity of shortening it, which at length offered in a manner unexpected.

(8) One of the pieces in our newspaper on some political point which I have now forgotten, gave offence to the Assembly. He [James] was taken up, censured, and imprisoned for a month by the Speaker's warrant, I suppose because he would not discover the author. I, too, was taken up and examined before the Council; but though I did not give them any satisfaction, they contented themselves with admonishing me and dismissed me, considering me, perhaps, as an apprentice who was bound to keep his master's secrets. During my brother's confinement, which I resented a good deal notwithstanding our private differences, I had the management of the paper, and I made bold to give our rulers some rubs in it, which my brother took very kindly, while others began to consider me in an unfavourable light as a young genius that had a turn for libeling and satire. My brother's discharge was accompanied with an order from the House (a very odd one) that "James Franklin should no longer print the paper called the *New England Courant*." There was a consultation held in our printing house amongst his friends in this conjecture. Some proposed to elude the order by changing the name of the paper; but my brother seeing inconveniences in that, it was finally concluded on as a better way to let it be printed for the future under the name of "Benjamin Franklin"; and to avoid the censure of the Assembly that might fall on him as still printing it by his apprentice, the contrivance was that my old indenture should be returned to me with a full discharge on the back of it, to show in case of necessity; but to secure to him the benefit of my service, I should sign new indentures for the remainder of

some political point—In 1722, an article in James Franklin's newspaper suggested that the British officials in Boston were cooperating with the local pirates.

gave offence (offense)—offended or insulted

taken up—arrested

the Speaker's warrant—an official order

discover—reveal

did not give them any satisfaction—did not satisfy them with any answers

notwithstanding—in spite of

made bold—was bold

rubs—insults

a turn for libeling and satire—a tendency or inclination for lies and ridicule

discharge—release, termination

in this conjecture—in this problem or plan

elude—avoid

contrivance—plan, scheme

indenture—the contract for the apprenticeship

to secure—to guarantee

the term, which were to be kept private. A very flimsy scheme it was, but, however, it was immediately executed, and the paper went on accordingly under my name for several months. At length a fresh difference arising between my brother and me, I took upon me to assert my freedom, presuming that he would **not venture to** produce the new indentures. It was not fair in me to take this advantage, and this I therefore reckon one of the first **errata** of my life. But the unfairness of it weighed little with me, when under the impressions of resentment for the blows his passion too often urged him to bestow upon me, though he was otherwise not an ill-natured man. Perhaps I was too **saucy** and provoking.

(9) When he found I would leave him, he took care to prevent my getting employment in any other printing house of the town by going round and speaking to every master, who accordingly refused to give me work. I then thought of going to New York as the nearest place where there was a printer; and I was the rather inclined to leave Boston when I reflected that I had already made myself a little obnoxious to the governing party; and from the arbitrary proceedings of the Assembly in my brother's case, it was likely [that] I might if I stayed soon bring myself **into scrapes**, and further that my indiscreet disputations about religion began to make me pointed at with horror by good people as an infidel or atheist. I **determined on the point**, but my father now siding with my brother, I was **sensible** that if I attempted to go openly, means would be used to prevent me. My friend Collins therefore undertook to manage my flight. He agreed with the captain of a New York **sloop** for my passage, under pretence of my being a young man of his acquaintance that had had **an intrigue** with a girl of

not venture to—not dare to, be afraid to

errata—a printer's word for mistakes (errors)

saucy—impertinent

into scrapes—into trouble

determined on the point—made a decision to go
sensible—aware

sloop—sailboat
an intrigue—a romantic relationship

bad character, whose parents would compel me to marry her and therefore I could not appear or come away publicly. I sold some of my books to raise a little money, was taken on board the sloop privately, had a fair wind, and in three days found myself at New York, near three hundred miles from my home, at the age of seventeen, without the least recommendation to or knowledge of any person in the place, and with very little money in my pocket.

PART 2: MORAL PERFECTION (Paragraphs 10–17)

A decade later, Franklin was a successful businessman in Philadelphia, the owner of a printing shop and bookstore.

(10) It was about this time I conceived the bold and arduous project of arriving at moral perfection. I wished to live without committing any fault at any time; I would conquer all that either natural inclination, custom, or company might lead me into. As I knew, or thought I knew, what was right or wrong, I did not see why I might not

arduous—difficult, strenuous

always do the one and avoid the other. But I soon found I had undertaken a task of more difficulty than I had imagined. While my attention was taken up and care employed in guarding against one fault, I was often surprized by another. Habit took the advantage of inattention. Inclination was sometimes too strong for reason. I concluded at length that the mere speculative conviction that it was our interest to be completely virtuous was not sufficient to prevent our slipping, and that the contrary habits must be broken and good ones acquired and established before we can have any dependence on a steady, uniform rectitude of conduct. For this purpose I therefore contrived the following method.

mere speculative conviction—only theoretical belief
slipping—making a mistake

rectitude—correctness

(11) In the various enumerations of the moral virtues I had met with in my reading, I found the catalogue more or less numerous, as different writers included more or fewer ideas under the same name. Temperance, for example, was by some confined to eating and drinking, while by others it was extended to mean the moderating [of] every other pleasure, appetite, inclination, or passion—bodily or mental, even to our avarice and ambition. I proposed to myself, for the sake of clearness, to use rather more names with fewer ideas; and I included under thirteen names of virtues all that at that time occurred to me as necessary or desirable, and annexed to each a short precept which fully expressed the extent I gave to its meaning.

enumerations, catalogue—lists

annexed—added
precept—instructions, directions

These names of virtues with their precepts were

1. Temperance

Eat not to dulness. Drink not to elevation.

2. Silence

Speak not but what may benefit others or yourself.
Avoid trifling conversation.

trifling—trivial

3. Order

Let all your things have their places.

Let each part of your business have its time.

4. Resolution

Resolve to perform what you ought.

Perform without fail what you resolve.

5. Frugality

Make no expence but do good to others or yourself;

i.e., waste nothing.

6. Industry

Lose no time. Be always employed in something useful.

Cut off all unnecessary actions.

7. Sincerity

Use no hurtful deceit. Think innocently and justly; and,

if you speak, speak accordingly.

8. Justice

Wrong none by doing injuries or omitting the benefits

that are your duty.

9. Moderation

Avoid extremes. Forbear resenting injuries so much

as you think they deserve.

10. Cleanliness

Tolerate no uncleanness in body, clothes or habitation.

11. Tranquility

Be not disturbed at trifles or at accidents common or unavoidable.

12. Chastity

Rarely use venery but for health or offspring—never to dulness, weakness, or the injury of your own or another's peace or reputation.

13. Humility

Imitate Jesus and Socrates.

forbear—refrain from

trifles—things of little importance

venery—sexual gratification

Jesus—a religious figure, whose followers established the Christian church

Socrates—a philosopher of Athens, Greece, in the fourth century B.C.

(12) My intention being to acquire the *habitude* of all these virtues, I judged it would be well not to distract my attention by attempting the whole at once but to fix it on one of them at a time, and when I should be master of that, then to proceed to another, and so on till I should have gone thro' the thirteen. And as the previous acquisition of some might facilitate the acquisition of certain others, I arranged them with that view as they stand above. *Temperance* first, as it tends to procure that coolness and clearness of head which is so necessary where constant vigilance was to be kept up, and guard maintained, against the unremitting attraction of ancient habits, and the force of perpetual temptations. This being acquired and established, *Silence* would be more easy, and my desire being to gain knowledge at the same time that I improved in virtue, and considering that in conversation it was obtained rather by the use of the ear than of the tongue, and therefore wishing to break a habit I was getting into of prattling, punning, and joking, which only made me acceptable to trifling company, I gave *Silence* the second place. This and the next, *Order*, I expected would allow me more time for attending to my project and my studies. *Resolution*, once become habitual, would keep me firm in my endeavours to obtain all the subsequent virtues; *Frugality* and *Industry*, freeing me from my remaining debt and, producing affluence and independence, would make more easy the practice of *Sincerity* and *Justice*, etc., etc. Conceiving then that agreeable to the advice of Pythagoras in his golden verses, daily examination would be necessary, I contrived the following method for conducting that examination.

(13) I made a little book in which I allotted a page for each of the virtues. I ruled each page with red ink so as to have seven columns,

habitude—habit

to procure—to provide, lead to

unremitting attraction of ancient habits—continual attraction of old habits

prattling—talking foolishly

Pythagoras—Greek philosopher and mathematician

allotted—used

one for each day of the week, marking each column with a letter for the day. I crossed these columns with thirteen red lines, marking the beginning of each line with the first letter of one of the virtues, on which line and in its proper column I might mark by a little black spot every fault I found upon examination to have been committed respecting that virtue upon that day.

(14) I determined to give a week's strict attention to each of the virtues successively. Thus in the first week my great guard was to avoid even the least offence against temperance, leaving the other virtues to their ordinary chance, only marking every evening the faults of the day. Thus if in the first week I could keep my first line marked "T." clear of spots, I supposed the habit of that virtue so much strengthened and its opposite weakened that I might venture extending my attention to include the next, and for the following week keep both lines clear of spots. Proceeding thus to the last, I could go thro' a course complete in thirteen weeks, and four courses in a year. And like him who, having a garden to weed, does not attempt to eradicate all the bad herbs at once, which would exceed his reach and his strength, but works on one of the beds at a time, and having accomplished the first, proceeds to a second; so I should have (I hoped) the encouraging pleasure of seeing on my pages the progress I made in virtue by clearing successively my lines of their spots, till in the end by a number of courses, I should be happy in viewing a clean book after a thirteen weeks' daily examination. . . .

offence (offense)—fault or mistake

	Form of the Pages						
	TEMPERANCE						
	Eat not to dullness. *Drink not to elevation.*						
	S	M	T	W	T	F	S
T							
S	✔✔	✔		✔		✔	
O	✔	✔	✔		✔	✔	✔
R			✔			✔	
F		✔			✔		
I			✔				
S							
J							
M							
Cl.							
T							
Ch.							
H							

(15) I entered upon the execution of this plan for self-examination and continued it with occasional intermissions for some time. I was surprised to find myself so much fuller of faults than I had imagined, but I had the satisfaction of seeing them diminish. To avoid the trouble of renewing now and then my little book, which by scraping out marks on the paper of old faults to make room for new ones in a new course became full of holes, I transferred my tables and precepts to the ivory leaves of a memorandum book on which the lines were drawn with red ink that made a durable stain, and on those lines I

marked my faults with a black lead pencil, which marks I could easily wipe out with a wet sponge. After a while I went thro' one course only in a year, and afterwards only one in several years, till at length I omitted them entirely, being employed in voyages and business abroad with a multiplicity of affairs that interfered; but I always carried my little book with me. . . .

(16) My list of virtues contained at first but twelve. But a Quaker friend having kindly informed me that I was generally thought proud, that my pride showed itself frequently in conversation, that I was not content with being in the right when discussing any point, but was overbearing and rather insolent—of which he convinced me by mentioning several instances—I determined endeavouring to cure myself if I could of this vice or folly among the rest, and I added *Humility* to my list, giving an extensive meaning to the word. I cannot boast of much success in acquiring the *reality* of this virtue, but I had a good deal with regard to the *appearance* of it. I made it a rule to forbear all direct contradiction to the sentiments of others and all positive assertion of my own. I even forbade myself . . . the use of every word or expression in the language that imported a fixed opinion, such as "certainly," "undoubtedly," etc.; and I adopted instead of them, "I conceive," "I apprehend," or "I imagine" a thing to be so or so, or "It appears to me at present." When another asserted something that I thought an error, I denied myself the pleasure of contradicting him abruptly and of showing immediately some absurdity in his proposition; and in answering I began by observing that in certain cases or circumstances his opinion would be right, but that in the present case there "appeared" or "seemed to me" some difference, etc. I soon

folly—foolishness

to forbear—avoid or refrain from

forbade—past tense of forbear

that imported a fixed opinion—that indicated an opinion that cannot be changed

found the advantage of this change in my manners: The conversations I engaged in went on more pleasantly; the modest way in which I proposed my opinions procured them a readier reception and less contradiction; I had less mortification when I was found to be in the wrong, and I more easily prevailed with others to give up their mistakes and join with me when I happened to be in the right. And this mode, which I at first put on with some violence to natural inclination, became at length so easy and so habitual to me that perhaps for these fifty years past no one has ever heard a dogmatical expression escape me. And to this habit (after my character of integrity) I think it principally owing that I had early so much weight with my fellow citizens when I proposed new institutions or alterations in the old, and so much influence in the public councils when I became a member. For I was but a bad speaker, never eloquent, subject to much hesitation in my choice of words, hardly correct in language, and yet I generally carried my point.

(17) In reality there is perhaps no one of our natural passions so hard to subdue as *pride*; disguise it, struggle with it, beat it down, stifle it, mortify it as much as one pleases, it is still alive and will every now and then peep out and show itself. You will see it perhaps often in this history. For even if I could conceive that I had completely overcome it, I should probably be proud of my humility.

procured them—got them, obtained for them
mortification—humiliation

mode—manner
with some violence to natural inclination—contrary to or against my natural tendency
dogmatical expression—an assertive or opinionated expression
weight—influence

mortify—subdue, restrain

THE FOUNDING FATHERS: BENJAMIN FRANKLIN

→ EXERCISES ←

Comprehension Questions

Answer these questions in paragraph form, using complete sentences in Modern English. Do not copy the answers directly from the reading passage. (See pages 218–21 in the Yellow Pages for a review of paragraph form.)

Part 1: "Early Years" (Paragraphs 1–9)

1. What kinds of books did young Franklin read?

2. Explain how Franklin used his copy of the *Spectator* to improve his writing.

3. Explain the disagreements between James and Benjamin Franklin.

4. How did Franklin begin to write articles for his brother's newspaper?

5. Explain the situation that put Benjamin in charge of the newspaper and later enabled him to escape from his apprenticeship.

6. What were Franklin's reasons for deciding to leave Boston?

Part 2: "Moral Perfection" (Paragraphs 10–17)

1. How did Franklin choose and organize his list of virtues?

2. Explain how Franklin used his chart.

3. Was Franklin successful in learning to live a morally perfect life?

Reading and Researching America

Vocabulary Development

Part 1: "Early Years" (Paragraphs 1–9)

1. Franklin uses several words related to the practice of *apprenticeship*, a historic system by which a boy learned a trade from an experienced tradesman. At a young age (Franklin was 12 years old), a boy and his parents would sign *indenture* papers pledging that the boy would work for the tradesman and in return the tradesman or *master* would teach the boy his trade. The boy and the master would both be *bound* by the terms of the contract, often for several years, until the contract was completed or *discharged*.

EXERCISE: Write a short explanation of Benjamin Franklin's apprenticeship to his brother James, using the vocabulary in italics in the preceding paragraph.

2. Franklin wrote that he and his friend John Collins were fond of argument, and he used many words in his autobiography that relate to argumentation. They are listed here along with the paragraph number where they appear in the reading:

- *to persuade* (2)
- *to dispute* (4), *dispute* (4, 7), *disputations* (9)
- *contradiction* (4), *contrary* (4)
- *antagonist* (4)
- *judgment* (7)
- *in my favor* (7)
- *to assert* (8)

EXERCISE: Write a short paragraph describing a recent argument that you have had, using several of these vocabulary words. Do you also enjoy a good argument?

3. Franklin writes that other people thought that he was vain (6), provoking (8), and obnoxious (9).

EXERCISE: Look up the meanings of these words and try to determine from the reading passage why people had these impressions of Franklin. Do you agree that he might have been vain, provoking, and obnoxious?

4. Here are more useful vocabulary words to study and use:

- *principal* (1, 3)
- *genius* (8)
- *ingenious* (3, 6)
- *ingenuity* (6)
- *propriety* (4)

20

The Founding Fathers: Benjamin Franklin

Part 2: "Moral Perfection" (Paragraphs 10–17)

These are the words that Franklin uses for the virtues he wants to acquire. Following the model, complete the sentences about a person with each virtue with a verb phrase that shows the meaning of the word. The first one has been done as an example.

a. **Temperance:** A person who is temperate <u>is careful not to eat or drink too much.</u>

b. **Silence:** A person who is silent _____

c. **Order:** A person who is orderly _____

d. **Resolution:** A person who is resolute _____

e. **Frugality:** A person who is frugal _____

f. **Industry:** A person who is industrious _____

g. **Sincerity:** A person who is sincere _____

h. **Justice:** A person who is just _____

i. **Moderation:** A person who is moderate _____

j. **Cleanliness:** A person who is clean _____

k. **Tranquility:** A person who is tranquil _____

l. **Chastity:** A person who is chaste _____

m. **Humility:** A person who is humble _____

Quotations and Paraphrases

Write the quotation with an introductory explanation of the source and the content, paying close attention to punctuation. Then paraphrase it in your own words. (See pages 246–52 in the Yellow Pages for help with quotations and paraphrases.)

READING AND RESEARCHING AMERICA

Part 1: "Early Years" (Paragraphs 1–9)

1. (paragraph 4) Argument "is apt to become a very bad habit, making people often extremely disagreeable in company . . . and thence . . . it is productive of disgusts and perhaps enmities where you may have occasion for friendship."

   _____
   _____
   _____
   _____

2. (paragraph 8) "I had the management of the paper, and I made bold to give our rulers some rubs in it, which my brother took very kindly, while others began to consider me in an unfavourable light as a young genius that had a turn for libeling and satire."

   _____
   _____
   _____
   _____

3. Choose your own quotation and follow the same directions.

   _____
   _____
   _____
   _____

Part 2: "Moral Perfection" (Paragraphs 10–17)

1. (paragraph 10) "While my attention was taken up and care employed in guarding against one fault, I was often surprized by another. Habit took the advantage of inattention. Inclination was sometimes too strong for reason." (In your paraphrase, use the modern spelling *surprised*.)

2. (paragraph 16) "My pride showed itself frequently in conversation, that I was not content with being in the right when discussing any point, but was overbearing and rather insolent . . . ."

3. Choose your own quotation and follow the same directions.

Writing Summaries

Write a one-paragraph summary in Modern English without plagiarism. (See pages 253–55 in the Yellow Pages for help in writing a summary.)

1. Summarize Franklin's attempts to improve his writing. (paragraphs 4–5)

2. Summarize Franklin's attempts to improve his character. (paragraphs 11–15)

Questions for Discussion and Writing

Discuss your answers to these questions with your classmates. These questions may also be used as essay topics. (See pages 221–24 in the Yellow Pages for a review of essay form.)

1. Franklin is a popular hero for Americans. What qualities make him an American hero? Would a person with these qualities be a hero in your country? What qualities do you think a hero should have?

2. Benjamin Franklin attended school for only two years and then educated himself by reading all the books he could find. Do you think that a person could educate himself or herself that way today? Would you prefer that kind of education?

3. The other point of view: Franklin wrote about his childhood and youth from his own point of view. What might someone in his family, such as his father or his brother James, say about Benjamin? (If you write an essay on this topic, you can write in your own voice or in the voice of one of his family members.)

4. Franklin wanted to lead a life of moral perfection. Do you think this is a reasonable goal? Is Franklin's method a good way to reach this goal? What other ways would you recommend?

5. Franklin wrote in his autobiography that the hardest fault to overcome is pride. From the evidence in these reading passages, do you think that Franklin was a proud man or a humble man?

THE FOUNDING FATHERS: BENJAMIN FRANKLIN

6. The words *pride* and *proud* have both positive and negative connotations in English. When do you think it is appropriate to feel proud, and when is it not appropriate? Do you think that Franklin was justified in feeling proud of himself?

7. Personal topic: Choose one of Franklin's 13 virtues (or choose another virtue) that you would like to achieve. Explain the problems that the lack of this virtue causes in your life, and explain what you can do to achieve it.

8. Read this description of Enlightenment philosophy taken from a book about American literature. In what ways does Benjamin Franklin embody these ideas?

> With its emphasis upon reason rather than authority, its encouragement of scientific inquiry, and its . . . belief in the perfectibility of man and his world, the Enlightenment . . . engendered a spirit of optimism . . . .
> (*Backgrounds of American Literary Thought*, p. 54)

Scanning for Specific Information

Scanning means looking over a page quickly to find a specific detail rather than beginning at the top of the page and reading every word. Working alone or with one or two other students, use a reference book to find the information to complete the sentences in the following reading. Try to work quickly to find just the information you need to fill in to complete the exercise. You may need to consult more than one source. Make sure that your answers fit the structure of the sentence.

Reference book(s) used _____

_____

REVOLUTION

During the early years of the American colonies, the British government allowed the colonists to make many of their own decisions in small local assemblies. Consequently, the American colonists were outraged when, in the mid-1700s, the British government began to assert more control over the colonies.

For the British, the maintenance of the North American colonies was becoming more expensive, as they had to support and protect the colonies from attacks from Native Americans and from other European countries that wanted to claim territory in North America. The French and Indian Wars in the years _____, for example, cost Britain _____ pounds.

The colonies were expected to pay back these expenses by sending valuable raw materials such as _____ back to England, but there were no direct taxes on the colonies until 1764, when the British parliament voted to impose a tax on molasses and sugar, called the _____. Another tax, called the _____, which passed in the year _____, required seals and stamps on legal documents, licenses, and newspapers. These taxes were passed by the members of Parliament in England, not by the local governments, so the colonists resolved to boycott English goods; their rallying cry was "No Taxation without Representation!" In 1773, Parliament passed the Tea Act, which enabled the British East India Company to sell tea at low prices. This act led to the Boston Tea Party, in which _____ threw 10,000 pounds worth of tea into the water of _____. In retaliation, the British government closed the harbor and began interfering with the local government. The American colonists were ready for a revolution.

The Founding Fathers: Benjamin Franklin

In the year _____, representatives of 12 colonies met in the city of _____ for the first Continental Congress and affirmed the independence of the colonies. The next year, 1775, the first shots of the Revolutionary War took place in the Massachusetts towns of _____ and _____, and in 1776, Thomas Paine wrote a pamphlet entitled _____ calling for a complete break with Britain. During the Second Continental Congress, on the date _____, 1776, the delegates from the colonies signed the _____, listing their complaints against Britain and declaring the colonies to be free and independent states, the United States of America.

Research Topics

Choose one of these topics or another topic that interests you to do one of the research exercises in the Yellow Pages. Share the results of your research with your classmates as you become experts in your own research areas.

George Washington	Thomas Jefferson	John Adams
Alexander Hamilton	James Madison	Thomas Paine
Boston	Philadelphia	*Poor Richard's Almanac*
Lexington and Concord	The Boston Tea Party	American Revolution
The Declaration of Independence	The Constitution	

Expansion Activities

1. In paragraph 5, Franklin describes a technique that he used to improve his writing. Try this method yourself, with a short passage from one of your textbooks or from another piece of writing that you think is well-written. Do you think this is an effective technique to improve your writing? What other benefits does this technique have?

2. In paragraph 16, Franklin describes the changes that he made in his style of conversation so that he would seem less proud and overbearing. With a partner, write a short dialogue in which one of you takes the part of the overbearing Franklin. Then rewrite the dialogue according to Franklin's recommendations. Read your dialogues aloud to your classmates, and ask them what they think of the changes.

3. Franklin's *Poor Richard's Almanac* was popular for the clever advice provided to the farmers and tradespeople of the mid-1700s. (The "Richard" in the title was an imaginary person, Richard Saunders, invented by Franklin.) This advice is still popular today: some examples are, *Haste makes waste* and *Early to bed, early to rise, makes a man healthy, wealthy, and wise.* Look up *Poor Richard's Almanac* on the Internet to find more of these sayings. What do you think of his advice? Is it still useful today?

4. **For further reading:** For the 25th anniversary of *Poor Richard's Almanac* in 1773, Franklin wrote a delightful essay entitled, "The Way to Wealth," in which he included many of his sayings. Look for this essay in an American literature anthology or on the Internet, and read it to find out what these people thought of Poor Richard's advice.

SLAVES
Frederick Douglass
(1818–1895)
★ ★ ★

INTRODUCTION

The use of slave labor was a part of the agricultural economy in the New World from the earliest days of colonization. In the 1600s Blacks were brought to America from Africa to work on tobacco, sugar cane, and rice plantations. At first, they were indentured servants who were often given their freedom after a period of time, but in the 1700s, slavery gradually developed into a system of property rights called chattel slavery, in which slaves could be bought, sold, and inherited like property. As farmers in the southern states began to grow cotton in the 1800s, they in particular became more dependent on the cheap labor provided by slaves, and the legal system of slavery became harsher and more established. By the 1850s, and into the 1860s, many huge plantation owners had hundreds of slaves.

Southerners defended the practice of slavery, claiming that human societies had always had slaves and that their slaves were treated better than free workers in the northern states. Northern reformers (called abolitionists) spoke out against slavery on the grounds that it was immoral for one person to own another and that all people have the same human rights to life and liberty. These abolitionists began an anti-slavery movement, calling for an end to slavery and helping slaves escape to the North.

It was illegal for slaves to learn to read and write, but one who did was Frederick Douglass, born a slave in the state of Maryland. Douglass lived on a plantation until he was eight years old, when he was sent to Baltimore to work for a family with a young son his age. There he learned to read and write, and his reading led him to understand the injustice of slavery and made him hope for his freedom. He was punished severely for his new attitude, but eventually he was able to escape slavery in 1838.

Douglass headed north to Massachusetts where he met people in the anti-slavery movement. When Douglass told them his own story of his life as a slave, they were impressed by his skills as a speaker and writer and invited him to join their movement. He gave many speeches, and in 1845 he wrote his autobiography, *Narrative of the Life of Frederick Douglass*.

Although Douglass was living in the North, he was still legally a slave and in danger of being captured and returned to his master. Eventually with the help of his friends, he was able to buy his freedom and establish an anti-slavery newspaper called *The North Star*. (When the slaves were escaping to the North, they followed the north star.)

During the Civil War (1861–1865), Douglass met with President Abraham Lincoln to discuss the future of Blacks after their release from slavery. Lincoln issued the Emancipation Proclamation in 1863, which basically freed all slaves, but many southern plantation owners refused to follow the new law. When the war ended, Douglass continued to work for the rights of Blacks. He also worked for the civil rights of women and held several offices in the government of the District of Columbia. He remained active in political life until he died in 1895. Because of his eloquence and determination in fighting oppression, Frederick Douglass is remembered as a hero for all oppressed people.

Pre-Reading Questions

Before you read, think about slavery and what you have heard about it: Who were the American slaves, and where did they come from? How were they treated, and how did they gain their freedom? Have other countries also had slavery? Does slavery still exist today?

READING PASSAGE

FREDERICK DOUGLASS:
From *Narrative of the Life of Frederick Douglass, an American Slave*

In terms of sentence structure, Frederick Douglass's writing is similar to Modern English. However, he uses a lot of old-fashioned vocabulary such as *deemed, recollect,* and *odiousness*. He also uses many more semi-colons than would be acceptable today.

One word that Douglass uses is extremely insulting today and **must never be used in any circumstances:** It is the word *nigger*. Douglass uses this word only in the speech of Mr. Auld, his master in Baltimore, but when he himself refers to his race, he uses the words *black man*. (Today, the term *African-American* is often the preferred term for *Black*.)

PART 1: CHILDHOOD (Paragraphs 1–23)

(1) I was born in Tuckahoe, near Hillsborough, and about twelve miles from Easton, in Talbot county, Maryland. I have no accurate knowledge of my age, never having seen any authentic record containing it. By far the larger part of the slaves know as little of their ages as horses know of theirs, and it is the wish of most masters within my knowledge to keep their slaves thus ignorant. I do not remember to have ever met a slave who could tell of his birthday. They seldom come nearer to it than planting-time, harvest-time, cherry-time, spring-time, or fall-time. A want of information concerning my own was a

want of—lack of

source of unhappiness to me even during childhood. The white children could tell their ages. I could not tell why I ought to be deprived of the same privilege. I was not allowed to make any inquiries of my master concerning it. He deemed all such inquiries on the part of a slave improper and impertinent, and evidence of a restless spirit. The nearest estimate I can give makes me now between twenty-seven and twenty-eight years of age. I come to this, from hearing my master say, some time during 1835, I was about seventeen years old.

deemed—considered, believed

(2) My mother was named Harriet Bailey. She was the daughter of Isaac and Betsey Bailey, both colored, and quite dark. My mother was of a darker complexion than either my grandmother or grandfather.

(3) My father was a white man. He was admitted to be such by all I ever heard speak of my parentage. The opinion was also whispered that my master was my father; but of the correctness of this opinion, I know nothing; the means of knowing was withheld from me. My mother and I were separated when I was but an infant—before I knew her as my mother. It is a common custom, in the part of Maryland from which I ran away, to part children from their mothers at a very early age. Frequently, before the child has reached its twelfth month, its mother is taken from it, and hired out on some farm a considerable distance off, and the child is placed under the care of an old woman, too old for field labor. For what this separation is done, I do not know, unless it be to hinder the development of the child's affection toward its mother, and to blunt and destroy the natural affection of the mother for the child. This is the inevitable result.

(4) I never saw my mother, to know her as such, more than four or five times in my life; and each of these times was very short in dura-

tion, and at night. She was hired by a Mr. Stewart, who lived about twelve miles from my home. She made her journeys to see me in the night, travelling the whole distance on foot, after the performance of her day's work. She was a field hand, and a whipping is the penalty of not being in the field at sunrise, unless a slave has special permission from his or her master to the contrary—a permission which they seldom get, and one that gives to him that gives it the proud name of being a kind master. I do not recollect of ever seeing my mother by the light of day. She was with me in the night. She would lie down with me, and get me to sleep, but long before I waked she was gone. Very little communication ever took place between us. Death soon ended what little we could have while she lived, and with it her hardships and suffering. She died when I was about seven years old, on one of my master's farms, near Lee's Mill. I was not allowed to be present during her illness, at her death, or burial. She was gone long before I knew any thing about it. Never having enjoyed, to any considerable extent, her soothing presence, her tender and watchful care, I received the tidings of her death with much the same emotions I should have probably felt at the death of a stranger.

a field hand—a slave that worked in the fields

tidings—news

(5) Called thus suddenly away, she left me without the slightest intimation of who my father was. The whisper that my master was my father, may or may not be true; and, true or false, it is of but little consequence to my purpose whilst the fact remains, in all its glaring odiousness, that slaveholders have ordained, and by law established, that the children of slave women shall in all cases follow the condition of their mothers; and this is done too obviously to administer to their own lusts, and make a gratification of their wicked desires profitable

intimation—hint or suggestion

glaring odiousness—shocking evil

ordained—commanded

as well as pleasurable; for by this cunning arrangement, the slaveholder, in cases not a few, sustains to his slaves the double relation of master and father.

(6) I know of such cases; and it is worthy of remark that such slaves invariably suffer greater hardships, and have more to contend with, than others. They are, in the first place, a constant offence to their mistress. She is ever disposed to find fault with them; they can seldom do any thing to please her; she is never better pleased than when she sees them under the lash, especially when she suspects her husband of showing to his mulatto children favors which he withholds from his black slaves. The master is frequently compelled to sell this class of his slaves, out of deference to the feelings of his white wife; and, cruel as the deed may strike any one to be, for a man to sell his own children to human flesh-mongers, it is often the dictate of humanity for him to do so; for, unless he does this, he must not only whip them himself, but must stand by and see one white son tie up his brother, of but few shades darker complexion than himself, and ply the gory lash to his naked back; and if he lisp one word of disapproval, it is set down to his parental partiality, and only makes a bad matter worse, both for himself and the slave whom he would protect and defend.

(7) Every year brings with it multitudes of this class of slaves. It was doubtless in consequence of a knowledge of this fact, that one great statesman of the south predicted the downfall of slavery by the inevitable laws of population. Whether this prophecy is ever fulfilled or not, it is nevertheless plain that a very different-looking class of people are springing up at the south, and are now held in slavery, from those originally brought to this country from Africa; and if their in-

sustains—has or holds

worthy of remark—worthwhile to point out

offence (offense)—injury or insult

ever disposed to—always ready to

under the lash—being whipped

mulatto—of mixed races, black and white

human flesh-mongers—slave traders

dictate of humanity—reasons of kindness

ply the gory lash—use the bloody whip

lisp—murmurs, says

parental partiality—favoritism of a parent

crease will do no other good, it will do away the force of the argument, that God cursed Ham, and therefore American slavery is right. If the lineal descendants of Ham are alone to be scripturally enslaved, it is certain that slavery at the south must soon become unscriptural; for thousands are ushered into the world, annually, who, like myself, owe their existence to white fathers, and those fathers most frequently their own masters.

Ham—a son of Noah, who sees his father naked and drunk. His punishment is to be forever a slave to his brothers. From a story in the Bible, Genesis 9:20–27. Blacks were considered to be the descendants of Ham, so this story served as justification for their slavery.

When Frederick Douglass was eight years old, he was chosen to go to the city of Baltimore to live with some relatives of his master Captain Lloyd, where he would be the personal slave of a young boy about his own age.

(8) We arrived at Baltimore early on Sunday morning, landing at Smith's Wharf, not far from Bowley's Wharf. We had on board the sloop a large flock of sheep; and after aiding in driving them to the slaughterhouse of Mr. Curtis on Louden Slater's Hill, I was conducted by Rich, one of the hands belonging on board of the sloop, to my new home in Alliciana Street, near Mr. Gardner's ship-yard, on Fells Point.

sloop—a sail boat

(9) Mr. and Mrs. Auld were both at home, and met me at the door with their little son Thomas, to take care of whom I had been given. And here I saw what I had never seen before; it was a white face beaming with the most kindly emotions; it was the face of my new mistress, Sophia Auld. I wish I could describe the rapture that flashed through my soul as I beheld it. It was a new and strange sight to me, brightening up my pathway with the light of happiness. Little Thomas was told, there was his Freddy,—and I was told to take care of little

rapture—great happiness

Thomas; and thus I entered upon the duties of my new home with the most cheering prospect ahead.

(10) I look upon my departure from Colonel Lloyd's plantation as one of the most interesting events of my life. It is possible, and even quite probable, that but for the mere circumstance of being removed from that plantation to Baltimore, I should have to-day, instead of being here seated by my own table, in the enjoyment of freedom and the happiness of home, writing this Narrative, been confined in the galling chains of slavery. Going to live at Baltimore laid the foundation, and opened the gateway, to all my subsequent prosperity. I have ever regarded it as the first plain manifestation of that kind providence which has ever since attended me, and marked my life with so many favors. I regarded the selection of myself as being somewhat remarkable. There were a number of slave children that might have been sent from the plantation to Baltimore. There were those younger, those older, and those of the same age. I was chosen from among them all, and was the first, last, and only choice.

mere circumstance—only chance

been confined in the galling chains of slavery—been still a slave

ever regarded it—always considered it

manifestation—a clear sign

providence—the care and protection of God

ever since attended me—has always accompanied me

(11) I may be deemed superstitious, and even egotistical, in regarding this event as a special interposition of divine Providence in my favor. But I should be false to the earliest sentiments of my soul, if I suppressed the opinion. I prefer to be true to myself, even at the hazard of incurring the ridicule of others, rather than to be false, and incur my own abhorrence. From my earliest recollection, I date the entertainment of a deep conviction that slavery would not always be able to hold me within its foul embrace; and in the darkest hours of my career in slavery, this living word of faith and spirit of hope departed not from me, but remained like ministering angels to cheer me through

deemed—considered to be

interposition—intervention

be false—be untrue, dishonest

incurring—bringing the bad result of

my own abhorrence—my self-hatred

I date the entertainment of—I began to have

departed not—did not depart

the gloom. This good spirit was from God, and to him I offer thanksgiving and praise.

(12) My new mistress proved to be all she appeared when I first met her at the door,—a woman of the kindest heart and finest feelings. She had never had a slave under her control previously to myself, and prior to her marriage she had been dependent upon her own industry for a living. She was by trade a weaver; and by constant application to her business, she had been in a good degree preserved from the blighting and dehumanizing effects of slavery. I was utterly astonished at her goodness. I scarcely knew how to behave towards her. She was entirely unlike any other white woman I had ever seen. I could not approach her as I was accustomed to approach other white ladies. My early instruction was all out of place. The crouching servility, usually so acceptable a quality in a slave, did not answer when manifested toward her. Her favor was not gained by it; she seemed to be disturbed by it. She did not deem it impudent or unmannerly for a slave to look her in the face. The meanest slave was put fully at ease in her presence, and none left without feeling better for having seen her. Her face was made of heavenly smiles, and her voice of tranquil music.

blighting—destructive

crouching servility—low posture suitable to a slave
did not answer—was not acceptable
manifested—shown plainly
deem it—consider it

(13) But, alas! this kind heart had but a short time to remain such. The fatal poison of irresponsible power was already in her hands, and soon commenced its infernal work. That cheerful eye, under the influence of slavery, soon became red with rage; that voice, made all of sweet accord, changed to one of harsh and horrid discord; and that angelic face gave place to that of a demon.

infernal work—the work of evil

(14) Very soon after I went to live with Mr. and Mrs. Auld, she very kindly commenced to teach me the A, B, C. After I had learned this,

the A, B, C—the alphabet

she assisted me in learning to spell words of three or four letters. Just at this point of my progress, Mr. Auld found out what was going on, and at once forbade Mrs. Auld to instruct me further, telling her, among other things, that it was unlawful, as well as unsafe, to teach a slave to read. To use his own words, further, he said, "If you give a nigger an inch, he will take an ell. A nigger should know nothing but to obey his master—to do as he is told to do. Learning would *spoil* the best nigger in the world. Now," said he, "if you teach that nigger (speaking of myself) how to read, there would be no keeping him. It would forever unfit him to be a slave. He would at once become unmanageable, and of no value to his master. As to himself, it could do him no good, but a great deal of harm. It would make him discontented and unhappy." These words sank deep into my heart, stirred up sentiments within that lay slumbering, and called into existence an entirely new train of thought. It was a new and special revelation, explaining dark and mysterious things, with which my youthful understanding had struggled, but struggled in vain. I now understood what had been to me a most perplexing difficulty—to wit, the white man's power to enslave the black man. It was a grand achievement, and I prized it highly. From that moment, I understood the pathway from slavery to freedom. It was just what I wanted, and I got it at a time when I the least expected it. Whilst I was saddened by the thought of losing the aid of my kind mistress, I was gladdened by the invaluable instruction which, by the merest accident, I had gained from my master. Though conscious of the difficulty of learning without a teacher, I set out with high hope, and a fixed purpose, at whatever cost of trouble, to learn how to read. The very decided manner with which he spoke, and strove to impress his wife with the evil consequences of

an ell—an old-fashioned measurement, about 4 feet

unfit him—make him unsuitable

slumbering—sleeping, resting
train of thought—set of ideas

to wit—that is to say, namely

strove—tried hard

giving me instruction, served to convince me that he was deeply sensible of the truths he was uttering. It gave me the best assurance that I might rely with the utmost confidence on the results which, he said, would flow from teaching me to read. What he most dreaded, that I most desired. What he most loved, that I most hated. That which to him was a great evil, to be carefully shunned, was to me a great good, to be diligently sought; and the argument which he so warmly urged, against my learning to read, only served to inspire me with a desire and determination to learn. In learning to read, I owe almost as much to the bitter opposition of my master, as to the kindly aid of my mistress. I acknowledge the benefit of both.

sensible—aware of

would flow from—would result from

(15) I had resided but a short time in Baltimore before I observed a marked difference, in the treatment of slaves, from that which I had witnessed in the country. A city slave is almost a freeman, compared with a slave on the plantation. He is much better fed and clothed, and enjoys privileges altogether unknown to the slave on the plantation. There is a vestige of decency, a sense of shame, that does much to curb and check those outbreaks of atrocious cruelty so commonly enacted upon the plantation. He is a desperate slaveholder, who will shock the humanity of his non-slaveholding neighbors with the cries of his lacerated slave. Few are willing to incur the odium attaching to the reputation of being a cruel master; and above all things, they would not be known as not giving a slave enough to eat. Every city slaveholder is anxious to have it known of him, that he feeds his slaves well; and it is due to them to say, that most of them do give their slaves enough to eat.

marked—easy to see

a vestige—a small reminder

lacerated—cut from whipping

incur the odium—bring hatred on themselves

due to them—in their credit, in their favor

(16) I lived in Master Hugh's family about seven years. During this time, I succeeded in learning to read and write. In accomplishing this, I was compelled to resort to various stratagems. I had no regular teacher. My mistress, who had kindly commenced to instruct me, had, in compliance with the advice and direction of her husband, not only ceased to instruct, but had set her face against my being instructed by any one else. It is due, however, to my mistress to say of her, that she did not adopt this course of treatment immediately. She at first lacked the depravity indispensable to shutting me up in mental darkness. It was at least necessary for her to have some training in the exercise of irresponsible power, to make her equal to the task of treating me as though I were a brute.

(17) My mistress was, as I have said, a kind and tenderhearted woman; and in the simplicity of her soul she commenced, when I first went to live with her, to treat me as she supposed one human being ought to treat another. In entering upon the duties of a slaveholder, she did not seem to perceive that I sustained to her the relation of a mere chattel, and that for her to treat me as a human being was not only wrong, but dangerously so. Slavery proved as injurious to her as it did to me. When I went there, she was a pious, warm, and tenderhearted woman. There was no sorrow or suffering for which she had not a tear. She had bread for the hungry, clothes for the naked, and comfort for every mourner that came within her reach. Slavery soon proved its ability to divest her of these heavenly qualities. Under its influence, the tender heart became stone, and the lamblike disposition gave way to one of tiger-like fierceness. The first step in her downward course was in her ceasing to instruct me. She now commenced

stratagems—tricks or strategies

depravity—wickedness, evil

a mere chattel—only a piece of property

pious—devout, religious

to divest her of—to take away from her

commenced—began

to practice her husband's precepts. She finally became even more violent in her opposition than her husband himself. She was not satisfied with simply doing as well as he had commanded; she seemed anxious to do better. Nothing seemed to make her more angry than to see me with a newspaper. She seemed to think that here lay the danger. I have had her rush at me with a face made all up of fury, and snatch from me a newspaper, in a manner that fully revealed her apprehension. She was an apt woman; and a little experience soon demonstrated, to her satisfaction, that education and slavery were incompatible with each other.

(18) From this time I was most narrowly watched. If I was in a separate room any considerable length of time, I was sure to be suspected of having a book, and was at once called to give an account of myself. All this, however, was too late. The first step had been taken. Mistress, in teaching me the alphabet, had given me the *inch*, and no precaution could prevent me from taking the *ell*.

(19) The plan which I adopted, and the one by which I was most successful, was that of making friends of all the little white boys whom I met in the street. As many of these as I could, I converted into teachers. With their kindly aid, obtained at different times and in different places, I finally succeeded in learning to read. When I was sent of errands, I always took my book with me, and by going one part of my errand quickly, I found time to get a lesson before my return. I used also to carry bread with me, enough of which was always in the house, and to which I was always welcome; for I was much better off in this regard than many of the poor white children in our neighborhood. This bread I used to bestow upon the hungry little urchins,

precepts—commandments, directions

apt—clever, adaptable

bestow—give as a gift
urchins—poor children

who, in return, would give me that more valuable bread of knowledge. I am strongly tempted to give the names of two or three of those little boys, as a testimonial of the gratitude and affection I bear them; but prudence forbids;—not that it would injure me, but it might embarrass them; for it is almost an unpardonable offence to teach slaves to read in this Christian country. It is enough to say of the dear little fellows, that they lived on Philpot Street, very near Durgin and Bailey's ship-yard. I used to talk this matter of slavery over with them. I would sometimes say to them, I wished I could be as free as they would be when they got to be men. "You will be free as soon as you are twenty-one, *but I am a slave for life!* Have not I as good a right to be free as you have?" These words used to trouble them; they would express for me the liveliest sympathy, and console me with the hope that something would occur by which I might be free.

prudence forbids—caution prevents

offence (offense)—mistake

(20) I was now about twelve years old, and the thought of being *a slave for life* began to bear heavily upon my heart. Just about this time, I got hold of a book entitled "The Columbian Orator." Every opportunity I got, I used to read this book. Among much of other interesting matter, I found in it a dialogue between a master and his slave. The slave was represented as having run away from his master three times. The dialogue represented the conversation which took place between them, when the slave was retaken the third time. In this dialogue, the whole argument in behalf of slavery was brought forward by the master, all of which was disposed of by the slave. The slave was made to say some very smart as well as impressive things in reply to his master—things which had the desired though unexpected effect; for the conversation resulted in the voluntary emancipation of the slave on the part of the master.

"The Columbian Orator"—popular 19th-century magazine of speeches used to teach reading and writing

disposed of—answered and declared wrong

(21) In the same book, I met with one of Sheridan's mighty speeches on and in behalf of Catholic emancipation. These were choice documents to me. I read them over and over again with unabated interest. They gave tongue to interesting thoughts of my own soul, which had frequently flashed through my mind, and died away for want of utterance. The moral which I gained from the dialogue was the power of truth over the conscience of even a slaveholder. What I got from Sheridan was a bold denunciation of slavery, and a powerful vindication of human rights. The reading of these documents enabled me to utter my thoughts, and to meet the arguments brought forward to sustain slavery; but while they relieved me of one difficulty, they brought on another even more painful than the one of which I was relieved. The more I read, the more I was led to abhor and detest my enslavers. I could regard them in no other light than a band of successful robbers, who had left their homes, and gone to Africa, and stolen us from our homes, and in a strange land reduced us to slavery. I loathed them as

Sheridan—Richard Brinsley Sheridan, 18th-century Irish writer, orator, and statesman

Catholic emancipation—18th–19th century movement to end restrictions placed against Roman Catholics in the British Isles

choice—significant, important

unabated—continued

gave tongue to—expressed

want of utterance—inability to express

denunciation—a public announcement that something is wrong or evil

vindication—justification, a statement that something is right

to sustain—to argue for

being the meanest as well as the most wicked of men. As I read and contemplated the subject, behold! that very discontentment which Master Hugh had predicted would follow my learning to read had already come, to torment and sting my soul to unutterable anguish. As I writhed under it, I would at times feel that learning to read had been a curse rather than a blessing. It had given me a view of my wretched condition, without the remedy. It opened my eyes to the horrible pit, but to no ladder upon which to get out. In moments of agony, I envied my fellow-slaves for their stupidity. I have often wished myself a beast. I preferred the condition of the meanest reptile to my own. Any thing, no matter what, to get rid of thinking! It was this everlasting thinking of my condition that tormented me. There was no getting rid of it. It was pressed upon me by every object within sight or hearing, animate or inanimate. The silver trump of freedom had roused my soul to eternal wakefulness. Freedom now appeared, to disappear no more forever. It was heard in every sound, and seen in every thing. It was ever present to torment me with a sense of my wretched condition. I saw nothing without seeing it, I heard nothing without hearing it, and felt nothing without feeling it. It looked from every star, it smiled in every calm, breathed in every wind, and moved in every storm.

(22) I often found myself regretting my own existence, and wishing myself dead; and but for the hope of being free, I have no doubt but that I should have killed myself, or done something for which I should have been killed. While in this state of mind, I was eager to hear any one speak of slavery. I was a ready listener. Every little while, I could hear something about the abolitionists. It was some time before I

unutterable—inexpressible
writhed—twisted in pain

the remedy—the solution

silver trump—the hope or dream
roused—awakened

found what the word meant. It was always used in such connections as to make it an interesting word to me. If a slave ran away and succeeded in getting clear, or if a slave killed his master, set fire to a barn, or did any thing very wrong in the mind of a slaveholder, it was spoken of as the fruit of *abolition*. Hearing the word in this connection very often, I set about learning what it meant. The dictionary afforded me little or no help. I found it was "the act of abolishing;" but then I did not know what was to be abolished. Here I was perplexed. I did not dare to ask any one about its meaning, for I was satisfied that it was something they wanted me to know very little about. After a patient waiting, I got one of our city papers, containing an account of the number of petitions from the north, praying for the abolition of slavery in the District of Columbia, and of the slave trade between the States. From this time I understood the words *abolition* and *abolitionist*, and always drew near when that word was spoken, expecting to hear something of importance to myself and fellow-slaves. The light broke in upon me by degrees. I went one day down on the wharf of Mr. Waters; and seeing two Irishmen unloading a scow of stone, I went, unasked, and helped them. When we had finished, one of them came to me and asked me if I were a slave. I told him I was. He asked, "Are ye a slave for life?" I told him that I was. The good Irishman seemed to be deeply affected by the statement. He said to the other that it was a pity so fine a little fellow as myself should be a slave for life. He said it was a shame to hold me. They both advised me to run away to the north; that I should find friends there, and that I should be free. I pretended not to be interested in what they said, and treated them as if I did not understand them; for I feared they might be treacherous. White men have been known to encourage slaves to escape, and then,

getting clear—getting free

the fruit of—the result of

perplexed—confused

satisfied that—knew that, realized that

a scow—a boat or barge

ye—you

to get the reward, catch them and return them to their masters. I was afraid that these seemingly good men might use me so; but I nevertheless remembered their advice, and from that time I resolved to run away. I looked forward to a time at which it would be safe for me to escape. I was too young to think of doing so immediately; besides, I wished to learn how to write, as I might have occasion to write my own **pass**. I consoled myself with the hope that I should one day find a good chance. Meanwhile, I would learn to write.

(23) The idea as to how I might learn to write was suggested to me by being in Durgin and Bailey's ship-yard, and frequently seeing the ship carpenters, after **hewing**, and getting a piece of **timber** ready for use, write on the timber the name of that part of the ship for which it was intended. When a piece of timber was intended for the **larboard** side, it would be marked thus—"L." When a piece was for the **starboard** side, it would be marked thus—"S." A piece for the larboard side **forward**, would be marked thus—"L. F." When a piece was for starboard side forward, it would be marked thus—"S. F." For larboard **aft**, it would be marked thus—"L. A." For starboard aft, it would be marked thus—"S. A." I soon learned the names of these letters, and for what they were intended when placed upon a piece of timber in the ship-yard. I immediately **commenced** copying them, and in a short time was able to make the four letters named. After that, when I met with any boy who I knew could write, I would tell him I could write as well as he. The next word would be, "I don't believe you. Let me see you try it." I would then make the letters which I had been so fortunate as to learn, and ask him to beat that. In this way I got a good many lessons in writing, which it is quite possible I should never

pass—a note giving permission to leave the master's house or plantation

hewing—chopping

timber—wood

larboard—left

starboard—right

forward, aft—front, back

commenced—began

have gotten in any other way. During this time, my copy-book was the board fence, brick wall, and pavement; my pen and ink was a lump of chalk. With these, I learned mainly how to write. I then commenced and continued copying the Italics in Webster's Spelling Book, until I could make them all without looking on the book. By this time, my little Master Thomas had gone to school, and learned how to write, and had written over a number of copy-books. These had been brought home, and shown to some of our near neighbors, and then laid aside. My mistress used to go to class meeting at the Wilk Street meetinghouse every Monday afternoon, and leave me to take care of the house. When left thus, I used to spend the time in writing in the spaces left in Master Thomas's copy-book, copying what he had written. I continued to do this until I could write a hand very similar to that of Master Thomas. Thus, after a long, tedious effort for years, I finally succeeded in learning how to write.

PART 2: ATTEMPT AT ESCAPE (Paragraphs 24–38)

In 1834, when Douglass was about 17 years old, he was sent to work for Mr. William Freeland, owner of a small plantation in the Maryland countryside.

(24) At the close of the year 1834, Mr. Freeland again hired me of my master, for the year 1835. But, by this time, I began to want to live *upon free land* as well as *with Freeland;* and I was no longer content, therefore, to live with him or any other slave-holder. I began, with the commencement of the year, to prepare myself for a final struggle,

hired me of—hired me from

which should decide my fate one way or the other. My tendency was upward. I was fast approaching manhood, and year after year had passed, and I was still a slave. These thoughts roused me—I must do something. I therefore resolved that 1835 should not pass without witnessing an attempt, on my part, to secure my liberty. But I was not willing to cherish this determination alone. My fellow-slaves were dear to me. I was anxious to have them participate with me in this, my life-giving determination. I therefore, though with great prudence, commenced early to ascertain their views and feelings in regard to their condition, and to imbue their minds with thoughts of freedom. I bent myself to devising ways and means for our escape, and meanwhile strove, on all fitting occasions, to impress them with the gross fraud and inhumanity of slavery. I went first to Henry, next to John, then to the others. I found, in them all, warm hearts and noble spirits. They were ready to hear, and ready to act when a feasible plan should be proposed. This was what I wanted. I talked to them of our want of manhood, if we submitted to our enslavement without at least one noble effort to be free. We met often, and consulted frequently, and told our hopes and fears, recounted the difficulties, real and imagined, which we should be called on to meet. At times we were almost disposed to give up, and try to content ourselves with our wretched lot; at others, we were firm and unbending in our determination to go. Whenever we suggested any plan, there was shrinking—the odds were fearful. Our path was beset with the greatest obstacles; and if we succeeded in gaining the end of it, our right to be free was yet questionable—we were yet liable to be returned to bondage. We could see no spot, this side of the ocean, where we could be free. We knew nothing about Canada. Our knowledge of the north did not extend far-

roused—awakened

prudence—caution

to ascertain—to determine, find out

to imbue—to inspire

I bent myself—I applied myself, I worked on

strove—tried hard

fitting—suitable, appropriate

gross—shameful, hateful

want of—lack of

disposed to—ready to

shrinking—a drawing back, a retreat

beset—blocked

ther than New York; and to go there, and be forever harassed with the frightful liability of being returned to slavery—with the certainty of being treated tenfold worse than before—the thought was truly a horrible one, and one which it was not easy to overcome. The case sometimes stood thus: At every gate through which we were to pass, we saw a watchman—at every ferry a guard—on every bridge a sentinel—and in every wood a patrol. We were hemmed in upon every side. Here were the difficulties, real or imagined—the good to be sought, and the evil to be shunned. On the one hand, there stood slavery, a stern reality, glaring frightfully upon us,—its robes already crimsoned with the blood of millions, and even now feasting itself greedily upon our own flesh. On the other hand, away back in the dim distance, under the flickering light of the north star, behind some craggy hill or snow-covered mountain, stood a doubtful freedom—half frozen—beckoning us to come and share its hospitality. This in itself was sometimes enough to stagger us; but when we permitted ourselves to survey the road, we were frequently appalled. Upon either side we saw grim death, assuming the most horrid shapes. Now it was starvation, causing us to eat our own flesh;—now we were contending with the waves, and were drowned;—now we were overtaken, and torn to pieces by the fangs of the terrible bloodhound. We were stung by scorpions, chased by wild beasts, bitten by snakes, and finally, after having nearly reached the desired spot,—after swimming rivers, encountering wild beasts, sleeping in the woods, suffering hunger and nakedness,—we were overtaken by our pursuers, and, in our resistance, we were shot dead upon the spot! I say, this picture sometimes appalled us, and made us

"rather bear those ills we had,
Than fly to others, that we knew not of."

tenfold worse—ten times worse

hemmed in—closed in

there stood slavery . . . its robes already crimsoned—a personification of slavery, standing in bloody robes

the north star—a bright star in the northern sky, marking the direction of freedom from slavery

stagger us—make us hesitate and almost stop

(25) In coming to a fixed determination to run away, we did more than Patrick Henry, when he resolved upon liberty or death. With us it was a doubtful liberty at most, and almost certain death if we failed. For my part, I should prefer death to hopeless bondage.

(26) Sandy, one of our number, gave up the notion, but still encouraged us. Our company then consisted of Henry Harris, John Harris, Henry Bailey, Charles Roberts, and myself. Henry Bailey was my uncle, and belonged to my master. Charles married my aunt: he belonged to my master's father-in-law, Mr. William Hamilton.

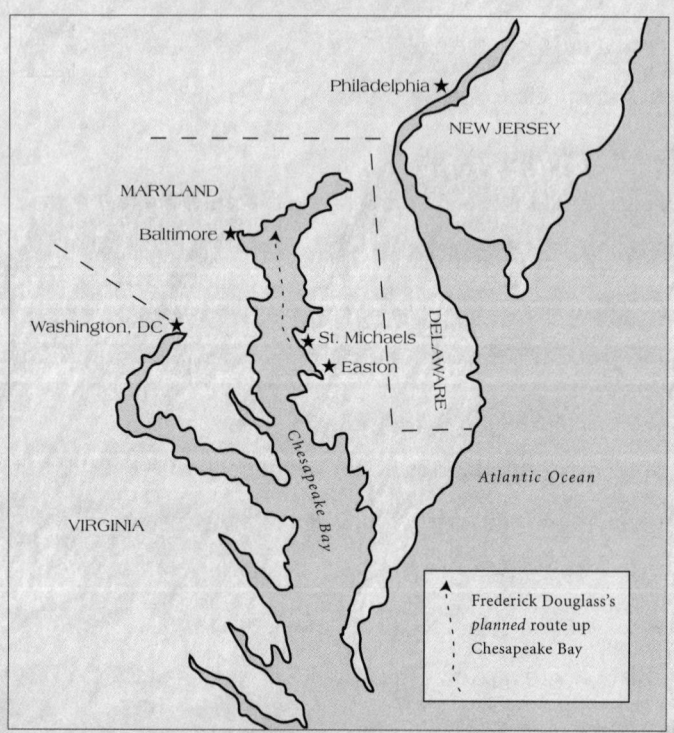

(27) The plan we finally concluded upon was, to get a large canoe belonging to Mr. Hamilton, and upon the Saturday night previous to Easter holidays, paddle directly up the Chesapeake Bay. On our arrival at the head of the bay, a distance of seventy or eighty miles from

where we lived, it was our purpose to turn our canoe adrift, and follow the guidance of the north star till we got beyond the limits of Maryland. Our reason for taking the water route was, that we were less liable to be suspected as runaways; we hoped to be regarded as fishermen; whereas, if we should take the land route, we should be subjected to interruptions of almost every kind. Any one having a white face, and being so disposed, could stop us, and subject us to examination.

liable to be—likely to be

and being so disposed—and if they wanted to

(28) The week before our intended start, I wrote several protections, one for each of us. As well as I can remember, they were in the following words, to wit:

to wit—that is to say, namely

> "This is to certify that I, the undersigned, have given the bearer, my servant, full liberty to go to Baltimore, and spend the Easter holidays. Written with mine own hand, &c., 1835.
>
> "WILLIAM HAMILTON,
>
> "Near St. Michael's, in Talbot county, Maryland."

We were not going to Baltimore; but, in going up the bay, we went toward Baltimore, and these protections were only intended to protect us while on the bay.

protections—passes or notes giving permission to leave the plantation

(29) As the time drew near for our departure, our anxiety became more and more intense. It was truly a matter of life and death with us. The strength of our determination was about to be fully tested. At this time, I was very active in explaining every difficulty, removing every doubt, dispelling every fear, and inspiring all with the firmness indispensable to success in our undertaking; assuring them

that half was gained the instant we made the move; we had talked long enough; we were now ready to move; if not now, we never should be; and if we did not intend to move now, we had as well fold our arms, sit down, and acknowledge ourselves fit only to be slaves. This, none of us were prepared to acknowledge. Every man stood firm; and at our last meeting, we pledged ourselves afresh, in the most solemn manner, that, at the time appointed, we would certainly start in pursuit of freedom. This was in the middle of the week, at the end of which we were to be off. We went, as usual, to our several fields of labor, but with bosoms highly agitated with thoughts of our truly hazardous undertaking. We tried to conceal our feelings as much as possible; and I think we succeeded very well.

(30) After a painful waiting, the Saturday morning, whose night was to witness our departure, came. I hailed it with joy, bring what of sadness it might. Friday night was a sleepless one for me. I probably felt more anxious than the rest, because I was, by common consent, at the head of the whole affair. The responsibility of success or failure lay heavily upon me. The glory of the one, and the confusion of the other, were alike mine. The first two hours of that morning were such as I never experienced before, and hope never to again. Early in the morning, we went, as usual, to the field. We were spreading manure; and all at once, while thus engaged, I was overwhelmed with an indescribable feeling, in the fulness of which I turned to Sandy, who was near by, and said, "We are betrayed!" "Well," said he, "that thought has this moment struck me." We said no more. I was never more certain of any thing.

---

half was gained—we would be halfway toward success

we had as well—we might as well

with bosoms highly agitated—with agitated feelings in our hearts

in the fulness of which—in the strength of which

(31) The horn was blown as usual, and we went up from the field to the house for breakfast. I went for the form, more than for want of any thing to eat that morning. Just as I got to the house, in looking out at the lane gate, I saw four white men, with two colored men. The white men were on horseback, and the colored ones were walking behind, as if tied. I watched them a few moments till they got up to our lane gate. Here they halted, and tied the colored men to the gate-post. I was not yet certain as to what the matter was. In a few moments, in rode Mr. Hamilton, with a speed betokening great excitement. He came to the door, and inquired if Master William was in. He was told he was at the barn. Mr. Hamilton, without dismounting, rode up to the barn with extraordinary speed. In a few moments, he and Mr. Freeland returned to the house. By this time, the three constables rode up, and in great haste dismounted, tied their horses, and met Master William and Mr. Hamilton returning from the barn; and after talking awhile, they all walked up to the kitchen door. There was no one in the kitchen but myself and John. Henry and Sandy were up at the barn. Mr. Freeland put his head in at the door, and called me by name, saying, there were some gentlemen at the door who wished to see me. I stepped to the door, and inquired what they wanted. They at once seized me, and, without giving me any satisfaction, tied me—lashing my hands closely together. I insisted upon knowing what the matter was. They at length said, that they had learned I had been in a "scrape," and that I was to be examined before my master; and if their information proved false, I should not be hurt.

(32) In a few moments, they succeeded in tying John. They then turned to Henry, who had by this time returned, and commanded him

horn—signal for meals

for the form—for form's sake, for appearance's sake

betokening—indicating

constables—policemen

any satisfaction—any answer

a "scrape"—a fight or quarrel

to cross his hands. "I won't!" said Henry, in a firm tone, indicating his readiness to meet the consequences of his refusal. "Won't you?" said Tom Graham, the constable. "No, I won't!" said Henry, in a still stronger tone. With this, two of the constables pulled out their shining pistols, and swore, by their Creator, that they would make him cross his hands or kill him. Each cocked his pistol, and, with fingers on the trigger, walked up to Henry, saying, at the same time, if he did not cross his hands, they would blow his damned heart out. "Shoot me, shoot me!" said Henry; "you can't kill me but once. Shoot, shoot,— and be damned! *I won't be tied!*" This he said in a tone of loud defiance; and at the same time, with a motion as quick as lightning, he with one single stroke dashed the pistols from the hand of each constable. As he did this, all hands fell upon him, and, after beating him some time, they finally overpowered him, and got him tied.

cocked—set ready to shoot

dashed—knocked

all hands—all of the men

(33) During the scuffle, I managed, I know not how, to get my pass out, and, without being discovered, put it into the fire. We were all now tied; and just as we were to leave for Easton jail, Betsy Freeland, mother of William Freeland, came to the door with her hands full of biscuits, and divided them between Henry and John. She then delivered herself of a speech, to the following effect:—addressing herself to me, she said, "*You devil! You yellow devil!* it was you that put it into the heads of Henry and John to run away. But for you, you long-legged mulatto devil! Henry nor John would never have thought of such a thing." I made no reply, and was immediately hurried off towards St. Michael's. Just a moment previous to the scuffle with Henry, Mr. Hamilton suggested the propriety of making a search for the protections which he had understood Frederick had written for himself and

scuffle—fight

yellow—mulatto, mixed race

the rest. But, just at the moment he was about carrying his proposal into effect, his aid was needed in helping to tie Henry; and the excitement attending the scuffle caused them either to forget, or to deem it unsafe, under the circumstances, to search. So we were not yet convicted of the intention to run away.

(34) When we got about half way to St. Michael's, while the constables having us in charge were looking ahead, Henry inquired of me what he should do with his pass. I told him to eat it with his biscuit, and own nothing; and we passed the word around, *"Own nothing;"* and *"Own nothing!"* said we all. Our confidence in each other was unshaken. We were resolved to succeed or fail together, after the calamity had befallen us as much as before. We were now prepared for any thing. We were to be dragged that morning fifteen miles behind horses, and then to be placed in the Easton jail. When we reached St. Michael's, we underwent a sort of examination. We all denied that we ever intended to run away. We did this more to bring out the evidence against us, than from any hope of getting clear of being sold; for, as I have said, we were ready for that. The fact was, we cared but little where we went, so we went together. Our greatest concern was about separation. We dreaded that more than any thing this side of death. We found the evidence against us to be the testimony of one person; our master would not tell who it was; but we came to a unanimous decision among ourselves as to who their informant was. We were sent off to the jail at Easton. When we got there, we were delivered up to the sheriff, Mr. Joseph Graham, and by him placed in jail. Henry, John, and myself, were placed in one room together—Charles, and Henry Bailey, in another. Their object in separating us was to hinder concert.

deem—consider

Own nothing!—Don't confess to anything!

after the calamity had befallen us—after the disaster had happened to us

so we went together—if we could go together

to hinder concert—to make cooperation difficult

(35) We had been in jail scarcely twenty minutes, when a swarm of slave traders, and agents for slave traders, flocked into jail to look at us, and to ascertain if we were for sale. Such a set of beings I never saw before! I felt myself surrounded by so many fiends from perdition. A band of pirates never looked more like their father, the devil. They laughed and grinned over us, saying, "Ah, my boys! we have got you, haven't we?" And after taunting us in various ways, they one by one went into an examination of us, with intent to ascertain our value. They would impudently ask us if we would not like to have them for our masters. We would make them no answer, and leave them to find out as best they could. Then they would curse and swear at us, telling us that they could take the devil out of us in a very little while, if we were only in their hands.

(36) While in jail, we found ourselves in much more comfortable quarters than we expected when we went there. We did not get much to eat, nor that which was very good; but we had a good clean room, from the windows of which we could see what was going on in the street, which was very much better than though we had been placed in one of the dark, damp cells. Upon the whole, we got along very well, so far as the jail and its keeper were concerned. Immediately after the holidays were over, contrary to all our expectations, Mr. Hamilton and Mr. Freeland came up to Easton, and took Charles, the two Henrys, and John, out of jail, and carried them home, leaving me alone. I regarded this separation as a final one. It caused me more pain than any thing else in the whole transaction. I was ready for any thing rather than separation. I supposed that they had consulted together, and had decided that, as I was the whole cause of the inten-

to ascertain—to determine

fiends from perdition—wicked men from damnation

taunting—teasing

than though—than if

tion of the others to run away, it was hard to make the innocent suffer with the guilty; and that they had, therefore, concluded to take the others home, and sell me, as a warning to the others that remained. It is due to the noble Henry to say, he seemed almost as reluctant at leaving the prison as at leaving home to come to the prison. But we knew we should, in all probability, be separated, if we were sold; and since he was in their hands, he concluded to go peaceably home.

(37) I was now left to my fate. I was all alone, and within the walls of a stone prison. But a few days before, and I was full of hope. I expected to have been safe in a land of freedom; but now I was covered with gloom, sunk down to the utmost despair. I thought the possibility of freedom was gone. I was kept in this way about one week, at the end of which, Captain Auld, my master, to my surprise and utter astonishment, came up, and took me out, with the intention of sending me, with a gentleman of his acquaintance, into Alabama. But, from some cause or other, he did not send me to Alabama, but concluded to send me back to Baltimore, to live again with his brother Hugh, and to learn a trade.

(38) Thus, after an absence of three years and one month, I was once more permitted to return to my old home at Baltimore. My master sent me away, because there existed against me a very great prejudice in the community, and he feared I might be killed.

✦ EXERCISES ✦

Comprehension Questions

Answer these questions in paragraph form, using complete sentences in Modern English. Do not copy the answers directly from the reading passage. (See pages 218–21 in the Yellow Pages for a review of paragraph form.)

Part 1: "Childhood" (Paragraph 1–23)

1. What did Douglass know about his family? What else did he want to know?

2. Explain the advantages and disadvantages of a master having children by his own slaves.

3. Explain the statesman of the South's idea about the future of slavery.

4. What did Douglass mean when he wrote that he had the benefit of both Mrs. Auld and Mr. Auld in learning to read?

Part 2: "Attempt at Escape" (Paragraphs 24–38)

1. Why was it so difficult to escape from slavery?

2. What plan did the men make to escape? What went wrong?

3. What was the result of the attempted escape?

Vocabulary Development

Part 1: "Childhood" (Paragraphs 1–23)
Douglass uses these words to explain his feelings about slavery and his wish to escape. Write a paragraph of your own about Douglass, using these words to explain his situation.

- *deprived of* (1)
- *privilege* (1)
- *improper* (1)
- *impertinent* (1)
- *restless* (1)
- *discontented* (14)
- *struggle* (14)
- *desire* (14)
- *determination* (14)

More useful vocabulary words to study and use:

- *inevitable* (3)
- *contend with* (6)
- *to impress* (14), *impressive* (20)
- *vestige* (15)
- *incompatible* (17)
- *abhor, detest, loathe* (21)
- *remedy* (21)

Part 2: "Attempt at Escape" (Paragraphs 24–38)

1. Douglass uses these words to describe the plan he made with his friends to escape from slavery. Write a paragraph of your own about their plan, using these words.

   - *resolved (24)*
   - *prudence (24)*
   - *devise (24)*
   - *feasible (24)*
   - *propose (24)*
   - *consult (24)*
   - *determination (24)*
   - *obstacles (24)*
   - *inspire (29)*
   - *hazardous (29)*

2. Here are more useful vocabulary words to study and learn:

   - *liable* (24, 27), *liability* (24)
   - *defiance* (32)

Quotations and Paraphrases

Write the quotation with an introductory explanation of the source and the content, paying close attention to punctuation. Then paraphrase it in your own words. (See pages 246–52 in the Yellow Pages for help with quotations and paraphrases.)

Part 1: "Childhood" (Paragraphs 1–23)

1. (paragraph 3) "For what this separation is done, I do not know, unless it be to hinder the development of the child's affection toward its mother, and to blunt and destroy the natural affection of the mother for the child. This is the inevitable result."

   _____

   _____

   _____

   _____

2. (paragraph 11) "From my earliest recollection, I date the entertainment of a deep conviction that slavery would not always be able to hold me within its foul embrace . . . ."

   _____

   _____

   _____

   _____

3. Choose your own quotation and follow the same directions.

   _____

   _____

   _____

   _____

Part 2: "Attempt at Escape" (Paragraphs 24–38)

1. (paragraph 24) "Whenever we suggested any plan, there was shrinking—the odds were fearful. Our path was beset with the greatest obstacles; and if we succeeded in gaining the end of it, our right to be free was yet questionable—we were yet liable to be returned to bondage."

2. (paragraph 36) "Mr. Hamilton and Mr. Freeland . . . had decided that, as I was the whole cause of the intention of the others to run away, it was hard to make the innocent suffer with the guilty; and that they had, therefore, concluded to take the others home, and sell me, as a warning to the others that remained."

3. Choose your own quotation and follow the same directions.

Writing Summaries

Write a one-paragraph summary in Modern English without plagiarism. (See pages 253–55 in the Yellow Pages for help in writing a summary.)

1. Summarize the ideas that Douglass learned from "The Columbian Orator" and Sheridan's speech. (paragraphs 20–21)

2. Summarize the dangers that Douglass faced in his attempt to escape slavery. (paragraph 24)

Questions for Discussion and Writing

Discuss your answers to these questions with your classmates. These questions may also be used as essay topics. (See pages 221–24 in the Yellow Pages for a review of essay form.)

1. Compare and contrast the experiences of Benjamin Franklin and Frederick Douglass as they learned to read and write.

2. Analyze the situations in which Douglass was treated well and those in which he was treated cruelly. Does there seem to be any pattern to these treatments?

3. In paragraph 10, Douglass writes that a "kind providence" had always marked his life with favors. What favors do you see in his life?

4. When Frederick Douglass's autobiography was first published, many people were surprised and refused to believe that a slave could write as well as he did. What features of his writing were surprising to you?

5. Douglass writes in paragraph 17 that Mrs. Auld learned that education and slavery are "incompatible with each other." Would Douglas agree? Do you agree?

6. The other point of view: Douglass's first master chose him to go to Baltimore, Mrs. Auld began to teach him to read, and Mr. Freeland decided not to send him to Alabama. What might these people have thought and felt about Douglass and about their roles in his life?

7. Throughout history, ruling classes have had ways to keep their oppressed people ignorant and powerless. Describe the situation of a group of oppressed people that you are familiar with (not American slaves), and explain how they are kept powerless.

8. Imagine that you are a member of a legislature that is discussing a bill that makes it unlawful to teach a slave to read. Write an essay arguing for or against the bill.

9. Read the following quotations defending the institution of slavery:

> "... there has never yet existed a wealthy and civilized society in which one portion of the community did not, in point of fact, live on the labor of the other...." (John C. Calhoun, *Disquisition of Government*, quoted in *Backgrounds of American Literary Thought*, p. 399.)

> "As for the Negro, who can deny that his life in the New World is preferable to that of his former state as a wild and naked heathen in the jungles of Africa? With his physical well-being guaranteed, his place in society securely determined, his spiritual welfare directed by the enlightened precepts of Christianity, is there any reason why the slave should not be the happiest of men?" (*Backgrounds of American Literary Thought*, p. 401)

Choose one or both of these quotations. What arguments can you present against their defenses of slavery?

Scanning for Specific Information

Scanning means looking over a page quickly to find a specific detail rather than beginning at the top of the page and reading every word. Working alone or with one or two other students, use a reference book to find the information to complete the sentences. Try to work quickly to find just the information you need to fill in to complete the exercise. You will probably need to consult more than one source. Make sure that your answers fit the structure of the sentence.

Reference book(s) used _____

_____

READING AND RESEARCHING AMERICA

SLAVERY IN THE UNITED STATES

In the years before the Civil War, there were about _____ million slaves in the southern states. They worked on huge plantations, providing the cheap labor that was necessary to grow crops such as _____. Living conditions for the slaves varied greatly, as Frederick Douglass described: Slaves who worked at skilled jobs, such as _____, were generally treated better than the field hands. However, whether slaves were treated well or cruelly, they had no control over their own lives, being unable to choose their work, their home, or sometimes even their spouse.

Actions to bring slavery to an end occurred on several different fronts in the years before the Civil War. In some cases, the slaves themselves revolted, such as the uprisings led by Denmark Vesey in the year _____ and Nat Turner in the year _____. The Abolitionist Movement began in the northern states at the time of the American Revolution when several states made slavery illegal and religious leaders began to speak out against slavery. In 1831, the abolitionist _____ began to publish a newspaper, called the _____, and in 1833, he founded the American Anti-Slavery Society. Anti-slavery literature became popular, such as the book *Uncle Tom's Cabin* by the author _____ _____. Northern abolitionists organized boycotts of southern goods and encouraged slaves to escape through networks of safe houses called the _____.

SLAVES: FREDERICK DOUGLASS

On a national level, the states were at first equally divided between free and slave states, but as new states began to be formed in the West, it didn't seem possible to maintain this balance. The Missouri Compromise of _____ and the Compromise of _____ were attempts by Congress to maintain the balance as new states entered the union, but it soon became clear that the economies of the western states were not suited to slavery. In 1854, Congress passed the _____, which allowed new states to make their own decisions about slavery; in the same year, the Supreme Court wrote the Dred Scott Decision, declaring that Blacks were not _____ and that laws to limit slavery were _____. These actions worsened already heated feelings and motivated abolitionists to form a new political party, the Republican Party, to fight slavery. The party's candidate in the presidential election of 1856 lost, but its candidate in 1860, _____, won the election, leading to the secession of the southern states and to the beginning of the Civil War in 1861.

Research Topics

Choose one of these topics or another topic that interests you to do one of the research exercises in the Yellow Pages. Share the results of your research with your classmates as you become experts in your own research areas.

slavery	southern states	plantations
Frederick Douglass	William Lloyd Garrison	Harriet Beecher Stowe
Abolitionist Movement	Fugitive Slave Act	Underground Railroad
Abraham Lincoln	Civil War	Emancipation Proclamation
13th and 14th Amendments		

Expansion Activities

1. The jazz, soul, and rock music that we listen to today has its roots in African-American music, including songs that the slaves sang as they worked or relaxed. Many people believe that these songs had hidden meanings about escaping from slavery to a better world. Two examples are "Go Down, Moses," about people who long for freedom from oppression, and "Follow the Dipping Gourd," which may refer to the Big Dipper, the constellation that includes the North Star. Look up slave songs in a book or on the Internet, and read a few songs to see if you can find any hidden meanings.

2. The route that slaves followed to escape to the northern states was called the Underground Railroad. This was not a real railroad but a system of safe houses where slaves could be protected as they made their way north by foot. Look up the Underground Railroad in the library or on the Internet to find out how this secret system worked and how many slaves used it to escape from their masters. Are there any Underground Railroad sites near you and your school?

3. Many people believe that slavery is a phenomenon of the past, something that doesn't exist in our modern world, but in fact, there exist many situations today that could be considered to be slavery. Look up slavery on the Internet to find some examples of modern slavery. In what ways does modern slavery seem similar to and different from the slavery experienced by Frederick Douglass? How are people working to stop slavery today?

4. If you would like to learn more about slavery, watch the popular mini-series *Roots* by Alex Haley or the movie *Glory* about a regiment of African-American soldiers who fought in the Civil War.

NATIVE AMERICANS
Black Elk

(1863–1950)
★ ★ ★

INTRODUCTION

When Americans began to explore the land west of the Mississippi River in the early 1800s, they found several million Native Americans already living there. Some lived as tribes in villages, and others lived a nomadic life to take advantage of seasonal food sources. The American settlers or pioneers considered the land to be undeveloped, underused, and available for them to live on.

At first, some Native American tribes were willing to share the land with the settlers and even to help them find food. However, soon the settlers and the Native Americans came into conflict because the settlers took the most productive lands in terms of food and resources. Recognizing the problem to some extent, the U.S. government signed numerous treaties with the tribes to reserve some land for them, but as more settlers moved west, the treaties were broken repeatedly. As their traditional ways of life broke down, many Native Americans died of starvation or from European diseases such as small pox, to which they had no resistance. The remaining Native Americans were forced to adapt more of a

European way of life, living in towns or on reservations where they were dependent on the government for supplies.

By the late 1800s, only a few tribes were able to live according to their traditional ways. One tribe was the Lakota Sioux of the Upper Plains states, a nomadic tribe highly dependant on herds of buffalo for their food, clothing, and equipment. Black Elk was born just at the time that settlers began to invade the lands of his tribe. One of his first memories was a battle in which his father fought, when the Sioux, led by their chief Red Cloud, attacked and killed several U.S. soldiers in 1866. This battle resulted in a treaty that allowed the Sioux to keep their territory.

However, the treaty was broken in 1874 when gold was discovered in the Black Hills, a sacred area in the middle of Sioux territory, and the pioneers again began to flood into that part of the country. Once more they were defeated: in 1876, the Sioux chief Crazy Horse attacked and killed General George Custer and his troops in a famous battle at Little Bighorn Creek. It was the Native Americans' final victory: With most of the buffalo gone, they could no longer continue their way of life, and many starved or froze to death during the following winter. In the last fight between settlers and Native Americans, a massacre of Sioux at the Battle of Wounded Knee in 1890, the remaining Indians were killed or forced onto the Pine Ridge Reservation in South Dakota.

Black Elk lived the remainder of his life on the reservation. In 1930, when Black Elk was an old man, he met John Neihardt, a poet who was interested in Native American traditions and spiritual life. Because Black Elk had been a medicine man with special powers to see the future and to heal people of illnesses, Neihardt interviewed him and recorded his memories of tribal life. Black Elk told Neihardt his story, including his visions of the future that he had never told anyone else. Neihardt published the story in the book *Black Elk Speaks*, now a classic account of Sioux Indian life and religion.

Pre-Reading Questions

Everyone is familiar with the way Native Americans have been shown in the movies, but what do you really know about them? Before you read, think about the Native Americans: What were the different tribes like? How did they live? Why did they come into conflict with the white settlers?

✦ READING PASSAGE ✦

BLACK ELK:
From *Black Elk Speaks:*
Being the Life Story of a Holy Man of the Oglala Sioux,
as Told through John G. Neihardt (Flaming Rainbow)

Black Elk uses some words from his language, such as *Wasichus* for Americans or white men, and words that are probably translated directly from his language, such as *yellow metal* for gold. When you write, use conventional English vocabulary and expressions.

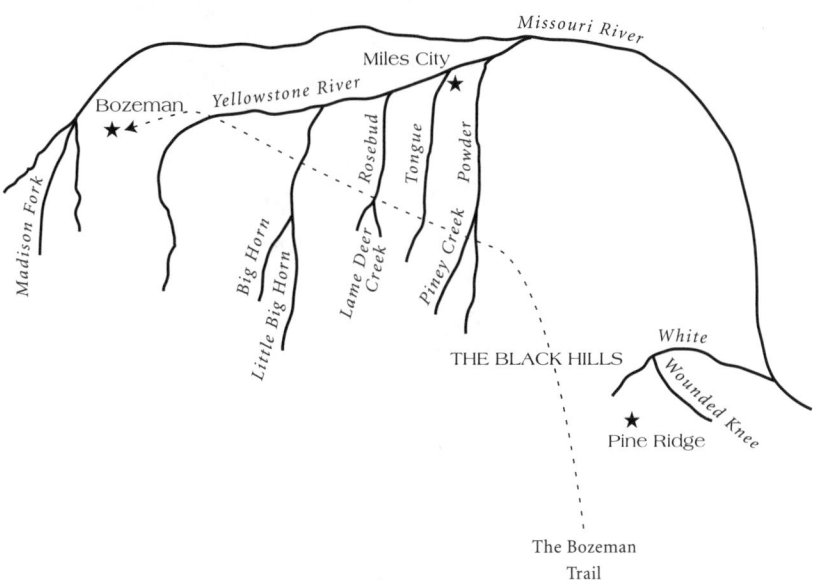

This map shows the area where Black Elk lived his life and where Nannie T. Alderson and her husband built their cattle ranch in the 1880s (see Chapter 4). Most of this area is now in the state of Montana; the Pine Ridge Reservation is in South Dakota. The Bozeman Trail began on the Platte River; today Interstate Highway 90 follows some of the route of this trail.

READING AND RESEARCHING AMERICA

PART 1: EARLY BOYHOOD (Paragraphs 1–26)

(1) I am a Lakota of the Ogalala band. My father's name was Black Elk, and his father before him bore the name, and the father of his father, so that I am the fourth to bear it. He was a medicine man and so were several of his brothers. Also, he and the great Crazy Horse's father were cousins, having the same grandfather. My mother's name was White Cow Sees; her father was called Refuse-to-Go, and her mother, Plenty Eagle Feathers. I can remember my mother's mother and her father. My father's father was killed by the Pawnees when I was too little to know, and his mother, Red Eagle Woman, died soon after.

medicine man—a man with supernatural powers

(2) I was born in the Moon of the Popping Trees (December) on the Little Powder River in the Winter When the Four Crows Were Killed (1863), and I was three years old when my father's right leg was broken in the Battle of the Hundred Slain. From that wound he limped until the day he died, which was about the time when Big Foot's band was butchered on Wounded Knee (1890). He is buried here in these hills.

Four Crows—a crow is a large black bird, but here Black Elk probably refers to the Crows, another Indian tribe

Battle of the Hundred Slain—the Fetterman Fight in 1866

Wounded Knee—the Battle of Wounded Knee

(3) I can remember that Winter of the Hundred Slain as a man may remember some bad dream he dreamed when he was little, but I can

not tell just how much I heard when I was bigger and how much I understood when I was little. It is like some fearful thing in a fog, for it was a time when everything seemed troubled and afraid.

(4) I had never seen a Wasichu then, and did not know what one looked like; but every one was saying that the Wasichus were coming and that they were going to take our country and rub us all out and that we should all have to die fighting. It was the Wasichus who got rubbed out in that battle, and all the people were talking about it for a long while; but a hundred Wasichus was not much if there were others and others without number where those came from.

Wasichu—Lakota word for a white man

rub out—kill

(5) I remember once that I asked my grandfather about this. I said: "When the scouts come back from seeing the prairie full of bison somewhere, the people say the Wasichus are coming; and when strange men are coming to kill us all, they say the Wasichus are coming. What does it mean?" And he said, "That they are many."

(6) When I was older, I learned what the fighting was about that winter and the next summer. Up on the Madison Fork the Wasichus had found much of the yellow metal that they worship and that makes them crazy, and they wanted to have a road up through our country to the place where the yellow metal was; but my people did not want the road. It would scare the bison and make them go away, and it would also let the other Wasichus come in like a river. They told us that they wanted only to use a little land, as much as a wagon would take between the wheels; but our people knew better. And when you look about now, you can see what it was they wanted.

yellow metal—gold

a road—the Bozeman Trail

(7) Once we were happy in our own country and we were seldom hungry, for then the two-leggeds and the four-leggeds lived together like relatives, and there was plenty for them and for us. But the Wasichus came, and they have made little islands for us and other little islands for the four-leggeds, and always these islands are becoming smaller, for around them surges the gnawing flood of the Wasichu; and it is dirty with lies and greed.

two-leggeds and four-leggeds—people and animals

islands—separate isolated areas

surges the gnawing flood—rushes a greedy mass of people

(8) A long time ago my father told me what his father told him, that there was once a Lakota holy man, called Drinks Water, who dreamed what was to be; and this was long before the coming of the Wasichus. He dreamed that the four-leggeds were going back into the earth and that a strange race had woven a spider's web all around the Lakotas. And he said: "When this happens, you shall live in square grey houses, in a barren land, and beside those square grey houses you shall starve." They say he went back to Mother Earth soon after he saw this vision, and it was sorrow that killed him. You can look about you now and see that he meant these dirt-roofed houses we are living in, and that all the rest was true. Sometimes dreams are wiser than waking.

(9) And so when the soldiers came and built themselves a town of logs there on Piney Fork of the Powder, my people knew they meant to have their road and take our country and maybe kill us all when they were strong enough. Crazy Horse was only about 19 years old then, and Red Cloud was still our great chief. In the Moon of the Changing Season (October) he called together all the scattered bands of the Lakota for a big council on the Powder River, and when we went on the warpath against the soldiers, a horseback could ride

a horseback—a man riding a horse

through our villages from sunrise until the day was above his head, so far did our camp stretch along the valley of the river; for many of our friends, the Shyela and the Blue Clouds, had come to help us fight.

Shyela and Blue Clouds— Cheyennes and Arapahoes

(10) And it was about when the bitten moon was delayed (last quarter) in the Time of the Popping Trees when the hundred were rubbed out. My friend, Fire Thunder here, who is older than I, was in that fight and he can tell you how it was.

Fire Thunder Speaks:

(11) I was 16 years old when this happened, and after the big council on the Powder we had moved over to the Tongue River where we were camping at the mouth of Peno Creek. There were many of us there. Red Cloud was over all of us, but the chief of our band was Big Road. We started out on horseback just about sunrise, riding up the creek toward the soldiers' town on the Piney, for we were going to attack it. The sun was about half way up when we stopped at the place where the Wasichu's road came down a steep, narrow ridge and crossed the creek. It was a good place to fight, so we sent some men ahead to coax the soldiers out. While they were gone, we divided into two parts and hid in the gullies on both sides of the ridge and waited. After a long while we heard a shot up over the hill, and we knew the soldiers were coming. So we held the noses of our ponies that they might not whinny at the soldiers' horses. Soon we saw our men coming back, and some of them were walking and leading their horses, so that the soldiers would think they were worn out. Then the men we had sent ahead came running down the road between us, and the soldiers on horseback followed, shooting. When they came to the flat at the bottom of the hill, the fighting began all at once. I had a sorrel

whinny—neigh (the sound a horse makes)

horse, and just as I was going to get on him, the soldiers turned around and began to fight their way back up the hill. I had a six-shooter that I had traded for, and also a bow and arrows. When the soldiers started back, I held my sorrel with one hand and began killing them with the six-shooter, for they came close to me. There were many bullets, but there were more arrows—so many that it was like a cloud of grasshoppers all above and around the soldiers; and our people, shooting across, hit each other. The soldiers were falling all the while they were fighting back up the hill, and their horses got loose. Many of our people chased the horses, but I was not after horses; I was after Wasichus. When the soldiers got on top, there were not many of them left and they had no place to hide. They were fighting hard. We were told to crawl up on them, and we did. When we were close, someone yelled: "Let us go! This is a good day to die. Think of the helpless ones at home!" Then we all cried, "Hoka hey!" and rushed at them. I was young then and quick on my feet, and I was one of the first to get in among the soldiers. They got up and fought very hard until not one of them was alive. They had a dog with them, and he started back up the road for the soldiers' town, howling as he ran. He was the only one left. I did not shoot at him because he looked too sweet; but many did shoot, and he died full of arrows. So there was nobody left of the soldiers. Dead men and horses and wounded Indians were scattered all the way up the hill, and their blood was frozen, for a storm had come up and it was very cold and getting colder all the time. We left all the dead lying there, for the ground was solid, and we picked up our wounded and started back; but we lost most of them before we reached our camp at the mouth of the Peno. There was a big blizzard that night; and some of the

a six-shooter—a revolver from which six shots can be fired without reloading

"Hoka hey!"—a battle cry

wounded who did not die on the way, died after we got home. This was the time when Black Elk's father had his leg broken.

Black Elk Continues:

(12) I am quite sure that I remember the time when my father came home with a broken leg that he got from killing so many Wasichus, and it seems that I can remember all about the battle too, but I think I could not. It must be the fear that I remember most. All this time I was not allowed to play very far away from our tepee, and my mother would say, "If you are not good the Wasichus will get you."

tepee—Indian tent, made of poles and animal skins

(13) We must have broken camp at the mouth of the Peno soon after the battle, for I can remember my father lying on a pony drag with bison robes all around him, like a baby, and my mother riding the pony. The snow was deep and it was very cold, and I remember sitting in another pony drag beside my father and mother, all wrapped in fur. We were going away from where the soldiers were, and I do not know where we went, but it was west.

pony drag—a frame pulled by a horse, made of poles and animal skins

(14) It was a hungry winter, for the deep snow made it hard to find the elk; and also many of the people went snowblind. We wandered a long time, and some of the bands got lost from each other. Then at last we were camping in the woods beside a creek somewhere, and the hunters came back with meat.

snowblind—temporary blindness caused by the glare of the sun on snow

(15) I think it was the same winter when a medicine man, by the name of Creeping, went around among the people curing snowblinds. He would put snow upon their eyes, and after he had sung a certain sacred song that he had heard in a dream, he would blow on the backs of their heads and they would see again, I have heard. It was

about the dragonfly that he sang, for that was where he got his power, they say.

(16) When it was summer again we were camping on the Rosebud, and I did not feel so much afraid, because the Wasichus seemed farther away and there was peace in the valley and there was plenty of meat. But all the boys from five or six years up were playing war. The little boys would gather together from the different bands of the tribe and fight each other with mud balls that they threw with willow sticks. And the big boys played the game called Throwing-Them-Off-Their-Horses, which is a battle all but the killing; and sometimes they got hurt. The horsebacks from the different bands would line up and charge upon each other, yelling; and when the ponies came together on the run, they would rear and flounder and scream in a big dust, and the riders would seize each other, wrestling until one side had lost all its men, for those who fell upon the ground were counted dead.

(17) When I was older, I, too, often played this game. We were always naked when we played it, just as warriors are when they go into battle if it is not too cold, because they are swifter without clothes. Once I fell off on my back right in the middle of a bed of prickly pears, and it took my mother a long while to pick all the stickers out of me. I was still too little to play war that summer, but I can remember watching the other boys, and I thought that when we all grew up and were big together, maybe we could kill all the Wasichus or drive them far away from our country.

(18) It was in the Moon When the Cherries Turn Black (August) that all the people were talking again about a battle, and our warriors

prickly pears—a pear-shaped cactus covered with spines

came back with many wounded. It was The Attacking of the Wagons, and it made me afraid again, for we did not win that battle as we did the other one, and there was much mourning for the dead. Fire Thunder was in that fight too, and he can tell you how it was that day.

Fire Thunder Speaks:

(19) It was very bad. There is a wide flat prairie with hills around it, and in the middle of this the Wasichus had put the boxes of their wagons in a circle, so that they could keep their mules there at night. There were not many Wasichus, but they were lying behind the boxes and they shot faster than they ever shot at us before. We thought it was some new medicine of great power that they had, for they shot so fast that it was like tearing a blanket. Afterwards I learned that it was because they had new guns that they loaded from behind, and this was the first time they used these guns. We came on after sunrise. There were many, many of us, and we meant to ride right over them and rub them out. But our ponies were afraid of the ring of fire the guns of the Wasichus made, and would not go over. Our women were watching us from the hills and we could hear them singing and mourning whenever the shooting stopped. We tried hard, but we could not do it, and there were dead warriors and horses piled all around the boxes and scattered over the plain. Then we left our horses in a gulch and charged on foot, but it was like green grass withering in a fire. So we picked up our wounded and went away. I do not know how many of our people were killed, but there were very many. It was bad.

The Attacking of the Wagons—the Wagon Box Fight of 1867

medicine of great power—a powerful advantage

READING AND RESEARCHING AMERICA

Black Elk Continues:

(20) I do not remember where we camped that winter but it must have been a time of peace and of plenty to eat.

Standing Bear Speaks:

(21) I am four years older than Black Elk, and he and I have been good friends since boyhood. I know it was on the Powder that we camped where there were many cottonwood trees. Ponies like to eat the bark of these trees and it is good for them. That was the winter when High Shirt's mother was killed by a big tree that fell on her tepee. It was a very windy night and there were noises that 'woke me, and then I heard an old woman had been killed, and it was High Shirt's mother.

Black Elk Continues:

(22) I was four years old then, and I think it must have been the next summer that I first heard the voices. It was a happy summer and nothing was afraid, because in the Moon When the Ponies Shed (May) word came from the Wasichus that there would be peace and that they would not use the road any more and that all the soldiers would go away. The soldiers did go away and their towns were torn down; and in the Moon of Falling Leaves (November), they made a treaty with Red Cloud that said our country would be ours as long as grass should grow and water flow. You can see that it is not the grass and the water that have been forgotten.

(23) Maybe it was not this summer when I first heard the voices, but I think it was, because I know it was before I played with bows and arrows or rode a horse, and I was out playing alone when I heard

them. It was like somebody calling me, and I thought it was my mother, but there was nobody there. This happened more than once, and always made me afraid, so that I ran home.

(24) It was when I was five years old that my Grandfather made me a bow and some arrows. The grass was young and I was horseback. A thunder storm was coming from where the sun goes down, and just as I was riding into the woods along a creek, there was a kingbird sitting on a limb. This was not a dream, it happened. And I was going to shoot at the kingbird with the bow my Grandfather made, when the bird spoke and said: "The clouds all over are one-sided." Perhaps it meant that all the clouds were looking at me. And then it said: "Listen! A voice is calling you!" Then I looked up at the clouds, and two men were coming there, headfirst like arrows slanting down; and as they came, they sang a sacred song and the thunder was like drumming. I will sing it for you. The song and the drumming were like this:

> "Behold, a sacred voice is calling you;
> All over the sky a sacred voice is calling."

horseback—riding horses

(25) I sat there gazing at them, and they were coming from the place where the giant lives (north). But when they were very close to me, they wheeled about toward where the sun goes down, and suddenly they were geese. Then they were gone, and the rain came with a big wind and a roaring.

wheeled—turned around suddenly

(26) I did not tell this vision to any one. I liked to think about it, but I was afraid to tell.

Black Elk continued to have visions, including a long powerful vision when he was nine years old and was sick and in a trance for 12 days. After a slow recovery from this illness, he seemed somehow different to other people and impressed them with his special insight and sensitivity.

PART 2: WASICHUS IN THE HILLS (Paragraphs 27–55)

(27) It was the next summer, when I was 11 years old (1874), that the first sign of a new trouble came to us. Our band had been camping on the Split-Toe Creek in the Black Hills, and from there we moved to Spring Creek, then to Rapid Creek where it comes out into the prairie. That evening just before sunset, a big thunder cloud came up from the west, and just before the wind struck, there were clouds of split-tail swallows flying all around above us. It was like a part of my vision, and it made me feel queer. The boys tried to hit the swallows with stones and it hurt me to see them doing this, but I could not tell

swallows—swift graceful birds

them. I got a stone and acted as though I were going to throw, but I did not. The swallows seemed holy. Nobody hit one, and when I thought about this I knew that of course they could not.

(28) The next day some of the people were building a sweat tepee for a medicine man by the name of Chips, who was going to perform a ceremony and had to be purified first. They say he was the first man who made a sacred ornament for our great chief, Crazy Horse. While they were heating the stones for the sweat tepee, some boys asked me to go with them and shoot squirrels. We went out, and when I was about to shoot at one, I felt very uneasy all at once. So I sat down, feeling queer, and wondered about it. While I sat there I heard a voice that said: "Go at once! Go home!" I told the boys we must go home at once, and we all hurried. When we got back, everyone was excited, breaking camp, catching the ponies and loading the drags; and I heard that while Chips was in the sweat tepee a voice had told him that the band must flee at once because something was going to happen there.

(29) It was nearly sundown when we started, and we fled all that night on the back trail toward Spring Creek, then down that creek to the south fork of the Good River. I rode most of the night in a pony drag because I got too sleepy to stay on a horse. We camped at Good River in the morning, but we stayed only long enough to eat. Then we fled again, upstream, all day long until we reached the mouth of Horse Creek. We were going to stay there, but scouts came to us and said that many soldiers had come into the Black Hills; and that was what Chips saw while he was in the sweat tepee. So we hurried on in the night towards Smoky Earth River (the White), and when we got there, I woke up and it was daybreak. We camped a while to eat, and

a sweat tepee—a tepee used as a sweat house

then went up the Smoky Earth, two camps, to Robinson, for we were afraid of the soldiers up there.

(30) Afterward I learned that it was Pahuska who had led his soldiers into the Black Hills that summer to see what he could find. He had no right to go in there, because all that country was ours. Also the Wasichus had made a treaty with Red Cloud (1868) that said it would be ours as long as grass should grow and water flow. Later I learned that Pahuska had found there much of the yellow metal that makes the Wasichus crazy; and that is what made the bad trouble, just as it did before, when the hundred were rubbed out.

Pahuska ("Long Hair")—General George Custer of the U.S. Army

(31) Our people knew there was yellow metal in little chunks up there; but they did not bother with it, because it was not good for anything.

(32) We stayed all winter at the Soldiers' Town, and all the while the bad trouble was coming fast; for in the fall we heard that some Wasichus had come from the Missouri River to dig in the Black Hills for the yellow metal, because Pahuska had told about it with a voice that went everywhere. Later he got rubbed out for doing that.

(33) The people talked about this all winter. Crazy Horse was in the Powder River country and Sitting Bull was somewhere north of the Hills. Our people at the Soldiers' Town thought we ought to get together and do something. Red Cloud's people said that the soldiers had gone in there to keep the diggers out, but we, who were only visiting, did not believe it. We called Red Cloud's people "Hangs-Around-The-Fort," and our people said they were standing up for the Wasichus, and if we did not do something we should lose the Black Hills.

Soldiers' Town—settlement around a fort of the U.S. Army

(34) In the spring when I was twelve years old (1875), more soldiers with many wagons came up from the Soldiers' Town at the mouth of the Laramie River and went into the Hills.

(35) There was much talk all summer, and in the Moon of Making Fat (June) there was a sun dance in there at the Soldiers' Town to give the people strength, but not many took part; maybe because everybody was so excited talking about the Black Hills. I remember two men who danced together. One had lost a leg in the Battle of the Hundred Slain and one had lost an eye in the Attacking of the Wagons, so they had only three eyes and three legs between them to dance with. We boys went down to the creek while they were sun dancing and got some elm leaves that we chewed up and threw on the dancers while they were all dressed up and trying to look their best. We did this even to some of the older people, and nobody got angry, because everybody was supposed to be in a good humor and to show their endurance in every kind of way; so they had to stand teasing too.

(36) In the Moon When the Calves Grow Hair (September) there was a big council with the Wasichus on the Smoky Earth River at the mouth of White Clay Creek. I can remember the council, but I did not understand much of it then. Many of the Lakotas were there, also Shyelas and Blue Clouds; but Crazy Horse and Sitting Bull stayed away. In the middle of the circle there was a shade made of canvas. Under this the councilors sat and talked and all around them there was a crowd of people on foot and horseback. They talked and talked for days, but it was just like wind blowing in the end. I asked my father what they were talking about in there, and he told me that the Grandfather at Washington wanted to lease the Black Hills so that the

the Grandfather at Washington—the president of the United States in Washington, DC

Wasichus could dig yellow metal, and that the chief of soldiers had said if we did not do this, the Black Hills would be just like melting snow held in our hands, because the Wasichus would take that country anyway.

(37) It made me sad to hear this. It was such a good place to play and the people were always happy in that country. Also I thought of my vision, and of how the spirits took me there to the center of the world.

(38) After the council we heard that creeks of Wasichus were flowing into the Hills and becoming rivers, and that they were already making towns up there. It looked like bad trouble coming, so our band broke up and started out to join Crazy Horse on Powder River. We camped on Horsehead Creek, then on the War Bonnet after we crossed the old Wasichus' road that made the trouble that time when the hundred were rubbed out. Grass was growing on it. Then we camped at Sage Creek, then on the Beaver, then on Driftwood Creek, and came again to the Plain of Pine Trees at the edge of the Hills.

Wasichus' road—the Bozeman Trail

(39) The nights were sharp now, but the days were clear and still; and while we were camping there I went up into the Hills alone and sat a long while under a tree. I thought maybe my vision would come back and tell me how I could save that country for my people, but I could not see anything clear.

(40) Afterwhile we came to the village on Powder River and went into camp at the downstream end. I was anxious to see my cousin, Crazy Horse, again, for now that it began to look like bad trouble coming, everybody talked about him more than ever and he seemed greater than before. Also I was getting older.

(41) Of course I had seen him now and then ever since I could remember, and had heard stories of the brave things he did. I remember the story of how he and his brother were out alone on horseback, and a big band of Crows attacked them, so that they had to run. And while they were riding hard, with all those Crows after them, Crazy Horse heard his brother call out; and when he looked back, his brother's horse was down and the Crows were almost on him. And they told how Crazy Horse charged back right into the Crows and fought them back with only a bow and arrows, then took his brother up behind him and got away. It was his sacred power that made the Crows afraid of him when he charged. And the people told stories of when he was a boy and used to be around with the older Hump all the time. Hump was not young anymore at the time, and he was a very great warrior, maybe the greatest we ever had until then. They say people used to wonder at the boy and the old man always being together; but I think Hump knew Crazy Horse would be a great man and wanted to teach him everything.

Crows—another Indian tribe, the traditional enemies of the Sioux

(42) Crazy Horse's father was my father's cousin, and there were no chiefs in our family before Crazy Horse; but there were holy men; and he became a chief because of the power he got in a vision when he was a boy. When I was a man, my father told me something about that vision. Of course he did not know all of it; but he said that Crazy Horse dreamed and went into the world where there is nothing but the spirits of all things. That is the real world that is behind this one, and everything we see here is something like a shadow from that world. He was on his horse in that world, and the horse and himself on it and the trees and the grass and the stones and everything were

made of spirit, and nothing was hard, and everything seemed to float. His horse was standing still there, and yet it danced around like a horse made only of shadow, and that is how he got his name, which does not mean that his horse was crazy or wild, but that in his vision it danced around in that queer way.

(43) It was this vision that gave him his great power, for when he went into a fight, he had only to think of that world to be in it again, so that he could go through anything and not be hurt. Until he was murdered by the Wasichus at the Soldiers' Town on White River, he was wounded only twice, once by accident and both times by some one of his own people when he was not expecting trouble and was not thinking; never by an enemy. He was fifteen years old when he was wounded by accident; and the other time was when he was a young man and another man was jealous of him because the man's wife liked Crazy Horse.

(44) They used to say too that he carried a sacred stone with him, like the one he had seen in some vision, and that when he was in danger, the stone always got very heavy and protected him somehow. That, they used to say, was the reason no horse he ever rode lasted very long. I do not know about this; maybe people only thought it; but it is a fact that he never kept one horse long. They wore out. I think it was only the power of his great vision that made him great.

(45) Now and then he would notice me and speak to me before this; and sometimes he would have the crier call me into his tepee to eat with him. Then he would say things to tease me, but I would not say anything back, because I think I was a little afraid of him. I was not

the crier—a messenger for the tribe

afraid that he would hurt me; I was just afraid. Everybody felt that way about him, for he was a queer man and would go about the village without noticing people or saying anything. In his own tepee he would joke, and when he was on the warpath with a small party, he would joke to make his warriors feel good. But around the village he hardly ever noticed anybody except little children. All the Lakotas like to dance and sing; but he never joined a dance, and they say nobody ever heard him sing. But everybody liked him, and they would do anything he wanted or go anywhere he said. He was a small man among the Lakotas and he was slender and had a thin face and his eyes looked through things and he always seemed to be thinking hard about something. He never wanted to have many things for himself, and did not have many ponies like a chief. They say that when game was scarce and the people were hungry, he would not eat at all. He was a queer man. Maybe he was always part way into that world of his vision. He was a very great man, and I think if the Wasichus had not murdered him down there, maybe we should still have the Black Hills and be happy. They could not have killed him in battle. They had to lie and murder him. And he was only thirty years old when he died.

(46) One day after we camped there on Powder River, I went upstream to see him again, but his tepee was empty and he was gone somewhere, maybe with a war-party against the Crows, for we were close to them now and had to look out for them all the time. Later I did see him. He put his arm across my shoulder and took me into his tepee and we sat down together. I do not remember what he said, but I know he did not say much, and he did not tease me. Maybe he was thinking about the trouble coming.

on the warpath—in a state of preparation for war

(47) During the winter, runners came from the Wasichus and told us we must come into the Soldiers' Town right away or there would be bad trouble. But it was foolish to say that, because it was very cold and many of our people and ponies would have died in the snow. Also, we were in our own country and doing no harm.

(48) Late in the Moon of the Dark Red Calves (February) there was a big thaw, and our little band started for the Soldiers' Town, but it was very cold again before we got there. Crazy Horse stayed with about a hundred tepees on Powder, and in the middle of the Moon of the Snowblind (March) something bad happened there. It was just daybreak. There was a blizzard and it was very cold. The people were sleeping. Suddenly there were many shots and horses galloping through the village. It was the cavalry of the Wasichus, and they were yelling and shooting and riding their horses against the tepees. All the people rushed out and ran, because they were not awake yet and they were frightened. The soldiers killed as many women and children and men as they could while the people were running toward a bluff. Then they set fire to some of the tepees and knocked the others down. But when the people were on the side of the bluff, Crazy Horse said something, and all the warriors began singing the death song and charged back upon the soldiers; and the soldiers ran, driving many of the people's ponies ahead of them. Crazy Horse followed them all that day with a band of warriors, and that night he took all the stolen ponies away from them, and some of their own horses, and brought them all back to the village.

cavalry—soldiers on horseback

a bluff—a broad cliff

(49) These people were in their own country and were doing no harm. They only wanted to be let alone. We did not hear of this until

quite awhile afterward; but at the Soldiers' Town we heard enough to make us paint our faces black.

paint our faces black—a way to indicate death and destruction

(50) We stayed at the Soldiers' Town this time until the grass was good in the Moon When the Ponies Shed (May). Then my father told me we were going back to Crazy Horse and that we were going to have to fight from then on, because there was no other way to keep our country. He said that Red Cloud was a cheap man and wanted to sell the Black Hills to the Wasichus; that Spotted Tail and other chiefs were cheap men too, and that the Hang-Around-the-Fort people were all cheap and would stand up for the Wasichus. My aunt, who was living at the Soldiers' Town, must have felt the way we did, because when we were breaking camp she gave me a six-shooter like the soldiers had, and told me I was a man now. I was thirteen years old and not very big for my age, but I thought I should have to be a man anyway. We boys had practiced endurance, and we were all good riders, and I could shoot straight with either a bow or a gun.

(51) We were a small band, and we started in the night and traveled fast. Before we got to War Bonnet Creek, some Shyelas (Cheyennes) joined us, because their hearts were bad like ours and they were going to the same place. Later I learned that many small bands were doing the same thing and coming together from everywhere.

(52) Just after we camped on the War Bonnet, our scouts saw a wagon train of the Wasichus coming up the old road that caused the trouble before. They had oxen hitched to their wagons and they were part of the river of Wasichus that was running into the Black Hills. They shot at our scouts, and we decided we would attack them.

When the war party was getting ready, I made up my mind that, small as I was, I might as well die there, and if I did, maybe I'd be known. I told Jumping Horse, a boy about my age, that I was going along to die, and he said he would too. So we went, and so did Crab and some other boys.

(53) When the Wasichus saw us coming, they put their wagons in a circle and got inside with their oxen. We rode around and around them in a wide circle that kept getting narrower. That is the best way to fight, because it is hard to hit ponies running fast in a circle. And sometimes there would be two circles, one inside the other, going fast in opposite directions, which made us still harder to hit. The cavalry of the Wasichus did not know how to fight. They kept together, and when they came on, you could hardly miss them. We kept apart in the circle. While we were riding around the wagons, we were hanging low on the outside of the ponies and shooting under their necks. This was not easy to do, even when your legs were long, and mine were not yet very long. But I stuck tight and shot with the six-shooter my aunt gave me. Before we started the attack I was afraid, but Big Man told us we were brave boys, and I soon got over being frightened. The Wasichus shot fast at us from behind the wagons, and I could hear bullets whizzing, but they did not hit any of us. I kept thinking of my vision, and maybe that helped. I do not know whether we killed any Wasichus or not. We rode around several times, and once we got close, but there were not many of us and we could not get at the Wasichus behind their wagons; so we went away. This was my first fight. When we were going back to camp, some Shyela warriors told us we were very brave boys, and that we were going to have plenty of fighting.

(54) We were traveling very fast now, for we were in danger and wanted to get back to Crazy Horse. He had moved over west to the Rosebud River, and the people were gathering there. As we traveled, we met other little bands all going to the same place, until there were a good many of us all mixed up before we got there. Red Cloud's son was with us, but Red Cloud stayed at Soldiers' Town.

(55) When we came to the ridge on this side of the Rosebud River, we could see the valley full of tepees, and the ponies could not be counted. Many, many people were there—Ogalalas, Hunkpapas, Minneconjous, Sans Arcs, Black Feet, Brules, Santees, and Yanktonais; also many Shyelas and Blue Clouds had come to fight with us. The village was long, and you could not see all the camps with one look. The scouts came out to meet us and bring us in, and everybody rejoiced that we had come. Great men were there: Crazy Horse and Big Road of the Ogalalas; Sitting Bull and Gall and Black Moon and Crow King of the Hunkpapas; Spotted Eagle of the Sans Arcs; the younger Hump and Fast Bull of the Minneconjous; Dull Knife and Ice Bear of the Shyelas; Inkpaduta with the Santees and Yanktonais. Great men were there with all those people and horses. Hetchetu aloh!

Hetchetu aloh!—It is so indeed!

Together the great chiefs of these tribes defeated General Custer at the Battle of Little Bighorn a few weeks later.

⇾ EXERCISES ⇽

Comprehension Questions

Answer these questions in paragraph form, using complete sentences in Modern English. Do not copy the answers directly from the reading passage. (See pages 218–21 in the Yellow Pages for a review of paragraph form.)

Part 1: "Early Boyhood" (Paragraphs 1–26)

1. What kinds of names did the Indians give to people, seasons, places, and events?

2. What did the holy man dream about the future of the Native Americans?

3. Describe the kinds of games that the Native American boys played.

Part 2: "Wasichus in the Hills" (Paragraphs 27–55)

1. Describe the events and visions that warned the Native Americans of trouble.

2. How was Crazy Horse different from the other Indians?

3. Why did Black Elk's people decide to leave the Soldiers' Town and join Crazy Horse again?

4. Describe the two attacks—the soldiers' attack on the Indian camp and the Indians' attack on the wagon train.

Vocabulary Development

Part 1: "Early Boyhood" (Paragraphs 1–26) and Part 2: "Wasichus in the Hills" (Paragraphs 27–55)

1. Black Elk describes the natural landscape of his homeland using the following words. Use these words to complete the labels on the drawing below.

   hills (2)   *ridge* (11)
   prairie (5)   *gully* or *gulch* (11, 19)
   fork (6)   *bluff* (48)
   creek (11)   *valley* (55)

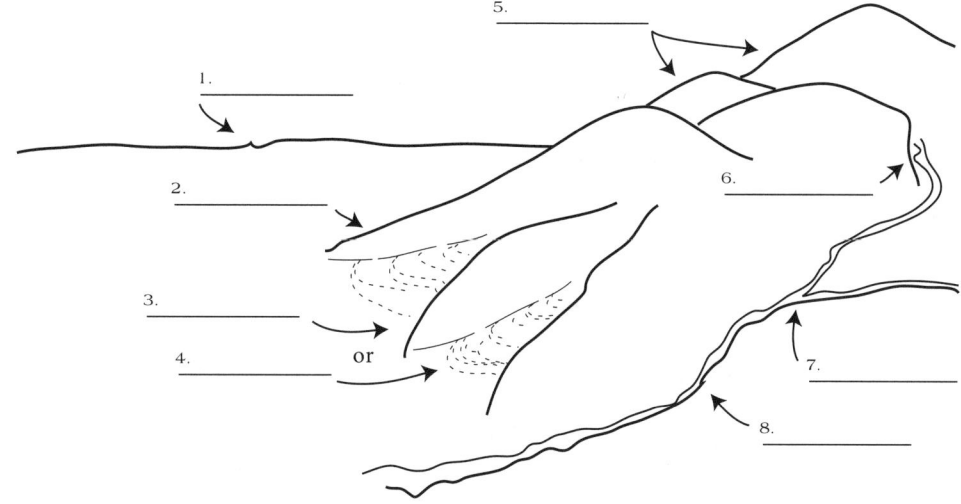

2. In Black Elk's language, the names of the months come from natural phenomena that happen during those months. For example, in May, when the weather gets warm, the ponies shed their warm winter hair. In September, as the weather grows cool again, the calves begin to grow their winter coats. Suppose we named months this way. What would be some appropriate names in the area where you live?

Month	Lakota Sioux Name	Your Name
January		
February	Month of the Dark Red Calves	
March	Moon of the Snowblind	
April		
May	Moon When the Ponies Shed	
June	Moon of Making Fat	
July		
August	Moon When the Cherries Turn Black	
September	Moon When the Calves Grow Hair	
October	Moon of the Changing Season	
November	Moon of Falling Leaves	
December	Moon of the Popping Trees	

NATIVE AMERICANS: BLACK ELK

3. Black Elk mentions a number of animals and plants that might be unfamiliar to you. Match these names to the drawings.

____ elk (1, 14)   ____ grasshopper (11)   ____ geese (25)
____ eagle (1)   ____ dragonfly (15)   ____ swallow (27)
____ bison (5)   ____ prickly pear (17)   ____ squirrel (28)
____ spider (8)   ____ cherries (18)   ____ oxen (52)

Illustration by Annie Heringer

Reading and Researching America

Quotations and Paraphrases

Write the quotation with an introductory explanation of the source and the content, paying close attention to punctuation. Then paraphrase it in your own words. (See pages 246–52 in the Yellow Pages for help with quotations and paraphrases.)

Part 1: "Early Boyhood" (Paragraphs 1–26)

1. (paragraph 7) "... [T]he Wasichus came, and they have made little islands for us and other little islands for the four-leggeds, and always these islands are becoming smaller, for around them surges the gnawing flood of the Wasichu; and it is dirty with lies and greed."

   _____
   _____
   _____
   _____

2. (paragraph 22) "It was a happy summer and nothing was afraid, because . . . [the Wasichus] made a treaty with Red Cloud that said our country would be ours as long as grass should grow and water flow. You can see that it is not the grass and the water that have been forgotten."

   _____
   _____
   _____
   _____

3. Choose your own quotation and follow the same directions.

   _____
   _____
   _____
   _____

Part 2: "Wasichus in the Hills" (Paragraphs 27–55)

1. (paragraph 31) "Our people knew there was yellow metal in little chunks up there; but they did not bother with it, because it was not good for anything."

2. (paragraph 36) "They [the leaders of the tribes] talked and talked for days, but it was just like the wind blowing in the end."

3. Choose your own quotation and follow the same directions.

Writing Summaries

Write a one-paragraph summary in Modern English without plagiarism. (See pages 253–55 in the Yellow Pages for help in writing a summary.)

1. Summarize the Americans' plan for the Native Americans' land, and the Native Americans' objections to the plan. (paragraphs 4–7)

2. Summarize the disagreement between Red Cloud's people and Black Elk's people. (paragraphs 30–33, 50)

Questions for Discussion and Writing

Discuss your answers to these questions with your classmates. These questions may also be used as essay topics. (See pages 221–24 in the Yellow Pages for a review of essay form.)

1. What kinds of games did the Native American boys play? To what extent would these games serve as a kind of education for Native American boys?

2. The Native Americans and the Europeans had different styles of fighting. What were the differences? What were the advantages and disadvantages of each?

3. At the big council in 1875, the Native American tribes could not agree on a way to deal with the Europeans' invasion of their land. Explain their different ideas. Can you think of other ideas that might have been more successful for the Native Americans to protect their lands?

4. Crazy Horse was a hero for the Native Americans. What qualities made him a hero? Would a person with these qualities be a hero for another group of people?

5. Black Elk describes several dreams and visions. What significance did these dreams and visions have for him? What significance do we give dreams and visions today?

> **Definitions**
>
> **Civilization**—an advanced state of human society in which a high level of culture, science, industry, and government has been reached
>
> **Manifest Destiny**—the belief that it was the destiny or fate of the United States to expand its territory over the whole of North America and to extend its political, social, and economic influence over this territory

6. Read the definition of civilization on page 98. To what extent does Black Elk's tribe meet these criteria of civilization?

7. Read the definition of Manifest Destiny on page 98. To what extent do the Europeans in Black Elk's account seem to believe in this idea?

Scanning for Specific Information

Scanning means looking over a page quickly to find a specific detail rather than beginning at the top of the page and reading every word. Working alone or with one or two other students, use a reference book to find the information to complete the sentences. Try to work quickly to find just the information you need to fill in to complete the exercise. You will probably have to consult more than one source. Make sure that your answers fit the structure of the sentence.

Reference book(s) used _____

_____

NATIVE AMERICANS

The Indians of the Americas came from Asia, crossing the Bering Strait between _____ over a land bridge that existed during the Ice Ages. They probably crossed in small bands, following animals they could hunt and extending farther into the American continent with each generation. No one knows the exact dates and numbers, but most migration is estimated to have taken place about _____ years ago, and in 1492, when Christopher Columbus landed in America, there may have been

_____ million people living there. Believing that he had landed close to India, Columbus called the people Indians.

The great native civilizations of Central and South America, the Aztecs and Incas, drew the immediate attention of the European explorers because of their vast wealth in _____. The Indians of North America, numbering _____ million, had little contact with Europeans until the 1700s and even 1800s, as Black Elk described. Their ways of life varied from the settled farmers of the Southwest who lived in adobe houses of several stories called _____ to the small nomadic bands that lived in _____ and wandered the Plains in search of _____. The Native Americans lived close to nature and believed that spirits lived in natural objects such as _____. They did not own land but only used it for _____. They did not have many material goods, but some tribes are known for their crafts; for example, the Northwest Indians are known for their _____, the Plains Indians for _____, the Desert Indians for _____, and the Pueblo Indians for _____. The Native Americans introduced Europeans to several new crops and animals, such as _____.

Today the Native American population of the United States is about _____ million. They were granted citizenship in _____ and have the same rights that all other American citizens do. Those who live on reservations have additional rights of self-government and support themselves using the lands' natural resources, but most today live modern lives in urban areas.

Research Topics

Choose one of these topics or another topic that interests you to do one of the research exercises in the Yellow Pages. Share the results of your research with your classmates as you become experts in your own research areas.

North American Indians
Sioux Indians
Crazy Horse
Battle of Little Bighorn
Western Expansion
Black Elk
General George Custer
Battle of Wounded Knee
Gold Rush
Red Cloud

Expansion Activities

1. The book *Black Elk Speaks* includes a song that Black Elk's tribe sang after its victory at the Battle of Little Bighorn. Black Elk calls it a "kill song." What does this song show about the Sioux Indians' attitudes toward General Custer and his soldiers?

    "Long Hair has never returned,
    So his woman is crying, crying.
    Looking over here, she cries."

    • • • • •

    "Long Hair, guns I had none.
    You brought me many. I thank you!
    You make me laugh!"

    • • • • •

    "Long Hair, horses I had none.
    You brought me many. I thank you!
    You make me laugh!"

    • • • • •

    "Long Hair, where he lies nobody knows.
    Crying, they seek him.
    He lies over here."

    • • • • •

    "Let go your holy irons (guns).
    You are not men enough to do any harm.
    Let go your holy irons!"

2. "Cowboys and Indians" has always been a popular topic in American movies throughout the years, but the portrayal of cowboys and Native Americans has changed over the years as Americans have begun to be more sympathetic to the plight of the Native Americans. Watch a "cowboys and Indians" movie, and talk with your classmates about how these groups are portrayed. One more recent movie that shows sympathy for the Native Americans is *Dances with Wolves* (1990).

3. Another example of changing attitudes concerns the name of the battlefield where Sioux Indians defeated the U.S. Army. The area was once named Custer Battlefield National Monument. Congress voted in 1991 to rename it the Little Bighorn Battlefield National Monument and to construct a memorial to the Native Americans who were killed in the battle. Look up this national monument in the library or on the Internet to learn about the ongoing controversy about how to recognize both the winners and the losers in this battle.

4. Some Americans traveling on the Great Plains during the nineteenth century were aware of the imminent destruction of the Native American way of life and made it their goal to record this way of life before it disappeared. Two such Americans were the artist George Catlin (1796–1872) and the photographer Edward Curtis (1868–1952). Both made many portraits of Native Americans and scenes of their lives. Look them up in the library or on the Internet to see examples of their work.

4

HOMESTEADERS
Nannie T. Alderson
(1860–1947)
★ ★ ★

INTRODUCTION

As Black Elk described in his autobiography, in the mid-1800s, Americans searching for gold flooded into the Great Plains, the homeland of Native Americans, an area of waving grass and huge herds of buffalo. By the 1880s, the buffalo herds had been destroyed for meat and hides, and the Native Americans who had depended on the buffalo for their livelihood were dead from war or starvation, or were living on reservations. The Great Plains, which earlier had seemed to be an undesirable place to settle, became more attractive: The thick grass that had fed huge herds of buffalo could be suitable for raising cattle.

Cattle ranching was well-established in the land south of the Great Plains that at one time belonged to Mexico; now it moved north. It seemed like an easy business: The ranchers bought cattle and turned them loose on the open range to feed themselves. The land was publicly owned, so the water and grass were free. There was little work to be done until spring, when cowboys rounded up the cattle and took the steers to market. These were the days of the Wild West, the days that made cowboys into American legends.

Many cattle ranchers were from the East Coast, like Walter and Nannie Alderson, or from England and Europe. Like the Aldersons, they were young and full of enthusiasm for the freedom and adventure of western life. The years from 1875 to 1885 were years of mild, rainy weather, so at first the ranchers were very successful. But then conditions changed: As more and more ranchers arrived, the plains became overcrowded, and the grass became thinner. Also, the weather changed. An especially cold winter in 1887 killed many cattle. The ranchers who managed to stay in business began to take a different approach to raising cattle: They fenced the cattle in and grew grass and hay to feed them during the winter. The days of the open range were over.

Nannie Alderson wrote in her book that the West was "a great country for men and horses, but hell on women and cattle." Although her life was hard, she was a woman with great vitality and resilience. She had had an unhappy childhood in West Virginia when the death of her father left her dependent on her mother's second husband, her stepfather. When she was 16, she visited an aunt in Atchison, Kansas, and loved the active, informal life there. A few years later, she married a man equally enthusiastic about the West, and they began a cattle ranch in Montana in 1883, just at the end of the good years. They did well at first, but after a lot of hard work and danger, finally gave up in 1893 and moved into town. During their years on the ranch, no one had ever been injured or killed. Ironically, Mr. Alderson was killed by a horse during their first months in town, leaving Mrs. Alderson to raise her family by herself. When she was in her eighties, she wrote, with the help of Helena Huntington Smith, an account of her life as a young bride on a Montana cattle ranch.

Pre-Reading Questions

The preceding reading passages (Chapters 1–3) in this book were written by men. Before you read, think about how a woman's autobiographical story might be different from a man's story: Would women write about different things? Would they have different experiences or face different kinds of problems?

✧ READING PASSAGE ✦

NANNIE T. ALDERSON:
From *A Bride Goes West*
(with Helena Huntington Smith)

Alderson's use of English is modern and casual in its style, maybe because she wrote her book in 1942 rather than during the 1880s when the events actually took place. Some terms that are glossed, such as *smattering* and *screw up*, are very informal and not used in academic writing.

PART 1: A NEW WORLD (Paragraphs 1–48)

(1) The year I was sixteen a new world opened up before me. My father's sister, Elizabeth Tiffany, had married a Mr. Symms and had pioneered in Kansas in the Fifties. On one of her periodic visits to Virginia she stopped to see me, because I wanted to know my father's people. The result was an invitation to visit her in Atchison, Kansas, from September to June.

(2) What an experience that was! Kansas then was the West. I felt that the very air there was easier to breathe. In Union you had to have your pedigree with you to be accepted anywhere, but in Atchison it didn't matter a bit who your ancestors were or what you did for a living; if you were nice you were nice. What impressed me most was the fact that a girl could work in an office or a store, yet that wouldn't keep her from being invited to the nicest homes or marrying one of the nicest boys. This freedom to work seemed to me a wonderful thing. I wanted to do something useful myself, as I felt keenly my dependence on my stepfather. But Auntie wouldn't let me; she knew my mother would never consent.

(3) So many little foolish conventions that we were brought up on at home didn't apply in Atchison. There was much less formality there; when people went visiting they took their darning or their knitting with them in the friendly old-fashioned way—but when I tried it after returning to West Virginia, mother was shocked. In Union on Sunday we were never allowed to open the piano nor visit anybody except relatives; in Kansas we all did as we pleased about these matters, and when I remonstrated with my cousin for playing a piece of popular music, she was able to retort: "I don't think it's any more wrong than it is for you to sit on the porch and talk to boys on a Sunday afternoon!"

(4) I had to admit that she was right. But the boys all worked, and Sunday was the only day they could come.

(5) On this visit I first met my husband. One evening in June, 1877, I was invited to take supper and spend the night with a Baptist preacher's family named Alderson, who were West Virginians like

Union (a town in West Virginia)—Nannie Alderson's birthplace

pedigree—an ancestry of importance and distinction

ourselves. There were several brothers in the home, and three or four girls had been invited. After a jolly supper one of the boys excused himself from the parlor and went out on the porch to smoke a cigar.

(6) In a minute he was back, saying excitedly: "Mother, Walt's home!"

(7) This announcement produced a great effect. "Walt," I learned, was a brother who had run away to Texas when he was twelve or thirteen years old, and they hadn't seen him for nine years.

(8) They made him come inside—a cowboy in sombrero and chaps. We girls were not impressed; we thought he was funny-looking. I remember that he was rather silent and ill at ease, and soon excused himself, saying he was going to bed. In the morning the brother brought the startling news that "Walt" had not slept in bed, but had gotten up in the night, taken a quilt, and lain down on the floor of the bedroom. This strange visitor, they said, had come up with a herd of cattle to Dodge City, the wild, tough cowtown which was then a northern terminus of the great cattle trail from Texas. He had left the house very early, before any of us were up, and I didn't see him again, except once at a crystal wedding party, before going back to Virginia.

(9) Texas in the late Sixties was wild and rough, the very place to appeal to rebellious spirits. I have often wished that I remembered more of Mr. Alderson's experiences there. I know that when he first went down there he got a job washing dishes for his keep. Later his boots gave out, and his first piece of luck was finding five dollars, with which he bought new ones. At one time he drove a stage coach during the night; I can't recall where, only that the little town at one end of his run was called Sweet Home. That has always seemed to me a

sombrero—Mexican-style cowboy hat

chaps—leggings of leather, worn by cowboys over their jeans to protect their legs

terminus—the end of a railroad line

lovely name. He told me that every morning at sunup, near the end of his long night's drive, a mocking bird would be singing in a certain liveoak tree when he went by. He came to look for it, and if the bird wasn't there, the day would be spoiled for him.

sunup—dawn (sun up)

(10) He had always been good with horses, so he drifted naturally into becoming a cowboy, and went up the trail to Kansas. He spoke of it as a hard school, with poor food and much exposure to the weather. I believe he had been up to Dodge City before, but on this trip, when he got up there with the herd, it came to him all of a sudden that he would go home and see his people.

(11) I spent a year at home in West Virginia after our first meeting; then, when I was seventeen, I went back to Atchison to stay with my aunt again, remaining this time for four years.

(12) I did not see Mr. Alderson at once on my second visit. Although he had stayed in Atchison, he didn't live at home, but had rooms downtown, where he went around with a fast horse-racing crowd. It may sound strange today to speak of horse-racing in Kansas, but the western part of the state at that time was not far from its wide-open frontier days, and the sporting element still held its own.

sporting element—people interested in racing horses
held its own—continued to be popular

(13) I should probably never have seen him again if his father had not taken ill. There were no nurses then; neighbors helped each other, and Auntie and I took turns at looking after the old gentleman. On a night when I was sitting up, Walter came home. He owned half interest in a race mare which he took on the circuit, and he had been in Kansas City racing this horse when his father grew worse, and they telegraphed him to come.

owned half interest in—shared ownership in
on the circuit—on a tour of race tracks

(14) For many nights after his arrival in Atchison we sat up together by the old gentleman's bedside, or talked quietly in the next room. In those talks he told me much about his early life, and one thing he said I have always remembered; that he had never known any pleasure in his home until I was in it. I believe that was one thing that gave him such a strong feeling for home afterwards. He told me, too, that he had made up his mind never to marry, but that I had changed it. He was already planning to go out and start a cattle ranch in Montana, and he asked me if I would be afraid to share that kind of life with him. I told him that I wasn't afraid, and we became engaged soon after his father died.

(15) My aunt and the relatives in Atchison did not approve the match at first. This was not because he was taking me to the unsettled West; they all thought the ranching business had a wealthy future, so that was looked upon as a good thing. No, they disapproved because of his wild reputation. But I had perfect confidence in him, believing then, as I do now, that it's not what a man has done before marriage that counts, it is what he does after.

the match—engagement

(16) I wanted to see my grandmother again before going so far away, so I went home to West Virginia and spent the next year there, getting ready to be married. How often I blessed Auntie in Atchison who had taught me to sew, and had also instilled what little smattering of common sense I had. I made all my trousseau myself. Thanks to Auntie I did have sense enough to make my underthings plain according to the standards of the day—so they had some pretense at suitability to the life I was planning to lead. When I had first arrived in Atchison my petticoats were like my mother's—a mass of lace, and frills upon

smattering—superficial knowledge
trousseau—a bride's clothing and household linen

petticoats—underskirts with lace and frills

frills. Auntie explained that this made too much ironing for one servant, and she taught me how to make simpler ones. So now I made my trousseau petticoats with just a single deep ruffle tucked solid to hold the starch, and a band of lace whipped to the ruffle. Mother thought them dreadfully plain, but when I had to iron them I thought them elaborate enough.

(17) I made my own wedding dress of white embroidered mull, and I earned the money to buy my wedding veil. This is how it happened. My grandfather had had a body servant, Alec, who was freed at the end of the war with the other slaves. He went North and prospered, becoming steward of a hotel in the White Mountains. In all those years, however, he never lost his loyal devotion to our family, and in 1882 he visited Union, bringing with him his wife, a smart young colored woman of whom he was very proud. She needed a new dress while in Union, and he was humiliated because none of the dressmakers, who of course were white, would make one for her. He told me about it one day, almost with tears in his eyes.

mull—a soft, fine fabric

(18) I said: "Why, Alec, I'll make your wife's dress gladly. And what's more, I'll let you pay me for it."

(19) He said: "Miss Nannie, would you do that?" I never have seen a man so touchingly grateful. So I made the dress, and earned my wedding veil.

(20) While I was at home making these preparations, Mr. Alderson was in Montana hunting for a site for a ranch. His partner was Mr. John Zook of St. Joe, Missouri, a young man who shared his interest in horses and the out-of-doors. The two of them had owned this race

St. Joe, Missouri—
St. Joseph, Missouri

mare together, and when they decided to go into ranching, the arrangement was that Mr. Zook was to provide the capital while my husband furnished the experience. The Northern Pacific was built as far as Miles City, Montana, and Mr. Alderson arrived on one of the first trains to come through the East.

Northern Pacific—Northern Pacific Railroad

(21) He stopped at a road ranch up Tongue River which was run by some people named Lays. That year the buffalo were still so thick that Mrs. Lays had only to say: "Mr. Alderson, we're out of meat"; and he would go out and find a herd and kill a calf, all just as easily as a man would butcher a yearling steer in his own pasture. Yet when I came out, one year later, there was nothing left of those great bison herds, which had covered the continent, but carcasses. I saw them on my first drive out to the ranch, and they were lying thick all over the flat above our house, in all stages of decay. So wasteful were the hunters, they had not even removed the tongues, though the latter were choice meat.

(22) The summer after I came out Mr. Alderson killed the last buffalo ever seen in our part of Montana. A man staying with us was out fishing when he saw this lonesome old bull wandering over the hills and gullies above our house—the first live buffalo seen in many months. He came home and reported it, saying: "Walt, why don't you go get him?" And next morning Mr. Alderson did go get him.

(23) That afternoon he suggested that we take the spring wagon and go up to where the old bull had fallen. There he lay in the green brush at the bottom of a draw—the last of many millions—with the bushes propping him up so that he looked quite lifelike. I had brought my scissors, and I snipped a sackfull of the coarse, curly hair from his mane to stuff a pillow with.

(24) I am afraid that the conservation of buffalo, or any other wild game, simply never occurred to the westerner of those days.

(25) The site Mr. Alderson chose for a ranch was near the mouth of Lame Deer Creek where it runs into the Rosebud, some sixty miles above the place where Rosebud joins the Yellowstone. Crook had fought the Indians on the Rosebud only six years before, and Custer had marched up it, to cross the divide and be slaughtered with all his command at the battle of Little Big Horn. I had read about all this when it happened, and had seen a picture of Custer with his long yellow hair in one of our Southern papers, when I was just a young girl. I had been terribly and painfully impressed, never dreaming that I should some day live so near the battlefield, even visit it, and walk on ground that had been stained by his blood.

Crook—General George Crook, an Indian fighter who later campaigned for Indian rights

Custer—General George Custer, who was killed in the Battle of Little Bighorn in 1876

divide—higher land between two streams or rivers, a ridge

(26) With the ranch selected and the cattle bought, Mr. Zook sold the race horse in Kansas and went out to the ranch to take over, while Mr. Alderson spent his share of the proceeds on coming East. We were married at my mother's house in Union, on April 4, 1883.

(27) On our way west we paid farewell visits to civilization in Chicago and St. Paul. Farther on the train stopped for an hour at Mandan, South Dakota, to enable the passengers to see a wonderful collection of mounted animals. The great heads and horns of the beasts of the prairie made a deep impression on me, since I was so soon to be living among them.

(28) I went with romantic ideas of being a helpmeet to a new man in a new country, but I was sadly ill-equipped when it came to carrying them out. Before I left Union a dear old lady taught me how to make

helpmeet—helpmate, a companion and helper

hot rolls, but except for that one accomplishment I knew no more of cooking than I did of Greek. Hot rolls, plus a vague understanding that petticoats ought to be plain, were my whole equipment for conquering the West.

(29) I had been prepared for Miles City ahead of time, so I was not surprised by the horses hitched to rails along the store fronts, the wooden sidewalks and unpaved streets, nor was I surprised that every other building was a saloon. Mr. Alderson had told me it was a pretty hoorah place. He didn't want me to go out alone, even in the daytime—not that I wouldn't be perfectly safe, but I might run into a drunken crowd or a fight.

hoorah—wild, exuberant

(30) Mr. Alderson had assured my mother and grandmother that I could go on to Bozeman where he had bought the cattle, and stay with friends there while our new house was being finished. I had different ideas, however, and on the train I had told him that I wanted to go on with him. He was very ready to be convinced.

(31) So we left Miles City April seventeenth, with a hundred-mile journey ahead of us which would take two days. We were driving behind two horses in a spring wagon, which was like buckboard but very much more comfortable. Already the grass had started, and the country was prettily tinged with green. But it was a big and bare country, with only scattering pine trees and the cottonwoods in the river bottoms to break its vast monotony. In all the years of my marriage, I never had trees over my head; they could have been planted, but we never lived long enough in one place for them to grow.

spring wagon—a wagon with springs

buckboard—a wagon without springs

(32) That night we stayed at a road ranch on Tongue River. We had a comfortable room to ourselves with a good bed, which the hostess must have given up to us, since the ordinary accommodations consisted of a kind of bunk room which was occupied that night by fully fifteen men. They were all young, nearly all seemed to be Easterners, and they were all going into the cattle business. Next morning at breakfast we all sat at one long table, and they all talked of nothing but cattle, horses, and prices. Everyone, it seemed, was making fabulous sums of money or was about to make them; no one thought of losses; and for the next year my husband and I were to breathe that air of optimism and share all those rose-colored expectations.

(33) For dinner we had a buffalo steak, cut from one of the last buffalo in that part of Montana. The rest of the week was the usual fare of boiled potatoes, dried fruit and sourdough bread. Dan [the owner of the road ranch] was supposed to be a woman-hater, but he was most kind, even to cooking the one egg for "the missus" which his hen had laid that day; and I dried the dishes for him while the team was being hitched. I was the first bride who had ever stopped there.

team—a group of horses

hitched—harnessed or tied to a wagon

(34) The second day of our trip was beautiful when we started out, though before we arrived it had clouded over and begun to snow. After coming sixty-five or seventy miles up Tongue River, we crossed over the divide to Rosebud, then went on down a long gulch to Lame Deer. One of my first lessons as a western wife was that location in that almost uninhabited country was not a matter of cities or roads, but of rivers and divides. Rivers, like women, were few, and they gained in importance proportionally, while the location of every tiny creek might be a matter of life-and-death importance to men and animals alike.

gulch—dry streambed or ravine

(35) We picnicked at noon, eating lunch beside Tongue River while the horses were fed oats and grazed on the new green grass. The scene was wild and picturesque enough, but I was feeling the effects of the journey, and besides was greatly troubled by a question which had begun to form in my mind. All that day and the day before we had kept passing low, cheerless-looking shacks, mud-daubed, with weeds sticking up out of dirt roofs. They looked primitive and uninviting enough to be the habitations of Indians, or of animals, and my heart sank lower and lower as I saw them.

mud-daubed—spread with mud

(36) Finally I screwed up the courage to ask: "Is ours as bad as that?"

screwed up—got up

(37) "Worse," Mr. Alderson answered. "Ours is as unattractive as a shack can be."

(38) Then he explained again what I already knew; that our house hadn't even been built for us but was just a maverick shack, as he called it, that had been thrown together as a shelter for some men who were getting out railroad ties. The tie cutters had been working in the Wolf Mountains, some miles above our home, and the idea was to float the ties down the Rosebud to the Yellowstone, where they would be used to build the Northern Pacific. A second group of men was camped near the mouth of Lame Deer to watch and see that they didn't jam. But there wasn't enough water in the Rosebud, and the scheme fell through. So an abandoned loggers' camp became my first Montana home.

maverick shack—an abandoned shack, far away from other houses ("maverick" usually refers to unbranded cattle)
railroad ties—boards used under railroad tracks
tie cutters—men who cut these boards

jam—get stuck

(39) In the late afternoon we came out of the mouth of a gulch down which we had been traveling. A huddle of log buildings lay below us on the flat, and as I watched, a man on horseback burst out of it,

galloping across the valley. I was told that it was one of our cowboys, and that he was probably going after the milk cow. Two men climbed down from a partly completed log house—our house-to-be. Then a fourth man whom I recognized as Johnny appeared in the door of a low cabin. So this was home.

(40) In a minute I was unfolding my cramped limbs and being helped out of the spring wagon, and then I was being introduced to "Old Uncle—the best logger in Montana," and to "Baltimore Bill—the best man ever seen on the end of a whipsaw." They were building our new house. Then the cowboy, Brown Taliaferro, came riding back and greeted me as "Miss Tiffany," which made everyone laugh and eased the stiffness.

whipsaw—a saw for two persons

(41) The first sight of my temporary home was not reassuring—a dirt-roofed cabin, hardly any taller than a man, with one door and only *one window*! In this country where windows had to be hauled many miles they were usually used sparingly, one being made to do the work of two—a half to each room. An immense pair of elk antlers hung over the door, one prong sporting a human skull which was perforated with bullet holes. The skull, I later learned, had been picked up on the battle ground of Lame Deer; whether it was Indian or white no one knew, but most of the bullet holes had been put there in the course of target practice by the boys.

antlers—horns of an animal

prong—the point of an antler

(42) Indoors waited a pleasant shock. On our arrival in Miles City Johnny Zook had met us, expecting to take my husband back to the ranch with him while I went on to Bozeman. As soon as he learned of my intention of coming to the ranch, he went on out ahead of us to fix

things up for my coming. He said merely: "I'm going to take down the variety actresses off the walls." But when I saw what a home he had made of that little shack, I had to admit that few women could have done as well.

variety actresses—posters of popular actresses

(43) A bright fire was burning in the stone fireplace, and the dirt floor was covered with a clean new wagon sheet of white canvas. Over that were laid several beautifully tanned skins—a buffalo robe, a mountain lion, a gray wolf, a coyote and two red fox pelts more worthy to be used for a lady's neckpiece than for rugs. (Later I hung those fox skins on the wall.) Johnny had even found a white bedspread—as I later had cause to regret, for our bedroom was also the family living room, the bed did double duty as a couch, and I never could keep that bedspread clean. A gray army blanket, hung across an opening in the logs, made a door between the bedroom and the kitchen. I was told to lie down and rest while the men got supper ready. I gratefully did so, but was too excited and tired to sleep.

tanned skins—animal skins made into leather

did double duty—served two functions

(44) Just before supper my husband came in, to explain that Uncle and Baltimore Bill (so called because he talked so much about Baltimore, where he had once been), had been worrying because neither possessed a coat other than the kind worn in winter for warmth. Going coatless was a custom of the country; would I excuse the boys if they came to the table in their shirtsleeves?

(45) I said Yes, of course I would. But when I did go out and sit down to table in the dirt-floored kitchen, with those grizzled coatless men in their grimy-looking flannel work shirts they had worn all day, a wave of homesickness came over me.

grizzled—unshaven

(46) It soon disappeared in enjoyment of one of the best suppers I ever ate—hot biscuits, venison and bacon, potato chips, evaporated fruit and coffee. That men could cook was something new under the sun to me, but the men in Montana could and did, and most of what I learned during my first years as a housewife I leaned from them.

(47) The first meal was a product of bachelor team work in the kitchen, as such was typical. My husband was the biscuit maker and meat cook; Brown made the gravy and coffee, while our partner's specialty was Saratoga chips, on which he spent all the care and artistry of a French chef, putting one or two in the fat at a time, and bringing them on the table piping hot.

Saratoga chips—potato chips or french fries

(48) The table was the let-down lid of a chuck box, such as was used on roundup wagons. This crude kitchen cabinet, the stove, and some home-made three-legged stools were the sole furnishings of the kitchen that night, but next day Uncle was turned over to me, to build a table and benches. I had brought enough white oilcloth to cover the top, and when it was set for our supper the second night with bright red doilies, my grandmother's silver, an old-fashioned "lazy Susan" in the center with vinegar, salt, pepper and mustard bottles; and two delicate china cups and saucers to raise the tone, I felt I had made a real stride toward home-making in the West.

chuck box—a wooden box for storing kitchen utensils

doilies—placemats
"lazy-Susan"—a large revolving tray

PART 2: BOOM AND BUST (Paragraphs 49–109)

(49) The ignorance of brides has been a subject of jokes probably ever since the days of Mother Eve. My own ignorance as I look back upon it seems incredible—and like Eve I had to learn housekeeping in a wilderness. If I had married at home in West Virginia I should at least have had kindly neighbor women to turn to for advice, and I should have had stores where I could buy things to cover a few of my mistakes. As it was I was a hundred horse-and-buggy miles from a loaf of baker's bread or a paper of pins.

Eve—according to the Bible, the first woman, wife of the first man, Adam

(50) For a guide to housekeeping in the West I had brought a cook book and housekeeping manual which our dear old pastor at home had given me for a wedding present. This book, written by a Southern gentlewoman for Southern gentlewomen, didn't contain a single cake recipe that called for fewer than six eggs. I now opened it to the section on laundry, and the first sentence that met my eye was as follows: "Before starting to wash it is essential to have a large, light, airy laundry with at least seven tubs."

pastor—minister of a church

(51) I had one tub, a boiler and a dishpan. But for air and light at least I was well off, since my laundry was the shady north end of the shack and took in the whole of Montana. I threw the book under the bunk bed and put all my best clothes in the boiler. I didn't use half enough soap, and the water was very alkaline. My white under-things turned a dingy yellow and came out covered with gummy black balls of alkali as big as a small pea and bigger, which stuck to the iron. I shall never forget that washing as long as I live.

under-things—underwear

(52) The boys did their best to help. One of them got dinner, and the others helped me to wring the clothes out of the hot water. I was grateful for their efforts and their sympathy, but as they didn't know any more about laundry than I did, it was a case of the blind leading the blind. I had so little sense. I didn't even know enough to pour cold water over the boiling clothes to cool them, and neither did the rest of them. We wrung them out hot, until my fingers were bleeding around the nails. There was no clothesline, so one of the boys stretched a lariat in the yard, but there were no clothespins either, and when a wind came up it blew down half of the wash into the sawdust which covered the premises.

lariat—a long rope used to catch horses

(53) Back home in West Virginia I had thought myself quite a housewife. Mother was ill a great deal and I carried the keys, feeling very proud as I went about with her key basket, unlocking closets and giving things out. But out here I found that I didn't know, as they say, straight up. On the ranch we had meat without end, milk, and butter (if I made it), and later a few vegetables. Every single other necessity of life came from Miles City. Once a year when the men went in to ship their cattle they laid in supplies—hundred-pound sacks of flour and sugar, huge tins of Arbuckle coffee, sides of bacon, evaporated fruits and canned goods by the case. What you forgot you did without. I don't know how many times in those first months I thought: "Oh, if we'd only remembered" this or that.

carried the keys—had the control of the keys to all of the cabinets and closets

straight up—the right way to do things

(54) There were Indians all around us. Hardly a day passed that they didn't visit us and beg for food. Often the shack would grow suddenly dark, and I would look up, to see the blanketed form of an Indian blocking the window, shading his eyes with his robe to peer

inside. It never dawned on me in that first year to be afraid of them, largely because I didn't know enough. Naively I thought them rather pathetic, with their dirt and queer travesty of white man's dress. How, I thought, could anyone fear such poor, miserable creatures? Yet these Indians were the Northern Cheyennes, known, until their surrender to General Miles a short two years before, as the deadliest fighters and most implacable foes of the white man. As neighbors in the early Eighties, they were scarcely more comfortable than a powder magazine. But it took time before I realized this.

(55) One of our steady visitors was old Chief Two Moons, who had played a leading part seven years before in chopping Custer's Command to pieces at the battle of Little Big Horn. Now he was just an old beggar who came around to our house asking for coffee. He was absurd and squalid-looking, with his dirty cotton shirt turned wrong side out, and his white man's pants with the seat cut out, which he wore like a pair of leggings over a breech clout. Two Moons' English was seemingly limited to "How," "Yes," and "No," but when he came for a meal he would always ask in signs how many horses my husband would take for me. Once when Mr. Alderson held up one finger, Two Moons laughed long and loud, so we concluded that he had a sense of humor, and that he asked the question more as flattery than with a serious view to trade. Next time he asked for my price in horses my husband began opening and shutting both hands very rapidly. Two Moons counted up to fifty or so and then said disgustedly: "God damn, too many." It was his longest English sentence.

---

it never dawned on me—I never thought

travesty—a ridiculous imitation

implacable foes—unsatisfied enemies

powder magazine—a container to store gun powder

squalid—dirty, miserable, neglected

breech clout—leather loin cloth

(56) The men of course knew the truth about our visitors, and I was never left alone at the ranch. No matter how much work there was to be done one man always had to stay with me.

(57) Sometimes I wonder if too much hasn't been said about the grim aspects of frontier life. Later on in my marriage I came down to hard, bare facts; to loneliness and poverty. But that first spring and summer I was anything but lonely in spite of the lack of women. I had much to learn and hard work to do. But I had no children to look after, I lived in surroundings of great beauty, I was happy in my marriage, and pioneering still seemed rather romantic.

(58) We had plenty of visitors. Although the ranches were far apart—our near neighbors being five to ten miles distant—the men were always riding around looking for lost horses or moving stock, and as summer time approached, reps from miles away—even hundreds of miles—would come riding by on their way to join the roundup, and they would stop with us. A rep was a cowboy sent out by his outfit to represent them on some other part of the range, and gather up stray cattle bearing their brand. There were no fences, the cattle drifted for many miles, and these riders came to us from long distances—from the Belle Fourche in South Dakota, from Sun Dance on the edge of the Black Hills. Each would be traveling with a string of horses, his bed packed across the back of one. He would ride in, turn his horses in with ours, and stay for a meal or a night. If for the night, he would just throw his bed down out of doors. Later I heard that quite a joke was made on the roundup about the number of reps who found it necessary to pass by the Zook and Alderson ranch.

stock—cattle

reps—men acting on behalf of their ranches (representatives)

roundup—each year the cowboys gathered the range cattle together (rounded them up) in order to brand the young cattle and separate out cattle to take to market

outfit—ranch

range—prairie, grass land

brand—a mark put on cattle to identify the ranch they belong to

(59) In 1883 we were all very young. Mr. Alderson was twenty-eight, and he was the oldest. I was twenty-three at the end of the summer; Johnny Zook and Hal were my age, Brown was a year younger. Our friends were in their twenties or early thirties. If we were empire builders we didn't feel like it or act the part. We made a game of everything, even the garden.

(60) In April Mr. Alderson and Johnny and Brown took the plough and started breaking ground for a garden plot on a level space near the house. I shall never forget how tough the sod was; it didn't want to be ploughed. For longer than human memory, the grass had grown and died and its roots had interlaced to form one of the strongest sods ever seen. Our little saddle horses weren't raised for such work, and besides they were only on grass, as we had no grain to give them, so they tired easily. The men could do just a few furrows at a time, and it took several days to make our small garden. But we planted it eventually with peas and lettuce and potatoes, and we turned the sod back over them, which was all we could do. We had fresh vegetables that summer, but the potatoes were quite flat.

sod—soil containing the roots of grass

on grass—eating only grass

furrows—rows to plant in

(61) While they were ploughing I would finish my housework—or just leave it unfinished, I'm afraid—and would go down there and watch them.

(62) No, we were not very serious then. We didn't mind the hard things because we didn't expect them to last. Montana in the early Eighties was booming just like the stock market in 1929, and the same feverish optimism possessed all of us. I believe the same thing was true of many other frontier communities. Our little dirt-roofed

shack didn't matter because our other house was building. And even the new house was to be only a stepping stone to something better. We didn't expect to live on a ranch all our lives—oh, my no! We used to talk and plan about where we would live when we were rich—we thought of St. Paul. It all looked so easy; the cows would have calves; and two years from now their calves would have calves, and we could figure it all out with a pencil and paper, how in no time at all we'd be cattle kings.

(63) Well, it wasn't so. But there was a glamour to it while it lasted. Raising cattle never was like working on a farm. It was always uncertain and exciting—you had plenty of money or you were broke—and then, too, work on horseback, while dangerous and often very hard, wasn't drudgery. There was more freedom to it. Even we women felt that, though the freedom wasn't ours.

(64) To me at first ranch life had endless novelty and fascination. There were horses to be broken and cattle to be branded, because new ones that we bought had to have our mark of ownership put on them before they were turned out on the range. Something was always going on in the corral, and I would leave the dishes standing in the kitchen and run down and watch, sometimes for hours. This having a Wild West show in one's back yard was absorbing but it was terrifying; I never could get used to the sight, but would marvel how anyone could stay on such a wild, twisting, plunging mass of horseflesh. The boys took it all quite calmly, and would call the rider to "Stay with him!" as though it were just a show. My husband always rode the ones that bucked the hardest. It was awful to see his head snap as if his neck would break, yet I never could stay away.

was building—was being built

to be broken—to be tamed
to be branded—to be marked with a symbol to indicate ownership

corral—a fenced yard for cattle or horses

bucked—kicked and jumped in order to throw off a rider

(65) In May Mr. Alderson left to go on the roundup, and for the second time in a few weeks I was minus a husband. This was to be the normal condition of affairs throughout my married life. The riding went on forever, but it was intensified in the summer and fall when they went on the roundup to brand the calves and gather the beef.

minus—without

(66) The old cattle range was divided up into districts, each of which was worked by its own crew of men, with horses and wagons, under the command of a captain. The roundup to which my husband belonged started May 1 near Miles City and worked its way slowly up the Rosebud toward us, Mr. Alderson joining them after they were in our territory. He had his own cowboys and horses, but he did not take a wagon, as ours was accounted one of the smaller outfits in this section of the country, and our boys joined one of the other wagons.

(67) On a beautiful Sunday morning in June they were camped only a few miles away, so I could ride over and pay them a visit. Mr. Zook, Hal and I started early. As we rode down into the valley of the Rosebud we saw a white patch—a wagon sheet stretched over the rear end of the chuck wagon. And from all sides the drives were coming in—cattle winding down from the hills, with riders following slowly on their flanks and at their rear, singing, calling or slapping their quirts against their chaps to make a noise; anything to keep the cattle moving. In the broad valley below were more cattle, thousands of them in one great herd, with more riders holding them, and over it all rose dust, and the noise of thousands of bawling throats. Men were at work in this big herd cutting out cows with calves into separate bunches, each according to the brand the mother wore. Mr. Alderson was in there cutting, and just as we

chuck wagon—wagon that serves as a kitchen
the drives—herds of cattle moved along (driven) by the cowboys
flanks—sides
quirts—whips

cutting out—separating

rode up his horse fell with him, but I didn't know it until somebody said to me: "He isn't hurt."

(68) Dinner time was ten o'clock, but the men had been up since before daybreak, and they were all hungry. A few were left to hold the herd, while the rest rode in, dismounted, and lined up before the cook's table with their tin plates and cups in their hands. Some of the company ate sitting on the ground. Others, myself among them, were enthroned on rolled-up cowboy beds, which made a perfect seat. My tin plate was piled with good beefsteak, potatoes, baked beans and stewed dried fruit; also canned tomatoes that tasted so good.

enthroned—seated as if on a throne

(69) The cowboys talked to me with shy good manners, explained things, and told me what to look for when the afternoon riding began. A Mexican cowboy who worked for one of the outfits was to ride his worst horse, a noted outlaw. After dinner when they all went to catch their fresh horses I fairly held my breath while this horse was blindfolded and saddled. Greatly to my surprise, and I think to the disappointment of the rider, he trotted meekly off with never a buck. Later on however he "blew up" in fine style, and there was a great exhibition of riding.

outlaw—usually a person outside the law, but in this case, a wild horse

a buck—a leap or jump

"blew up"—suddenly began to buck

(70) Later on in the summer I again visited the roundup, even taking a little tent along and spending several nights and days. This was partly to release Hal, who would otherwise have had to stay at the ranch for my protection. I rode less than a modern girl would do, sleeping late in my tent instead of getting up at dawn and going on the long morning rides with the men, but when they came back with the cattle I would mount and help hold the herd.

mount—get on a horse

(71) After the calf branding was finished there was a lull in midsummer when the roundup stopped working, and the men came home and put up hay. That kept them all busy for awhile, too busy to help me. For the first time in three months of married life I had to do all the work myself. And I felt horribly abused! When I had to dress my first chicken, I thought the end of the world had come. I didn't realize then that the spring, when we had all had such gay times together, was a slack season on the ranch, while haying time was one of the busiest of the whole year. I didn't realize how badly I'd been spoiled. I only knew that for the first time the wood box sometimes went unfilled. Instead of recognizing it for an oversight and saying, "Don't forget the wood," I brooded over it, waited until they were gone, carried the wood and water myself, and was sure my husband didn't love me. I needn't add that this was only a passing phase, and I soon came to my senses. I think many women are foolishly oversensitive in their first year of married life.

to dress—to prepare for cooking

slack (time)—quiet time, not busy

brooded—thought sadly

came to my senses—became reasonable

(72) One January night the dog barked so long and loud that my husband decided to go out, to see if a wolf or coyote could be nearby. He found two Indians in the angle of the house, slumped in their saddles and almost frozen. They were afraid of the dog and, in their stolid way, just sat there, not making a sound. They had started across the divide, but the snow was so deep their horses floundered till they were worn out, and I suppose the lights from our windows attracted them. Mr. Alderson brought them in by the fire and put their hands and feet into cold water. I got them a meal by the open fire in our room, as the kitchen fire was out. These Indians knew no English words to express themselves, but they drank the coffee and devoured

stolid—without emotions

huge helpings of steak. We put down a bed for them on the kitchen floor and gave their horses a feed of oats. In the morning they went on their way. I had heard it said that Indians never forget a kindness, and at that time I still believed it.

(73) I was busy packing up for a stay of a month or six weeks in Miles City, putting my grandmother's silver away in the bureau drawers, because the boys insisted they were afraid to use it. I hated to leave the dog, he was so human and so devoted to us. But it was a pleasure to look forward to his joy on our return. He had shown when little Charlie came to visit how fond he was of children, and we would be bringing a baby back with us.*

(74) Miles City was something of a problem, as there were no hospitals and no nurses. However, I knew one woman who lived there; I had met her on the train, coming out here from St. Paul, so when I knew I was to go to Miles City I wrote and asked her to find a place for me. She wrote back that no one was willing to take **a woman in that condition**. "But," she added "my mother was a midwife and I know a good deal about nursing." And she went on to say that she would take me if I didn't object to the small back bedroom which was all they had. She and her husband would sleep on a couch in the sitting room, but she would have to share my closet in the bedroom as it was the only one.

(75) At the time this sounded like the best arrangement we could make and doubtless it was, but it had many flaws. Because of the

a woman in that condition—a pregnant woman

The Aldersons were expecting a baby, so Mrs. Alderson had to go to Miles City where there was a doctor to help her. Little Charlie was a neighbor boy who came for a visit and played with the dog.

closet arrangement there was a good deal of going out and in, and very little privacy. Later the landlady was very little help with the baby. I don't think she was the type to care for nursing.

(76) As it was the slack season at the ranch, my husband was able to be with me most of the time. I had about three weeks to wait before the baby was born in March.

(77) The doctor was a nice old Kentuckian, and I fared, I suppose, as well as the average young mother. Then, when we had had barely two days in which to rejoice over the birth of our baby girl, a telegram came, addressed to Mr. Alderson. He had gone up to town, and the landlady brought it to me. I thought it was a wire of congratulation from his brother-in-law in Kansas, and asked her to read it.

(78) It said: "Indians have burned your house. Come immediately with sheriff and posse."

(79) It seemed ages before a messenger located my husband and he returned, accompanied by the doctor who said, "Your husband has been deputized and it is very necessary that he go and see about this, but if you are going to worry yourself sick over it he won't go."

(80) I said that of course he must go. During that long afternoon I listened to repeated warnings about the bad effect my worrying and grieving might have on the baby, and I gave myself many a mental shake and tried to think of our loss as one only of material things. But I never can forget the four days and nights, especially the nights, that I lay in that small back room wondering why the Indians had turned against us, what was happening, and if there would be an Indian outbreak and my husband would be killed.

posse—men given the legal authority to help the sheriff

deputized—made a deputy, given legal authority to act as a sheriff

(81) My husband returned at last to report that the house was a total loss, that the Indians had surrendered, but that he found nothing of value belonging to us in the tepees he had searched, that the ashes of the house had been sifted but my Grandmother's silver was not recovered. Bad as all this was, the worst was learning that the Indians had shot our dog out of pure meanness—shot him so full of holes that the boys couldn't even save his beautiful furry hide.

(82) The disaster had come upon us through Hal's fault. Here was how it had happened.

(83) The northern Cheyennes, now that the buffalo were all gone, were poor, wandering from river to river visiting their kin, begging and maybe killing a beef now and then. A lodge consisted of a chief's or sub-chief's relatives and his squaw's relatives, which made a big family. An Indian sub-chief named Black Wolf, living on a tributary to Tongue River across the divide from us, had brought his lodge to visit on the Rosebud not far from our ranch. On a day of melting snow, he had come round begging for food and tobacco; the boys fed him, and afterwards he sat down to smoke on a pile of fence posts, some yards from our door. There was a man named Reinhart who had been working for us the latter part of the winter, getting out poles for the fences. When Hal looked out the door and saw the Indian sunning himself, he said to Reinhart:

(84) "I'll bet you five dollars I can put a hole through that old Indian's hat without touching his head."

(85) The other man of course replied: "I'll bet you can't."

kin—relatives
a beef—a cow or steer
squaw—an Indian woman

(86) Hal drew his six shooter and fired, just nicking the Indian's scalp. Black Wolf could not and would not believe that Hal had not meant to kill him. When they found they could not pacify him they let him go, and rode hurriedly to Young's store ten miles away to get help in defending the property, for they knew what was coming. They got three or four cowboys and some arms, but Mr. Young was so sure there would be an uprising, he wouldn't let his guns go. They had intended to get inside the house and hold it, but when they got back after several hours they were too late; the Indians, the whole lodge, were in possession. Squaws and papooses were seated in a semicircle in the front yard, while the bucks were carrying out bureau drawers and emptying the contents in the midst of them for them to help themselves, afterward tossing the empty drawers against the side of the house. Hal, realizing that they meant to set fire to it, rode up to them as near as he dared, promising them beef, coffee, ponies, and tobacco. But when they started shooting at him, tearing up the earth under his horse, he realized it was no use, and the men could do nothing but ride up on top of a hill and watch while the house roared into flames. It was chinked with oakum between the logs, which made it burn all the faster.

(87) This was Tuesday, March 18th, the day the baby was born. Distances were great and travel difficult, and it was not until Sunday morning that the sheriff and posse from Miles City, with many settlers and cowboys, had the Indians surrounded on the Rosebud and persuaded them to stack their arms and surrender. Afterwards my husband went with the interpreter through the tepees. He found Black Wolf reposing on one of my feather pillows, a red cord from off my

six shooter—a gun that holds six bullets

papooses—Indian children

bucks—Indian men

chinked with oakum—the spaces between the logs of the house were filled with old pieces of rope.

best pin cushion around his hat. Hal's bullet had done him no harm. The Indians had camped by our house from Tuesday till Saturday, had eaten a year's supply of groceries, ten deer hams I was curing for summer use and all our chickens, besides burning the corral posts and poles, and cutting up the saddles.

(88) The silver, as I say, was never found, and I feel sure that the Indians divided it among themselves and maybe beat it into bracelets and other jewelry. This same silver that I lost in the fire had been through a fire before, when my grandmother's home in Union was burned to the ground before the Civil War. She and the children barely escaped with their lives, but every piece of silver had been counted and put away the night before the fire as it was every night in good old Southern fashion, locked in a cabinet; and afterwards the ashes were taken up and sifted and the melted bullion recovered, and she and my grandfather took it to Philadelphia, and had it made over into spoons which I brought out to Montana and lost.

(89) After my husband shipped his beef in August he brought the baby and me to our new home on Tongue River. Again it was a hundred-mile trip from Miles City, and the baby and I had been out of the hotel so little that our faces blistered the first half day, though I carried an umbrella. We stopped at a new road ranch where a kindly woman gave us fresh cream to relieve the sunburn. She also furnished material and helped me make a dark blue sunbonnet for the baby, lined with white paper around the face. All in all she was so nice and kind and clean, I didn't care if people did say she wasn't married to the man of the place.

shipped his beef—sent his beef to market in Chicago

(90) The men had built our new house on high ground above the river, where there were no trees. It looked bleak to me after our lovely, sheltered valley of the Lame Deer, and of course I wanted to know why they hadn't built among the cottonwoods on the river bottom. I was told that it was because of cloudbursts, which occasionally sent floods sweeping down the riverbeds in this rough country. One afternoon a year or two later there were thunderheads above the Wolf Mountains, so big and black that a man who was staying with us remarked: "I shouldn't wonder if we hear a cloudburst tomorrow." He had hardly finished speaking when a wall of water swept down a tributary which we called Zook Creek, right beside the house. It came boiling along at a fearful speed, great trees bouncing on its crest, and I'll never forget the stench of mud and decay which rose from it. One of the boys jumped on his horse bareback and galloped out to cut the stake ropes of two or three of our saddle horses, which were picketed in the creek bottom right in the path of the flood.

(91) The men liked the new location because the hay bottoms were much bigger than they were in Lame Deer valley. I was already learning to keep my feelings to myself.

(92) While we were on Tongue River the Cheyennes were all around us, the same Indians with whom we had twice had trouble through no fault of our own. One of our neighbors was Black Wolf, whom Hal shot and whose lodge burned our home. One winter morning a few months after my arrival, just as we were finishing breakfast, Black Wolf came in. He announced that he had a sick papoose, and wanted milk. Mr. Alderson invited him to sit down and have some coffee while I was straining the milk into the bottle. There was a piece of steak on

cloudbursts—sudden rain storms

thunderheads—large clouds

crest—the highest part of a wave

picketed—tied up to wooden stakes or pickets

hay bottoms—the bottom of the creek where hay was grown

the platter in front of him, and when I set his coffee down he pointed first to the steak and then to the stove, as a sign that he wished me to cook it some more. This made me so mad—when I knew the old heathen often ate meat raw, with the blood running down his chin—that I told him I wasn't going to cook it for him; he could eat it the way it was or go without. Although he didn't understand English he appeared to catch the drift, for he concluded to eat the steak "as is."

heathen—someone who does not believe in God

catch the drift—understand the meaning

(93) It was two braves of Black Wolf's lodge who admitted at the trial that they were the ones who set fire to our home, and were sent to the penitentiary. One of them died in prison, and the Indian Bureau later circulated a petition to have the other one pardoned, with the result that he was given his freedom. As soon as he reached home, he walked ten miles to spend the day with us! We wouldn't have known him from any other Indian, but he made us understand, with the sign language and a few English words, that he had burned our "tepee." He further informed us, with gestures, the he had had his hands tied together and had gone for a long ride on a train ("Choo-choo-choo"); that his comrade had "gone to sleep"; that he himself had now come home to stay. He seemed to believe we would be glad to see him!

circulated a petition—passed around a document for people to sign

(94) Other Indians told us that one of the bucks who set fire to our house was one of the two whom we took in and fed and sheltered that stormy night. Somehow words fail me at this point. Our relations with our Indian neighbors were, to say the least, perplexing.

(95) I persuaded one of them, a squaw named Rattlesnake, to come (when the spirit moved her) and do our washing, while her daughter, a comely, tidy looking . . . sixteen-year-old girl looked after the baby.

when the spirit moved her—whenever she wanted

comely—pretty

I had quite a time over this girl's name. Whenever I asked it she would look sullen, and she and the mother would jabber away at each other, without answering me. One day the interpreter from the agency came over with them, so I asked him to find out what the young squaw's name was. He talked with them a minute and then said: "She doesn't want you to know her name. She doesn't like it."

jabber—talk quickly

agency—the Indian Bureau, a federal agency to take care of Indian concerns

(96) I said: "Tell her we white folks often don't like our names either, and if she will tell me hers I will give her a pretty one."

(97) Her name was Bob-Tailed Horse. No wonder the child objected! I told the interpreter to tell her I would call her Minnehaha. She and her mother tried out the first part of this name, repeating it several times with a pleased expression. "Mee-nee!" So that was settled.

(98) Minnie made a good and faithful nurse, when she chose to come, carrying the baby on her back as she was carried when she was a papoose, and crooning songs to her. Indians are unquestionably fond of children. They will snatch them out of mischief, give them a little shake and grunt at them, and there it ends. After that the child is simply removed from temptation, and I have never seen one of them spank a small child.

papoose—a Native American word that means baby

crooning—singing

(99) Our baby started walking at fourteen months, but her little shoes were so slick on the soles, from the polishing they got on the dry grass, that she fell until she grew discouraged. So I asked Minnie to make her a pair of moccasins. A few days later she brought a prettily beaded pair and put them on the baby, who was so delighted to find she could walk without falling, that she walked a hundred miles, I'm sure, the first day.

moccasins—soft Indian shoes made of animal skin

(100) It was all very kindly up to a point, but beyond the kindness there was a blank wall. In view of the cruelties that had been exchanged between white man and Indian, it was no wonder if real warmth was lacking between them, or if the Indian attitude toward us was one of complete cynicism. I can understand this now, but at the time I was terribly disappointed. I came from the South, and despite the burning of our house I looked, unconsciously perhaps, for the same affectionate relationship with the Indians that had existed in my old home between the colored people and the whites. One of the hard lessons I had to learn in Montana was that the affection I sentimentally wanted just simply was not there.

(101) Spring had come to Montana when I took the baby and went home for a long visit to my mother and grandmother.

(102) Our second little girl was born in West Virginia in August, and we called her Fay Sue. I didn't go back to Montana until the following March, and in that way I missed the hard winter, the worst in the history of the West. But I found nothing the same afterwards. From then onwards, even the illusion of prosperity vanished.

(103) There had been signs even before the hard winter that the cattle business was not all we thought it. In '84 or '85 there was a stockyards strike in Chicago and the cattle couldn't be shipped; after Mr. Zook and Mr. Alderson had gathered all their steers and brought them into Miles City they had to take them all the way home again and turn them back out on the range. So there were no profits from the sale of beef steers that year; and the next year prices began to slip.

stockyards—cattle yards in Chicago, where the meat-packing plants were located

(104) Then too we had hard luck in our first year, and heavy expenses with our first two children. When I went to Miles City and the first baby was born, our house was burned, and I had to stay and board for seven months. Meanwhile there was all the expense of moving the outfit and building the new house; a log house cost a lot to build even in those days, even though our second one was of inferior cottonwood logs instead of pine. The firm had to borrow money to pay for all this. Part of the time they were paying eighteen percent for it. Finally, because I'd had such a miserable time in Miles City before, I went home to West Virginia for my second baby. We would never have decided on that expense if we had known what hard times were ahead.

(105) Mr. Alderson came east to join me after Thanksgiving, but when reports of the winter began reaching him he became horribly worried and anxious to get back. We started home in March, as soon as he felt we could get through to the ranch. As it was, we were the first to try to break trail. Coming through North Dakota, the snow was so deep that we had to have a snow plow and two engines most of the time, and often the only way we knew the train had stopped at a town was by seeing the tops of houses above the great drifts. When we reached Miles City everyone told us we could never make it. But my husband knew that if we hoped to get to the ranch we must start now or be indefinitely delayed, for the bright sun was already softening the ice in the rivers, and threatening to unleash spring floods, and we had countless river and creek crossings to make.

break trail—open a path through the snow

(106) It was a depressing trip; Miles City had been full of talk about the dreadful losses, and we passed by several places where the cattle were piled up in frozen heaps. I remember one place in particular

where the road followed around a bank, with rocks and a small shelf up above. They had squeezed in under the rocks for shelter until no more could squeeze in, and had died.

(107) My husband began riding the range at once—and now we found something to encourage us. For we had not lost as heavily as most of our neighbors. My husband had weaned his calves the previous November, thus giving the cows a chance to get stronger before the snow got so deep. He was the first man to wean in our part of Montana; not only that, but he winter-fed too. He had a lot of good grass on the divide at the head of Muddy. He had stacked this and built corrals up there in the fall, and when the snow covered all the feed Mr. Zook and Brown rode out when they could, and gathered up what cattle they could find and fed them. This saved many of our cattle—more than most people saved—but we lost heavily nevertheless.

✦ EXERCISES ✦

Comprehension Questions

Answer these questions in paragraph form, using complete sentences in Modern English. Do not copy your answers directly from the reading passage. (See pages 218–21 in the Yellow Pages for a review of paragraph form.)

Part 1: "A New World" (Paragraphs 1–48)

1. Why did Nannie prefer life in Kansas to life in West Virginia?

2. How did Nannie prepare for her life on a cattle ranch?

3. What were some things that made her feel homesick at first?

Part 2: "Boom and Bust" (Paragraphs 49–109)

1. What were the many difficulties of housekeeping on a ranch in Montana?

2. What aspects helped Nannie to enjoy her life in spite of the difficulties?

3. Describe the Aldersons' encounters with the Indians.

4. Why did the Indians attack the house?

5. What problems made the cattle business harder than the Aldersons had thought?

Vocabulary Development

Part 1: "A New World" (Paragraphs 1–48) and Part 2: "Boom and Bust" (Paragraphs 49–109)

1. Alderson writes about ranch life in detail, mentioning that there was both *novelty* and *drudgery* in her life. Look up the meanings of these two words, and

write them below. Then put checkmarks on the lines below to indicate which of the ranch tasks in the list were novelty for Alderson and which were drudgery.

novelty (64): _____

drudgery (63): _____

ranch tasks	novelty	drudgery
a. doing the ironing (16)	_____	_____
b. doing the laundry (50)	_____	_____
c. rounding up the cattle (58)	_____	_____
d. ploughing (plowing) the garden (60, 61)	_____	_____
e. breaking the horses (64)	_____	_____
f. branding the cattle (64)	_____	_____
g. dressing a chicken (71)	_____	_____
h. filling the wood box (71)	_____	_____

2. Here are a few more useful vocabulary words to study and learn:

Part 1
impress (2), *impressed* (25)
consent (2)
conventions (3)
humiliated (17)
decay (21)
conservation (24)

Part 2
double duty (43)
sole (48)
pathetic (54)
concluded (55)
flattery (55)
lull (71)
pacify (86)
illusion (102)

Quotations and Paraphrases

Write the quotation with an introductory explanation of the source and the content, paying close attention to punctuation. Then paraphrase it in your own words. (See pages 246–52 in the Yellow Pages for help with quotations and paraphrases.)

Part 1: "A New World" (Paragraphs 1–48)

1. (paragraph 2) "In Union you had to have your pedigree with you to be accepted anywhere, but in Atchison it didn't matter a bit who your ancestors were or what you did for a living; if you were nice you were nice."

2. (paragraph 32) "Everyone, it seemed, was making fabulous sums of money or was about to make them; no one thought of losses; and for the next year my husband and I were to breathe that air of optimism and share all those rose-colored expectations."

3. Choose your own quotation and follow the same directions.

READING AND RESEARCHING AMERICA

Part 2: "Boom and Bust" (Paragraphs 49–109)

1. (paragraph 54) ". . . [T]hese Indians were the Northern Cheyennes, known, until their surrender to General Miles a short two years before, as the deadliest of fighters and most implacable foes of the white man . . . . But it took time before I realized this."

   _____
   _____
   _____
   _____

2. (paragraph 62) "It all looked so easy; the cows would have calves; and two years from now their calves would have calves, and we could figure it all out with a pencil and paper, how in no time at all we'd be cattle kings."

   _____
   _____
   _____
   _____

3. Choose your own quotation and follow the same directions.

   _____
   _____
   _____
   _____

Writing Summaries

Write a one-paragraph summary in Modern English without plagiarism. (See pages 253–55 in the Yellow Pages for help in writing a summary.)

1. Summarize the good and bad aspects of life on a cattle ranch. (paragraphs 57–64)

2. Summarize the Aldersons' "perplexing" relations with the Native Americans. (paragraphs 92–100)

Questions for Discussion and Writing

Discuss your answers to these questions with your classmates. These questions may also be used as essay topics. (See pages 221–24 in the Yellow Pages for a review of essay form.)

1. Mrs. Alderson writes about the demise of the buffalo and the Native Americans. To what extent does she seem to believe in the idea of Manifest Destiny as defined in Chapter 3?

2. Mrs. Alderson writes that women, like rivers, were important in the West because there were so few of them. What evidence does she give that women were valued and respected?

3. Mrs. Alderson says that cattle-ranching was not so hard because she and her husband and friends were young. How did their youth help them to enjoy their lives? Do you agree that young people are generally more able to bear a hard life?

4. Mrs. Alderson mentions several lessons she learned as a young ranch wife. What were the lessons she learned? Are these lessons still important today?

5. Mrs. Alderson was surprised that the affection that she felt between the blacks and whites in the South did not exist between the Native Americans and whites in the West. Does this difference surprise you? Use information from Frederick Douglass and Black Elk in your answer.

6. Mrs. Alderson wrote that the West was "a great country for men . . . , but hell on women . . . ." But in fact the Western states were the first states to give women the rights to hold property in their own names and to vote. What conditions in Western life might have helped Western women to get these rights sooner than women in other areas of the country?

7. Read again the Lakota holy man's vision of the future (paragraph 8 in Chapter 3, Black Elk). To what extent did the vision come true?

8. A 19th century historian, Frederick Jackson Turner, wrote that the people of the West were individualistic, egalitarian, and idealistic. To what extent do you think the Aldersons seem to fit this description?

Scanning for Specific Information

Scanning means looking over a page quickly to find a specific detail rather than beginning at the top of the page and reading every word. Working alone or with one or two other students, use a reference book to find the information to complete the sentences. Try to work quickly to find just the information you need to fill in to complete the exercise. You will probably need to consult more than one source. Make sure that your answers fit the structure of the sentence.

Reference book(s) used _____
_____

MANIFEST DESTINY

As the United States acquired lands beyond the Mississippi River, there was a shared belief among Americans that the country would eventually reach the Pacific Coast. A New York journalist, _____, gave this belief the name Manifest Destiny when he wrote in a magazine article in the year _____ that Americans had the right to spread their democratic ideals and prosperous way of life westward across the continent.

The West, thought at first to be a wasteland of deserts and grasslands, was soon discovered to have a variety of rich natural resources. The first resource to be exploited was the furs of animals such as _____. Then, in the year _____, gold was discovered in California, and a decade later, the Comstock Lode of _____ was discovered in the state of _____. After the rush for these precious minerals, families began to settle in the rich agricultural lands of Texas, Oregon, and California, traveling together across the plains in _____.

The lands of the West belonged to the government and were distributed to settlers at low prices. In the late 1700s, the government surveyed the land and passed the Northwest Ordinances of _____ and _____, allowing the purchase of sections of land of the size _____ for about $ _____ a section. In the year _____, Congress passed the Homestead Act, providing 160 acres of land free to any settler who _____.

The resources of the West could also be used for free by ranchers, miners, and loggers. Many poor people, including immigrants, found opportunities to become successful through hard work and luck. Still, the lives of the settlers were not easy, as Alderson describes.

145

READING AND RESEARCHING AMERICA

Although historian Frederick Jackson Turner declared in 1893 that the frontier days were over, the West lives on today in the American ideals of self-reliance and egalitarianism that were characteristic of these pioneers.

Research Topics

Choose one of these topics or another topic that interests you to do one of the research exercises in the Yellow Pages. Share the results of your research with your classmates as you become experts in your own research areas.

the Great Plains	Kansas	Montana
pioneers	Western land policies	homesteading
cattle ranching	cowboys	women in the West
Cheyennes	cattle ranching	Dodge City

Expansion Activities

1. Although the "open range" days of cattle ranching lasted only a few short years, this period of history has a mythological significance for Americans. Even if we live in the city, we still eat beef, wear blue jeans, and dream about the open spaces. Look for advertisements in magazines and on television that make use of the images of the Old West. Do you think you would have enjoyed life as a cowboy or homesteader?

2. Artists also presented a romantic view of the West. Albert Bierstadt (1830–1902) and Thomas Moran (1837–1926) painted large landscapes of western mountains, often lit with a symbolic golden glow as the sun set in the west. Frederick Remington (1861–1909) and Charles M. Russell (1864–1926) were inspired by the action of cowboys and horses. To better understand their visions, look up the works of these artists in the library or on the Internet.

3. Cowboy songs and movies are popular all over the world. Look up the words to these two songs in the library or on the Internet: *Home on the Range* and *Don't Fence Me In,* and sing along if you can find the music. Watch a classic western movie, such as *High Noon* (1952), about a sheriff who has to face an old enemy, or *Shane* (1953), about the conflict between ranchers and open range cattlemen. A newer movie, called *Open Range* (2003), may also be of interest.

4. Look up the Homestead Act of 1862 in the library or on the Internet, and read it carefully to determine the exact procedure for establishing a homestead. Who was eligible? Where was the land? How much did homesteaders have to pay, and what did they have to do? How long did this act remain in effect? Is there any evidence of abuse of this act to acquire free land?

5

GREAT INDUSTRIALISTS
Andrew Carnegie

(1835–1919)

★ ★ ★

INTRODUCTION

Industrialization began in the United States in the early 1800s and brought many rapid changes to people's lives. Prior to the Civil War (1861–1865), most people farmed or did craftswork and produced their own goods by hand at home. However, after the war, more and more people began to work in huge factories where steam and water power were used to produce goods quickly and cheaply. Large amounts of capital were necessary to build these factories and the necessary transportation systems to deliver raw materials and manufactured goods, leading to the development of the investment banking business. The men who were able to generate this money and put it to use were called the great Industrial Capitalists, or "Captains of Industry." Their names are still known today: John D. Rockefeller, Collis P. Huntington, Leland Stanford, J. P. Morgan, Cornelius Vanderbilt, and the author of the reading in this chapter, Andrew Carnegie.

The fast-developing industries of the late 1800s provided many opportunities for young men who were clever and hard-working. Andrew Carnegie is a good example: He began working at the age of 12 and advanced rapidly in telegraph and railroad companies. With an acute business sense, he recognized the importance of steel to the railroad industries, and with money invested by his family and friends, he started his own company to make steel for rails and bridges. He was an aggressive businessman whose tactics might seem ruthless or even illegal today. In fact, workers at a Carnegie steel plant in Homestead, Pennsylvania, staged one of the largest and most violent labor strikes of the time. The laws of that era, however, tended to put the interests of the great factory owners ahead of the interests of the workers.

The Carnegie Steel Company was very successful, so successful that Carnegie was able to sell it in 1899 to the great industrial banker J. P. Morgan for $400 million.

Then Carnegie retired and did something very different from the other capitalists of his day: He began to give his money away, according to the principles he described in his book, *The Gospel of Wealth and Other Timely Essays*. He established more than 2,500 free public libraries in towns all over the United States and established foundations to support education, scientific research, and world peace. His name is still found on Carnegie Libraries throughout the United States, Carnegie Hall in New York, and Carnegie-Mellon University in Pittsburgh. By the time of his death in 1919, he had given away more than $350 million of his wealth.

Carnegie's philanthropy helped to temper his reputation as an aggressive businessman so that today he is remembered as a positive example of the great Captains of Industry. His "rags to riches" story was an inspiration to many boys in the early 20th century and still has an influence on young people today. In *The Gospel of Wealth and Other Timely Essays*, Carnegie wrote about the childhood experiences that led him to become a businessman and his ideas about the accumulation and distribution of wealth.

Pre-Reading Questions

These are names of some of the wealthiest families in the United States in the late 1800s: Rockefeller, Huntington, Stanford, Morgan, Vanderbilt, and Carnegie. Which names do you recognize, and what do you associate them with? Who are some of the wealthiest people today, and how did they make their fortunes?

✣ READING PASSAGE ✣

ANDREW CARNEGIE:
From *The Gospel of Wealth and Other Timely Essays*

Part 1, "Introduction: How I Served My Apprenticeship," was first published in 1896 in a magazine for young people called *Youth's Companion*. In a simple, straightforward style, Carnegie tells the story of how he became a businessman. He uses some words that seem old-fashioned today, such as *tussle* and *akin to;* as usual, avoid using these old-fashioned words in your own writing. He also uses an old-fashioned spelling for the name of his city, *Pittsburg,* now spelled *Pittsburgh.*

Carnegie originally wrote Part 2, "The Gospel of Wealth—The Problem of the Administration of Wealth," for the *North American Review* in 1889. It is intended for adults and is written in a formal, academic style with specialized vocabulary used in economics and law. When you write for academic purposes, it is appropriate to use this kind of vocabulary.

PART 1: HOW I SERVED MY APPRENTICESHIP
(Paragraphs 1–63)

(1) It is a great pleasure to tell how I served my apprenticeship as a business man. But there seems to be a question preceding this: Why did I become a business man? I am sure that I should never have selected a business career if I had been permitted to choose.

apprenticeship—period of time spent as an apprentice, working with a master in order to learn a trade

(2) The eldest son of parents who were themselves poor, I had, fortunately, to begin to perform some useful work in the world while still very young in order to earn an honest livelihood, and was thus shown even in early boyhood that my duty was to assist my parents and, like them, become, as soon as possible, a bread-winner in the family. What I could get to do, not what I desired, was the question.

a bread-winner—someone who earns wages to support a family

GREAT INDUSTRIALISTS: ANDREW CARNEGIE

(3) When I was born my father was a well-to-do master weaver in Dunfermline, Scotland. He owned no less than four damask-looms and employed apprentices. This was before the days of steam-factories for the manufacture of linen. A few large merchants took orders, and employed master weavers, such as my father, to weave the cloth, the merchants supplying the materials.

master—a skilled workman qualified to train apprentices
damask—a fabric woven in reversible patterns

(4) As the factory system developed hand-loom weaving naturally declined, and my father was one of the sufferers by the change. The first serious lesson of my life came to me one day when he had taken in the last of his work to the merchant, and returned to our little home greatly distressed because there was no more work for him to do. I was then just about ten years of age, but the lesson burned into my heart, and I resolved then that the wolf of poverty should be driven from our door some day, if I could do it.

(5) The question of selling the old looms and starting for the United States came up in the family council, and I heard it discussed from day to day. It was finally resolved to take the plunge and join relatives already in Pittsburg. I well remember that neither father nor mother thought that the change would be otherwise a great sacrifice for them, but that "it would be better for the two boys."

(6) In after life, if you can look back as I do and wonder at the complete surrender of their own desires which parents make for the good of their children, you must reverence their memories with feelings akin to worship.

reverence—treat with deep respect
akin to—similar to

(7) On arriving in Allegheny City (there were four of us: father, mother, my younger brother, and myself), my father entered a cotton

Allegheny City—a town near Pittsburgh

factory. I soon followed, and served as a "bobbin-boy," and this is how I began my preparation for subsequent apprenticeship as a business man. I received one dollar and twenty cents a week, and was then just about twelve years old.

(8) I cannot tell you how proud I was when I received my first week's own earnings. One dollar and twenty cents made by myself and given to me because I had been of some use in the world! No longer entirely dependent upon my parents, but at last admitted to the family partnership as a contributing member and able to help them! I think this makes a man out of a boy sooner than almost anything else, and a real man, too, if there be any germ of true manhood in him. It is everything to feel that you are useful.

(9) I have had to deal with great sums. Many millions of dollars have since passed through my hands. But the genuine satisfaction I had from that one dollar and twenty cents out-weighs any subsequent pleasure in money-getting. It was the direct reward of honest, manual labor; it represented a week of very hard work—so hard that, but for the aim and end which sanctified it, slavery might not be much too strong a term to describe it.

(10) For a lad of twelve to rise and breakfast every morning, except the blessed Sunday morning, and go into the streets and find his way to the factory and begin to work while it was still dark outside, and not be released until after darkness came again in the evening, forty minutes' interval only being allowed at noon, was a terrible task.

(11) But I was young and had my dreams, and something within always told me that this would not, could not, should not last—I should

---

bobbin—a spool to hold yarn or thread

a bobbin-boy—boy responsible for replacing bobbins when needed

germ—seed, the initial stage of development

sanctified—made respectable or holy

some day get into a better position. Besides this, I felt myself no longer a mere boy, but quite a little man, and this made me happy.

(12) A change soon came, for a kind old Scotsman, who knew some of our relatives, made bobbins, and took me into his factory before I was thirteen. But here for a time it was even worse than in the cotton factory, because I was set to fire a boiler in the cellar, and actually to run the small steam-engine which drove the machinery. The firing of the boiler was all right, for fortunately we did not use coal, but the refuse wooden chips; and I always liked to work in wood. But the responsibility of keeping the water right and of running the engine, and the danger of my making a mistake and blowing the whole factory to pieces, caused too great a strain, and I often awoke and found myself sitting up in bed through the night, trying the steam-gauges. But I never told them at home that I was having a hard tussle. No, no! everything must be bright to them.

a hard tussle—a difficult struggle
bright—enthusiastic, cheerful
a point of honor—something that affects one's honor or reputation

(13) This was a point of honor, for every member of the family was working hard, except, of course, my little brother, who was then a child, and we were telling each other only all the bright things. Besides this, no man would whine and give up—he would die first.

(14) There was no servant in our family, and several dollars per week were earned by the mother by binding shoes after her daily work was done! Father was also hard at work in the factory. And could I complain?

binding—fastening, sewing

(15) My kind employer, John Hay,—peace to his ashes!—soon relieved me of the undue strain, for he needed some one to make out bills and keep his accounts, and finding that I could write a plain

his ashes—the remains of his body

school-boy hand and could "cipher," he made me his only clerk. But still I had to work hard upstairs in the factory, for the clerking took but little time.

a school-boy hand—the neat handwriting of a school boy

"cipher"—do accounts

(16) You know how many people moan about poverty as being a great evil, and it seems to be accepted that if people had only plenty of money and were rich, they would be happy and more useful, and get more out of life.

(17) As a rule, there is more genuine satisfaction, a truer life, and more obtained from life in the humble cottages of the poor than in the palaces of the rich. I always pity the sons and daughters of rich men, who are attended by servants, and have governesses at a later age, but am glad to remember that they do not know what they have missed.

(18) They have kind fathers and mothers, too, and think that they enjoy the sweetness of these blessings to the fullest: but this they cannot do; for the poor boy who has in his father his constant companion, tutor, and model, in his mother—holy name!—his nurse, teacher, guardian angel, saint, all in one, has a richer, more precious fortune in life than any rich man's son who is not so favored can possibly know, and compared with which all other fortunes count for little.

(19) It is because I know how sweet and happy and pure the home of honest poverty is, how free from perplexing care, from social envies and emulations, how loving and how united its members may be in the common interest of supporting the family, that I sympathize with the rich man's boy and congratulate the poor man's boy; and it is for these reasons that from the ranks of the poor so many strong, eminent, self-reliant men have always sprung and always must spring.

(20) If you will read the list of the immortals who "were not born to die," you will find that most of them have been born to the precious heritage of poverty.

(21) It seems, nowadays, a matter of universal desire that poverty should be abolished. We should be quite willing to abolish luxury, but to abolish honest, industrious, self-denying poverty would be to destroy the soil upon which mankind produces the virtues which enable our race to reach a still higher civilization than it now possesses.

(22) I come now to the third step in my apprenticeship, for I had already taken two, you see—the cotton factory and then the bobbin factory; and with the third—the third time is the chance, you know—deliverance came. I obtained a situation as messenger boy in the telegraph office of Pittsburg when I was fourteen. Here I entered a new world.

(23) Amid books, newspapers, pencils, pens and ink and writing-pads, and a clean office, bright windows, and the literary atmosphere, I was the happiest boy alive.

(24) My only dread was that I should some day be dismissed because I did not know the city; for it is necessary that a messenger boy should know all the firms and addresses of men who are in the habit of receiving telegrams. But I was a stranger in Pittsburg. However, I made up my mind that I would learn to repeat successively each business house in the principal streets, and was soon able to shut my eyes and begin at one side of Wood Street, and call every firm to the bottom. Before long I was able to do this with the business streets generally. My mind was then at rest upon that point.

immortals—people whose fame continues after death

(25) Of course every messenger boy wants to become an operator, and before the operators arrived in the early mornings the boys slipped up to the instruments and practised. This I did, and was soon able to talk to the boys in the other offices along the line, who were also practising.

(26) One morning I heard Philadelphia calling Pittsburg and giving the signal, "Death message." Great attention was then paid to "death messages," and I thought I ought to try to take this one. I answered and did so, and went off and delivered it before the operator came. After that the operators sometimes used to ask me to work for them.

(27) Having a sensitive ear for sound, I soon learned to take messages by ear, which was then very uncommon—I think only two persons in the United States could then do it. Now every operator takes by ear, so easy it is to follow and do what any other boy can—if you only have to. This brought me into notice, and finally I became an operator, and received the, to me, enormous recompense of twenty-five dollars per month—three hundred dollars a year!

(28) This was a fortune—the very sum that I had fixed when I was a factory-worker as the fortune I wished to possess, because the family could live on three hundred dollars a year and be almost or quite independent. Here it was at last! But I was soon to be in receipt of extra compensation for extra work.

(29) The six newspapers of Pittsburg received telegraphic news in common. Six copies of each despatch were made by a gentleman who received six dollars per week for the work, and he offered me a gold dollar every week if I would do it, of which I was very glad indeed, because I always liked to work with news and scribble for newspapers.

---

an operator—a telegraph operator

"death message"—a message about the death of an important person

despatch (dispatch)—a message written and sent quickly

(30) The reporters came to a room every evening for the news which I had prepared, and this brought me into most pleasant intercourse with these clever fellows, and besides, I got a dollar a week as pocket-money, for this was not considered family revenue by me.

intercourse—conversation, association

(31) I think this last step of doing something beyond one's task is fully entitled to be considered "business." The other revenue, you see, was just salary obtained for regular work; but here was a little business operation upon my own account, and I was very proud indeed of my gold dollar every week.

upon my own account—in my own interest

(32) The Pennsylvania Railroad shortly after this was completed to Pittsburg, and that genius, Thomas A. Scott, was its superintendent. He often came to the telegraph office to talk to his chief, the general superintendent, at Altoona, and I became known to him in this way.

Thomas A. Scott—a railroad executive who advised President Lincoln about the use of railroads to support the northern troops during the Civil War

(33) When that great railway system put up a wire of its own, he asked me to be his clerk and operator; so I left the telegraph office—in which there is great danger that a young man may be permanently buried, as it were—and became connected with the railways.

buried—put in an obscure or insignificant position

(34) The new appointment was accompanied by what was, to me, a tremendous increase in salary. It jumped from twenty-five to thirty-five dollars per month. Mr. Scott was then receiving one hundred and thirty-five dollars per month, and I used to wonder what on earth he could do with so much money.

(35) I remained for thirteen years in the service of the Pennsylvania Railroad Company, and was at last superintendent of the Pittsburg division of the road, successor to Mr. Scott, who had in the meantime risen to the office of vice-president of the company.

(36) One day Mr. Scott, who was the kindest of men, and had taken a great fancy to me, asked if I had or could find five hundred dollars to invest.

a great fancy—a strong liking or preference

(37) Here the business instinct came into play. I felt that as the door was opened for a business investment with my chief, it would be wilful flying in the face of providence if I did not jump at it; so I answered promptly:

came into play—began to have an influence

flying in the face of providence—going against fate

(38) "Yes, sir; I think I can."

(39) "Very well," he said, "get it; a man has just died who owns ten shares in the Adams Express Company which I want you to buy. It will cost you fifty dollars per share, and I can help you with a little balance if you cannot raise it all."

balance—the remainder of the money

(40) Here was a queer position. The available assets of the whole family were not five hundred dollars. But there was one member of the family whose ability, pluck, and resource never failed us, and I felt sure the money could be raised somehow or other by my mother.

queer—awkward, difficult

pluck—courage

(41) Indeed, had Mr. Scott known our position he would have advanced it himself; but the last thing in the world the proud Scot will do is to reveal his poverty and rely upon others. The family had managed by this time to purchase a small house and pay for it in order to save rent. My recollection is that it was worth eight hundred dollars.

Scot—a person from Scotland

(42) The matter was laid before the council of three that night and the oracle spoke: "Must be done. Mortgage our house. I will take the steamer in the morning for Ohio, and see uncle, and ask him to

oracle—a person with authority, in this case Carnegie's mother

arrange it. I am sure he can." This was done. Of course her visit was successful—where did she ever fail?

(43) The money was procured, paid over; ten shares of Adams Express Company stock was mine; but no one knew our little home had been mortgaged to "give our boy a start."

procured—gotten, obtained

(44) Adams Express stock then paid monthly dividends of one per cent, and the first check for five dollars arrived. I can see it now, and I well remember the signature of "J. C. Babcock, Cashier," who wrote a big "John Hancock" hand.

a big "John Hancock" hand—a big signature like that of John Hancock on the Declaration of Independence

(45) The next day being Sunday, we boys—myself and my ever-constant companions—took our usual Sunday afternoon stroll in the country, and sitting down in the woods, I showed them this check, saying, "Eureka! We have found it."

Eureka!—Greek for "I have found it!"

(46) Here was something new to all of us, for none of us had ever received anything but from toil. A return from capital was something strange and new.

toil—hard physical work

(47) How money could make money, how, without any attention from me, this mysterious golden visitor should come, led to much speculation upon the part of the young fellows, and I was for the first time hailed as a "capitalist."

(48) You see, I was beginning to serve my apprenticeship as a business man in a satisfactory manner.

(49) A very important incident in my life occurred when, one day in a train, a nice, farmer-looking gentleman approached me, saying that the conductor had told him I was connected with the Pennsylvania

Railroad, and he would like to show me something. He pulled from a small green bag the model of the first sleeping-car. This was Mr. Woodruff, the inventor.

Mr. Woodruff—Theodore Tuttle Woodruff, inventor of the sleeping car

struck me like a flash—was clear to me in an instant

(50) Its value struck me like a flash. I asked him to come to Altoona the following week, and he did so. Mr. Scott, with his usual quickness, grasped the idea. A contract was made with Mr. Woodruff to put two trial cars on the Pennsylvania Railroad. Before leaving Altoona Mr. Woodruff came and offered me an interest in the venture, which I promptly accepted. But how I was to make my payments rather troubled me, for the cars were to be paid for in monthly installments after delivery, and my first monthly payment was to be two hundred and seventeen dollars and a half.

(51) I had not the money, and I did not see any way of getting it. But I finally decided to visit the local banker and ask him for a loan, pledging myself to repay at a rate of fifteen dollars per month. He promptly granted it. Never shall I forget his putting his arm over my shoulder, saying, "Oh, yes, Andy; you are all right!"

(52) I then and there signed my first note. Proud day this; and surely now no one will dispute that I was becoming a "business man." I had signed my first note, and, most important of all,—for any fellow can sign a note,—I had found a banker willing to take it as "good."

(53) My subsequent payments were made by the receipts from the sleeping-cars, and I really made my first considerable sum from this investment in the Woodruff Sleeping-car Company, which was afterward absorbed by Mr. Pullman—a remarkable man whose name is now known over all the world.

Mr. Pullman—George Pullman, owner of the Palace Car Company, whose name is now associated with sleeping cars, commonly known as Pullman cars

(54) Shortly after this I was appointed superintendent of the Pittsburg division, and returned to my dear old home, smoky Pittsburg. Wooden bridges were then used exclusively upon the railways, and the Pennsylvania Railroad was experimenting with a bridge built of cast-iron. I saw that wooden bridges would not do for the future, and organized a company in Pittsburg to build iron bridges.

(55) Here again I had recourse to the bank, because my share of the capital was twelve hundred and fifty dollars, and I had not the money; but the bank lent it to me, and we began the Keystone Bridge Works, which proved a great success. This company built the first great bridge over the Ohio River, three hundred feet span, and has built many of the most important structures since.

(56) This was my beginning in manufacturing; and from that start all our other works have grown, the profits of one building the other. My "apprenticeship" as a business man soon ended, for I resigned my position as an officer of the Pennsylvania Railroad Company to give exclusive attention to business.

(57) I was no longer merely an official working for others upon a salary, but a full-fledged business man working upon my own account.

(58) I never was quite reconciled to working for other people. At the most, the railway officer has to look forward to the enjoyment of a stated salary, and he has a great many people to please; even if he gets to be president, he has sometimes a board of directors who cannot know what is best to be done; and even if this board is satisfied, he has a board of stockholders to criticize him, and as the property is not his own he cannot manage it as he pleases.

(59) I always liked the idea of being my own master, of manufacturing something and giving employment to many men. There is only one thing to think of manufacturing if you are a Pittsburger, for Pittsburg even then had asserted her supremacy as the "Iron City," the leading iron-and-steel-manufacturing city in America.

(60) So my indispensable and clever partners, who had been my boy companions, I am delighted to say,—some of the very boys who had met in the grove to wonder at the five-dollar check,—began business, and still continue extending it to meet the ever-growing and ever-changing wants of our most progressive country, year after year.

(61) Always we are hoping that we need expand no farther; yet ever we are finding that to stop expanding would be to fall behind; and even to-day the successive improvements and inventions follow each other so rapidly that we see just as much yet to be done as ever.

(62) When the manufacturer of steel ceases to grow he begins to decay, so we must keep on extending. The result of all these developments is that three pounds of finished steel are now bought in Pittsburg for two cents, which is cheaper than anywhere else on earth, and that our country had become the greatest producer of iron in the world.

(63) And so ends the story of my apprenticeship and graduation as a business man.

PART 2: "THE GOSPEL OF WEALTH—THE PROBLEM OF THE ADMINISTRATION OF WEALTH"
(Paragraphs 64–81)

(64) The problem of our age is the proper administration of wealth, that the ties of brotherhood may still bind together the rich and poor in harmonious relationship. The conditions of human life have not only been changed, but revolutionized, within the past few hundred years. In former days there was little difference between the dwelling, dress, food, and environment of the chief and those of his retainers. The Indians are to-day where civilized man then was. When visiting the Sioux, I was led to the wigwam of the chief. It was like the others in external appearance, and even within the difference was trifling between it and those of the poorest of his braves. The contrast between the palace of the millionaire and the cottage of the laborer with us to-day measures the change which has come with civilization. This change, however, is not to be deplored, but welcomed as highly beneficial. It is well, nay, essential, for the progress of the race that the houses of some should be homes for all that is highest and best in literature and the arts, and for all the refinements of civilization, rather than that none should be so. Much better this great irregularity than universal squalor. Without wealth there can be no Maecenas. The "good old times" were not good old times. Neither master nor servant was as well situated then as to-day. A relapse to old conditions would be disastrous to both—not the least so to him who serves—and would sweep away civilization with it. But whether the change be for good or ill, it is upon us, beyond our power to alter, and, therefore, to be accepted and made the best of. It is a waste of time to criticize the inevitable.

Sioux—North American Indian tribe
wigwam—Indian hut or lodge
trifling—insignificant

nay—indeed, in fact

Maecenas—a patron, a supporter of the arts

(65) It is easy to see how the change has come. One illustration will serve for almost every phase of the cause. In the manufacture of products we have the whole story. It applies to all combinations of human industry, as stimulated and enlarged by the inventions of this scientific age. Formerly, articles were manufactured at the domestic hearth, or in small shops which formed part of the household. The master and his apprentices worked side by side, the latter living with the master, and therefore subject to the same conditions. When these apprentices rose to be masters, there was little or no change in their mode of life, and they, in turn, educated succeeding apprentices in the same routine. There was, substantially, social equality, and even political equality, for those engaged in industrial pursuits had then little or no voice in the State.

domestic hearth—at home

(66) The inevitable result of such a mode of manufacture was crude articles at high prices. To-day the world obtains commodities of excellent quality at prices which even the preceding generation would have deemed incredible. In the commercial world similar causes have produced similar results, and the race is benefited thereby. The poor enjoy what the rich could not before afford. What were the luxuries have become the necessaries of life. The laborer has now more comforts than the farmer had a few generations ago. The farmer has more luxuries than the landlord had, and is more richly clad and better housed. The landlord has books and pictures rarer and appointments more artistic than the king could then obtain.

commodities—products

deemed—believed

clad—dressed

appointments—equipment, furnishings

(67) The price we pay for this salutary change is, no doubt, great. We assemble thousands of operatives in the factory, and in the mine, of whom the employer can know little or nothing, and to whom he is lit-

salutary—favorable, beneficial

operatives—workers

tle better than a myth. All intercourse between them is at an end. Rigid castes are formed, and, as usual, mutual ignorance breeds mutual distrust. Each caste is without sympathy with the other, and ready to credit anything disparaging in regard to it. Under the law of competition, the employer of thousands is forced into the strictest economies, among which the rates paid to labor figure prominently, and often there is friction between the employer and the employed, between capital and labor, between rich and poor. Human society loses homogeneity.

(68) The price which society pays for the law of competition, like the price it pays for cheap comforts and luxuries, is also great; but the advantages of this law are also greater still than its cost—for it is to this law that we owe our wonderful material development, which brings improved conditions in its train. But, whether the law be benign or not, we must say of it, as we say of the change in the conditions of men to which we have referred: It is here; we cannot evade it;

intercourse—conversation, association
castes—social classes
breeds—causes

disparaging—insulting

in its train—as a result

no substitutes for it have been found; and while the law may be sometimes hard for the individual, it is best for the race, because it insures the survival of the fittest in every department. We accept and welcome, therefore, as conditions to which we must accommodate ourselves, great inequality of environment; the concentration of business, industrial and commercial, in the hands of a few; and the law of competition between these, as being not only beneficial, but essential to the future progress of the race. Having accepted these, it follows that there must be great scope for the exercise of special ability in the merchant and in the manufacturer who has to conduct affairs upon a great scale. That this talent for organization and management is rare among men is proved by the fact that it invariably secures enormous rewards for its possessor, no matter where or under what laws or conditions. The [people who are] experienced in affairs always rate the MAN whose services can be obtained as a partner as not only the first consideration, but such as render the question of his capital scarcely worth considering: for able men soon create capital; in the hands of those without the special talent required, capital soon takes wings. Such men become interested in firms or corporations using millions; and, estimating only simple interest to be made upon the capital invested, it is inevitable that their income must exceed their expenditure and that they must, therefore, accumulate wealth. Nor is there any middle ground which such men can occupy, because the great manufacturing or commercial concern which does not earn at least interest upon its capital soon becomes bankrupt. It must either go forward or fall behind; to stand still is impossible. It is a condition essential to its successful operation that it should be thus far profitable, and even that, in addition to interest on capital, it should make

the race—the human race

survival of the fittest—the evolutionary principle that the plants and animals best suited to the environment survive over those that are not as well suited

in every department—in every area of life

such as render—a consideration that makes

able—capable

takes wings—goes quickly, disappears

profit. It is a law, as certain as any of the others named, that men possessed of this peculiar talent for affairs, under the free play of economic forces must, of necessity, soon be in receipt of more revenue than can be judiciously expended upon themselves; and this law is as beneficial for the race as the others.

(69) Objections to the foundations upon which society is based are not in order, because the condition of the race is better with these than it has been with any other which has been tried. Of the effect of any new substitutes proposed we cannot be sure. The Socialist or Anarchist who seeks to overturn present conditions is to be regarded as attacking the foundation upon which civilization itself rests, for civilization took its start from the day when the capable, industrious workman said to his incompetent and lazy fellow, "If thou dost not sow, thou shalt not reap," and thus ended primitive Communism by separating the drones from the bees. One who studies this subject will soon be brought face to face with the conclusion that upon the sacredness of property civilization itself depends—the right of the laborer to his hundred dollars in the savings-bank, and equally the legal right of the millionaire to his millions. Every man must be allowed "to sit under his own vine and fig-tree, with none to make afraid," if human society is to advance, or even to remain so far advanced as it is. To those who propose to substitute Communism for this intense Individualism, the answer therefore is: The race has tried that. All progress from that barbarous day to present time has resulted from its displacement. Not evil, but good, has come to the race from the accumulation of wealth by those who have had the ability and energy to produce it. But even if we admit for a moment

judiciously—with good judgment
expended—spent

"If thou does not sow, thou shalt not reap."—If you do not plant, you shall not harvest.
drones—bees that do no useful work

with none to make afraid—with no one to fear

that it might be better for the race to discard its present foundation, Individualism,—that it is a nobler ideal that man should labor, not for himself alone, but in and for a brotherhood of his fellows, and share with them all in common—even admit all this, and a sufficient answer is, This is not evolution, but revolution. It necessitates the changing of human nature itself—a work of eons, even if it were good to change it, which we cannot know.

(70) It is not practicable in our day or in our age. Even if desirable theoretically, it belongs to another and long-succeeding sociological stratum. Our duty is with what is practicable now—with the next step possible in our day and generation. It is criminal to waste our energies in endeavoring to uproot, when all we can profitably accomplish is to bend the universal tree of humanity a little in the direction most favorable to the production of good fruit under existing circumstances. We might as well urge the destruction of the highest existing type of man because he failed to reach our ideal as to favor the destruction of Individualism, Private Property, the Law of Accumulation of Wealth, and the Law of Competition; for these are the highest result of human experience, the soil in which society, so far, has produced the best fruit. Unequally or unjustly, perhaps, as these laws sometimes operate, and imperfect as they appear to the Idealist, they are nevertheless, like the highest type of man, the best and most valuable for all that humanity has yet accomplished.

long-succeeding sociological stratum— some future society

(71) We start, then, with a condition of affairs under which the best interests of the race are promoted, but which inevitably gives wealth to the few. Thus far, accepting conditions as they exist, the situation can be surveyed and pronounced good. The question then arises,—

and if the foregoing be correct, it is the only question with which we have to deal,—What is the proper mode of administering wealth after the laws upon which civilization is founded have thrown it into the hands of a few? And it is of this great question that I believe I offer the true solution. It will be understood that fortunes are here spoken of, not moderate sums saved by many years of effort, the returns from which are required for the comfortable maintenance and education of families. This is not wealth, but only competence, which it should be the aim of all to acquire, and which it is for the best interest of society should be acquired.

(72) There are but three modes in which surplus wealth can be disposed of. It can be left to the families of the decedents; or it can be bequeathed for public purposes; or, finally, it can be administered by its possessors during their lives. Under the first and second modes most of the wealth of the world that has reached the few has hitherto been applied. Let us in turn consider each of these modes. The first is the most injudicious. In monarchical countries, the estates and the greatest portion of the wealth are left to the first son, that the vanity of the parent may be gratified by the thought that his name and title are to descend unimpaired to succeeding generations. The condition of this class in Europe to-day teaches the failure of such hopes or ambitions. The successors have become impoverished though their follies, or from the fall in the value of the land. Even in Great Britain the strict law of entail has been found inadequate to maintain an hereditary class. Its soil is rapidly passing into the hands of the stranger. Under republican institutions the division of property among the children is much fairer; but the question which forces itself upon

the most injudicious—the most lacking in good judgment, the worst

monarchial—having a monarch or king

follies—foolish actions

law of entail—laws that determine inheritance

thoughtful men in all lands is, Why should men leave great fortunes to children? If this is done from affection, is it not misguided affection? Observation teaches that, generally speaking, it is not well for the children that they should be so burdened. Neither is it well for the State. Beyond providing for the wife and daughters moderate sources of income, and very moderate allowances indeed, if any, for the sons, men may well hesitate; for it is no longer questionable that great sums bequeathed often work more for the injury than for the good of the recipients. Wise men will soon conclude that, for the best interests of the members of their families, and of the State, such bequests are an improper use of their means.

(73) It is not suggested that men who have failed to educate their sons to earn a livelihood shall cast them adrift in poverty. If any man sees fit to rear his sons with a view to their living idle lives, or, what is highly commendable, has instilled in them the sentiment that they are in a position to labor for public ends without reference to pecuniary considerations, then, of course, the duty of the parent is to see that such are provided for in moderation. There are instances of millionaires' sons unspoiled by wealth, who, being rich, still perform great services to the community. Such are the very salt of the earth, as valuable as, unfortunately, they are rare. It is not the exception, however, but the rule, that men must regard; and, looking at the usual result of enormous sums conferred upon legatees, the thoughtful man must shortly say, "I would as soon leave to my son a curse as the almighty dollar," and admit to himself that it is not the welfare of the children, but family pride, which inspires these legacies.

bequeathed—inherited

cast them adrift—send them away

pecuniary considerations—concerns about money

the very salt of the earth—the most noble people on the earth

legatees—children who receive a legacy or inheritance

(74) As to the second mode, that of leaving wealth at death for public uses, it may be said that this is only a means for the disposal of wealth, provided a man is content to wait until he is dead before he becomes of much good in the world. Knowledge of the results of legacies bequeathed is not calculated to inspire the brightest hopes of much posthumous good being accomplished by them. The cases are not few in which the real object sought by the testator is not attained, nor are they few in which his real wishes are thwarted. In many cases the bequests are so used as to become only monuments of his folly. It is well to remember that it requires the exercise of not less ability than that which acquires it, to use wealth so as to be really beneficial to the community. Besides this, it may fairly be said that no man is to be extolled for doing what he cannot help doing, nor is he to be thanked by the community to which he only leaves wealth at death. Men who leave vast sums in this way may fairly be thought men who would not have left it at all had they been able to take it with them. The memories of such cannot be held in grateful remembrance, for there is no grace in their gifts. It is not to be wondered at that such bequests seems so generally to lack the blessing.

(75) The growing disposition to tax more and more heavily large estates left at death is a cheering indication of the growth of a salutary change in public opinion. The State of Pennsylvania now takes—subject to some exceptions—one tenth of the property left by its citizens. The budget presented in the British Parliament the other day proposes to increase the death duties; and, most significant of all, the new tax is to be a graduated one. Of all forms of taxation this seems the wisest. Men who continue hoarding great sums all their

legacies bequeathed—property left after death
posthumous good—good deeds done after death
sought—looked for, intended
testator—a person who makes a will
not attained—not accomplished
thwarted—opposed, blocked
bequests—property left after death
folly—foolish act
extolled—praised

estates—the property of a person who has died

hoarding—accumulating

lives, the proper use of which for public ends would work good to the community from which it chiefly came, should be made to feel that the community, in the form of the State, cannot thus be deprived of its proper share. By taxing estates heavily at death, the State marks its condemnation of the selfish millionaire's unworthy life.

(76) There remains, then, only one mode of using great fortunes; but in this we have the true antidote for the temporary unequal distribution of wealth, the reconciliation of the rich and poor—a reign of harmony, another ideal, differing, indeed, from that of the Communist in requiring only the further evolution of existing conditions, not the total overthrow of our civilization. It is founded upon the present most intense Individualism, and the race is prepared to put it in practice by degrees whenever it pleases. Under its sway we shall have an ideal State, in which the surplus wealth of the few will become, in the best sense, the property of the many, because administered for the common good; and this wealth, passing through the hands of the few, can be made a much more potent force for the elevation of our race than if distributed in small sums to the people themselves. Even the poorest can be made to see this, and to agree that great sums gathered by some of their fellow-citizens and spent for public purposes, from which the masses reap the principal benefit, are more valuable to them than if scattered among themselves in trifling amounts through the course of many years.

(77) This, then, is held to be the duty of the man of wealth: To set an example of modest, unostentatious living, shunning display or extravagance; to provide moderately for the legitimate wants of those dependent upon him; and, after doing so, to consider all surplus

antidote—solution

under its sway—under its influence

reap—get

revenues which come to him simply as trust funds, which he is called upon to administer, and strictly bound as a matter of duty to administer in the manner which, in his judgment, is best calculated to produce the most beneficial results for the community—the man of wealth thus becoming the mere trustee and agent for his poorer brethren, bringing to their service his superior wisdom, experience, and ability to administer, doing for them better than they would or could do for themselves.

brethren—fellow people (literally brothers)

(78) The best uses to which surplus wealth can be put have already been indicated. Those who would administer wisely must, indeed, be wise; for one of the serious obstacles to the improvement of our race is indiscriminate charity. It were better for mankind that the millions of the rich were thrown into the sea than so spent as to encourage the slothful, the drunken, the unworthy. Of every thousand dollars spent in so-called charity to-day, it is probable that nine hundred and fifty dollars is unwisely spent—so spent, indeed, as to produce the very evils which it hopes to mitigate or cure. A well-known writer of philosophic books admitted the other day that he had given a quarter of a dollar to a man who approached him as he was coming to visit the house of his friend. He knew nothing of the habits of the beggar, knew not the use that would be made of his money, although he had every reason to suspect that it would be spent improperly. This man professed to be a disciple of Herbert Spencer; yet the quarter-dollar given that night will probably work more injury than all the money will do good which its thoughtless donor will ever be able to give in true charity. He only gratified his own feelings, saved himself from annoyance—and this was probably one of the most selfish and very worst actions of his life, for in all [other] respects he is most worthy.

indiscriminate—careless, haphazard
It were better—It would be better
the slothful—the lazy (people)

mitigate—alleviate, to make less severe

Herbert Spencer—English philosopher who applied the principles of evolution to the human race, a theory called Social Darwinism

(79) In bestowing charity, the main consideration should be to help those who will help themselves; to provide part of the means by which those who desire to improve may do so; to give those who desire to rise the aids by which they may rise; to assist, but rarely or never to do all. Neither the individual nor the race is improved by almsgiving. Those worthy of assistance, except in rare cases, seldom require assistance. The really valuable men of the race never do, except in case of accident or sudden change. Every one has, of course, cases of individuals brought to his own knowledge where temporary assistance can do genuine good, and these he will not overlook. But the amount which can be wisely given by the individual for individuals is necessarily limited by his lack of knowledge of the circumstances connected with each. He is the only true reformer who is as careful and as anxious not to aid the unworthy, and, perhaps, even more so, for in almsgiving more injury is probably done by rewarding vice than by relieving virtue.

bestowing—giving

almsgiving—giving charity

vice—bad behavior
virtue—good behavior

(80) . . . The best means of benefiting the community is to place within its reach the ladders upon which the aspiring can rise—free libraries, parks, and means of recreation, by which men are helped in body and mind; works of art, certain to give pleasure and improve the public taste; and public institutions of various kinds, which will improve the general condition of the people; in this manner returning their surplus wealth to the mass of their fellows in the forms best calculated to do them lasting good.

(81) Such, in my opinion is the true gospel concerning wealth, obedience to which is destined some day to solve the problem of the rich and the poor, and to bring "Peace on earth, among men good will."

GREAT INDUSTRIALISTS: ANDREW CARNEGIE

⇾ EXERCISES ⇽

Comprehension Questions

Answer these questions in paragraph form, using complete sentences in Modern English. Do not copy the answers directly from the reading passage. (See pages 218–21 in the Yellow Pages for a review of paragraph form.)

Part 1: "Introduction: How I Served My Apprenticeship" (Paragraphs 1–63)

1. Explain the situation in Scotland that made the Carnegie family decide to come to America. What did they look forward to in America?

2. Describe Carnegie's first three jobs.

3. Carnegie writes that it is an advantage to grow up in poverty. Explain his reasons.

4. Why was Carnegie especially proud of his investments in the Adams Express Company, the Woodruff Sleeping car Company, and the Keystone Bridge Company?

Part 2: "The Gospel of Wealth" (Paragraphs 64–81)

1. How were the lives of the master and the workers in the past different from their lives today?

2. Why should we accept the situation that some people are much richer than other people?

3. Why did Carnegie think that we cannot change the foundations of society?

4. Explain the duty of a man of wealth in your own words. (See paragraph 77.)

5. Why did Carnegie think that it is a bad idea to give money to poor people?

Vocabulary Development

Part 1: "Introduction: How I Served My Apprenticeship" (Paragraphs 1–63)

1. Carnegie uses a variety of idioms and expressions that are still common in conversation today. To find out what these expressions mean, look them up in a dictionary or ask a native speaker of English. Then use each expression in a sentence of your own.

    a. *bread-winner* (2)
    b. *burned into my heart* (4)
    c. *to drive the wolf of poverty from the door* (4)
    d. *takes the plunge* (5)
    e. *a germ of* (true manhood) (8)
    f. *deliverance came* (22)
    g. *pocket-money* (30)
    h. *struck me like a flash* (50)
    i. *grasp the idea* (50)

2. Here are more useful words to study and learn:

    livelihood (1)
    resolve (4)
    humble (17)
    reveal (41)
    promptly (51)

Part 2: "The Gospel of Wealth" (Paragraphs 64–81)

1. In paragraph 69, Carnegie mentions several "ism's"—socialism, anarchism, communism, and individualism. Look up the definitions of these political systems to determine their central ideas and differences. Which one does Carnegie prefer? Which do your prefer?

GREAT INDUSTRIALISTS: ANDREW CARNEGIE

2. Carnegie uses many vocabulary words in his essay that are worth learning and using. Here is a selection. Write a paragraph about Carnegie's ideas about the distribution of wealth using at least eight to ten of these words.

bind together (64)	*harmonious* (64)	*to deplore* (64)
squalor (64)	*benign* (68)	*evade* (68)
barbarous (69)	*endeavor* (70)	*uproot* (70)
to promote (71)	*inevitably* (71)	*to survey* (71)
dispose of (72)	*unimpaired* (72)	*commendable* (73)
to instill (73)	*in moderation* (73)	*reconciliation* (76)

Quotations and Paraphrases

Write the quotation with an introductory explanation of the source and the content, paying close attention to punctuation. Then paraphrase it in your own words. (See pages 246–52 in the Yellow Pages for help with quotations and paraphrases.)

Part 1: "Introduction: How I Served My Apprenticeship" (Paragraphs 1–63)

1. (paragraph 9) "I have had to deal with great sums.... But the genuine satisfaction I had from [my first] dollar and twenty cents out-weighs any subsequent pleasure in money-getting."

   _____
   _____
   _____
   _____

2. (paragraph 17) "As a rule, there is more genuine satisfaction, a truer life, and more obtained from life in the humble cottages of the poor than in the palaces of the rich."

   _____
   _____
   _____
   _____

READING AND RESEARCHING AMERICA

3. Choose your own quotation and follow the same directions.

_____
_____
_____
_____

Part 2: "The Gospel of Wealth" (Paragraphs 64–81)

1. (paragraph 64) "The problem of our age is the proper administration of wealth, that the ties of brotherhood may still bind together the rich and poor in harmonious relationship."

_____
_____
_____
_____

2. (paragraph 77) "This . . . is held to be the duty of the man of wealth: To set an example of modest, unostentatious living, shunning display or extravagance; to provide moderately for the legitimate wants of those dependent upon him; and . . . consider all surplus revenues . . . as trust funds, which he is called upon to administer . . . in the manner which . . . is best calculated to produce the most beneficial results for the community . . . ."

_____
_____
_____
_____

3. Choose your own quotation and follow the same directions.

_____

_____

_____

Writing Summaries

Write a one-paragraph summary in Modern English without plagiarism. (See pages 253–55 in the Yellow Pages for help in writing a summary.)

1. Summarize Carnegie's argument that it is an advantage to grow up in poverty. (paragraphs 16–21)

2. Summarize Carnegie's argument in paragraphs 64–71 in which he justifies the accumulation of great wealth in the hands of a few men.

3. Summarize Carnegie's three ways of disposing of great wealth and the advantages and disadvantages of each one. (paragraphs 71–81)

Questions for Discussion and Writing

Discuss your answers to these questions with your classmates. These questions may also be used as essay topics. (See pages 221–24 in the Yellow Pages for a review of essay form.)

1. What personal qualities enabled Carnegie to become successful in business? Are these qualities the same ones that are needed to be successful in business today? Would these qualities help you to become successful in your country? Are there other qualities that you think are important to success?

2. In paragraph 9, Carnegie wrote that the work he did as a child in the cotton factory was like slavery. Compare his work to Frederick Douglass's work as a child slave in Baltimore. Do you agree that Carnegie's work was like slavery?

3. Carnegie wrote, "I know how sweet and happy and pure the home of honest poverty is, how free from perplexing care, from social envies and emulations, how loving and how united its members may be in the common interest of supporting the family . . . ." (paragraph 19)

   To what extent do you agree with Carnegie's description of a poor family?

4. Here are two common American sayings. Would Carnegie agree with either of them? Do you agree with either of them?

   "Neither a borrower nor a lender be."
   "God helps those who help themselves."

5. Carnegie wrote that the Law of Competition may be "hard for the individual (but) it is best for the race . . . ." (paragraph 68). Explain Carnegie's idea. To what extent do you agree with it?

6. Carnegie writes about the "nobler ideal" (paragraph 69) that man should work for his fellows and share the wealth with them, but he says that this ideal is against human nature. Carnegie also says that we can't change human nature. To what extent do you agree with these ideas?

7. Carnegie says that we should not give charity to people indiscriminately (paragraph 78). What are his reasons? To what extent do you agree with him?

Definitions

Darwinism—the theory in biology that living things change over time and that the living things that survive are the ones that are best suited to their environment. Often called Survival of the Fittest.

Social Darwinism—the belief that Darwin's ideas can be applied to human beings and that some human beings are more fit to survive than others.

---

8. Read these definitions. Does Carnegie seem to believe in Social Darwinism? To what extent do you agree with Social Darwinism?

GREAT INDUSTRIALISTS: ANDREW CARNEGIE

9. The "Captains of Industry" mentioned in the Introduction are sometimes called "Robber Barons" instead, because of the ways in which they exploited their workers, their investors, and the government with their aggressive competition. Do some research on one of these men and decide for yourself which name is more appropriate.

Scanning for Specific Information

Scanning means looking over a page quickly to find a specific detail rather than beginning at the top of the page and reading every word. Working alone or with one or two other students, use a reference book to find the information to complete the sentences. Try to work quickly to find just the information you need to fill in to complete the exercise. You will probably need to consult more than one source. Make sure that your answers fit the structure of the sentence.

Reference book(s) used _____

_____

GREAT CAPITALISTS OR ROBBER BARONS?

In the early 1900s, the GNP (_____) of the United States surpassed that of any other country, and Americans became the wealthiest people in the world. The nation had rich natural resources that contributed to this wealth, but equally important were the businessmen who invented or developed new technology and organized and managed growing industries.

Examples include Thomas Edison, the inventor of the _____

_____. The Edison Company was the first to

install a central system to _____ to a neighborhood in New York City. Gustavus Swift used assembly line techniques and refrigerated railroad cars to produce inexpensive _____ products. Andrew Carnegie made cheap, high-quality steel using new technology such as the _____ processes and investing in sources of raw materials like _____.

J. P. Morgan, an investment banker and financier, reorganized industries by merging small competing companies into larger companies that could operate more efficiently. He began with railroads and later merged the Edison Company with other electric companies to form _____ and the Carnegie Steel Company with other steel companies to form _____, the world's largest corporation at the time.

These giant corporations, called trusts or monopolies, were run by small groups of men: The president of one company would sit on the board of directors of several other companies so that these men could work together to control prices and competition. This concentration of wealth and power in just a few individuals frequently led to corrupt business practices, but the government, following a capitalist policy called *laissez-faire*, which means _____, did nothing to limit the power of the trusts.

With no _____ taxes, these powerful men became extremely wealthy while their workers lived in poverty. This inequality was justified by the theory of Charles Darwin, who wrote in his 1859 book, _____, that competition leads to the survival of the fittest; his biological principle was applied to human society to explain that the more intelligent and aggressive men should be more successful than the weaker. But some people were appalled by the cruel cut-throat methods of the capitalists and their lack of sympathy for the workers, hence the other common name for the Great Capitalists—the Robber Barons.

In the late 1800s, the government began to take action to control business practices and maintain competition. In the year _____, Congress established the first federal regulatory agency, the Interstate Commerce Commission, with powers to regulate _____. In the year _____, the Sherman Antitrust Act was passed, making it illegal for businesses to _____. Since then, much legislation has been enacted in the United States to control the relationships between workers, business owners, and consumers.

Research Topics

Choose one of these topics or another topic that interests you to do one of the research exercises in the Yellow Pages. Share the results of your research with your classmates as you become experts in your own research areas.

Industrial Revolution	capitalism	individualism
investment banking	iron and steel industries	railroads
Captains of Industry	Charles Darwin	Social Darwinism
Andrew Carnegie	J. P. Morgan	John D. Rockefeller
Collis P. Huntington	Leland Stanford	Cornelius Vanderbilt
Interstate Commerce Commission	Sherman Antitrust Act	

Expansion Activities

1. The Parker Brothers board game Monopoly® is very popular among American children: The game ends when one person controls so much property on the board that the other players go bankrupt trying to pay their rents. In fact, one property that you can buy is the Pennsylvania Railroad. Play this game with your classmates or friends to see if you have the talent to be a "great capitalist."

2. "Rags to Riches" stories like Carnegie's were very popular in the early 1900s. An American author of the time, Horatio Alger, wrote a series of books intended to show young men the way to success by "pulling themselves up by their bootstraps." A typical title is *The Errand Boy: or, How Phil Brent Won Success*. Look for one of these books in your local library or at a used book store, or look up Horatio Alger on the Internet. You might try writing a short "Horatio Alger" story of your own.

3. The names of the Captains of Industry are still well known today because there are so many colleges, museums, libraries, hospitals, and other institutions that were established by them and have their names, such as Stanford University, Carnegie Hall, Vanderbilt University, and the Huntington Library. Find out if there is an institution in your area that you or your class can visit. If no institution is close enough to visit, you might be able to take a "virtual tour" on a website.

6

REFORMERS
Jane Addams
(1860–1935)
★ ★ ★

INTRODUCTION

*I*n the late 1800s, the population of the United States doubled as a result of increased immigration from the countries of eastern and southern Europe, such as Poland, Hungary, Italy, and Greece. The new immigrants settled in the industrial cities of the Northeast and Midwest—New York, Boston, Cleveland, Pittsburgh, and Chicago—where they could find work easily in huge factories. Coming from small country villages in Europe, they found American city life difficult because of the differences in language and culture. They typically lived with people from their own countries in small rooms in apartment buildings called tenements that did not have heat, electricity, or plumbing. They worked together in the meat-packing plants, textile factories, and steel mills, and were often exploited by factory owners because of their lack of education and English language skills.

Many Americans were alarmed at the swelling numbers of poor, uneducated foreigners in their cities, but a few people wanted to help them. One was Jane Addams, a young woman who grew up in a middle-class family in the small town of Cedarville, Illinois. Her father, the miller for the town and later a state senator, and her education at a local women's college gave her a strong sense of idealism, but at that time there were very few opportunities for young women to put their education and ideals to work. After graduation from college (Rockford Seminary, now Rockford College), Jane Addams traveled to Europe, as many young women of the time did to finish their education. There Addams became interested in the settlement houses in the big cities of England. These houses, located in the slums, acted as social welfare agencies to provide cultural and educational opportunities for the impoverished working classes. She decided to start a settlement house in Chicago and enlisted the help of her father and her college friends to find a house and to fund the project.

Hull-House opened on the south side of Chicago in 1889 with a kindergarten for little children and classes and clubs for older children and adults. Many of Addams' idealistic young friends from college were eager to help, teaching classes in English, nutrition, child care, and household management. The women soon realized that their neighbors needed more than educational and cultural opportunities. Because many of the problems of the neighborhood—such as inadequate plumbing, lack of garbage collection, unsafe buildings, and dirty food and water—needed a government solution, the women became political activists on behalf of the poor. With their family connections to people with money and influence, they were able to bring needed changes to state and city laws.

As Hull-House became more and more successful, Jane Addams gave speeches and wrote articles and books on the immigrant urban poor and their needs. She became active in the World Peace Movement at the time of World War I and was awarded the Nobel Peace Prize in 1935. Since her death in 1935, Hull-House has continued its work with Chicago's working poor.

Pre-Reading Questions

Many people are aware of the problems of the poor, but few people do anything about them. Before you read, think about people you have heard about or know who try to help poor people: Why do they help, and what do they do to help? What kinds of help do you think are worthwhile?

REFORMERS: JANE ADDAMS

→ READING PASSAGE ←

JANE ADDAMS:
From *Twenty Years at Hull-House*

A well-educated, idealistic woman, Jane Addams wrote in a style that today would be called old-fashioned, flowery, sentimental, and Victorian. Expressions such as *such meager preparation* and *in lieu of the wider advantage which an eastern college is supposed to afford* in paragraph 1 are understandable, but more elaborate than the words we would use in Modern English. When you write about Jane Addams, use a simple modern style.

PART 1: THE BEGINNINGS OF HULL-HOUSE
(Paragraphs 1–16)

(1) As my three older sisters had already attended the seminary at Rockford, of which my father was trustee, without any question I entered there at seventeen, with such meager preparation in Latin and algebra as the village school had afforded. I was very ambitious to go to Smith College, although I well knew that my father's theory in regard to the education of his daughters implied a school as near at

seminary—a religious college

trustee—member of the governing board of the college

such meager—only a little

Smith College—a women's college in Massachusetts

home as possible, to be followed by travel abroad in lieu of the wider advantages which the eastern college is supposed to afford. I was much impressed by the recent return of my sister from a year in Europe, yet I was greatly disappointed at the moment of starting to humdrum Rockford. After the first weeks of homesickness were over, however, I became very much absorbed in the little world which the boarding school in any form always offers to its students.

(2) The school at Rockford in 1877 had not changed its name from seminary to college, although it numbered, on its faculty and among its alumnae, college women who were most eager that this should be done, and who really accomplished it during the next five years. The school was one of the earliest efforts for women's higher education in the Mississippi Valley, and from the beginning was called "The Mount Holyoke of the West." It reflected much of the missionary spirit of that pioneer institution, and the proportion of missionaries among its early graduates was almost as large as Mount Holyoke's own. In addition there had been thrown about the founders of the early western school the glamour of frontier privations, and the first students, conscious of the heroic self-sacrifice made in their behalf, felt that each minute of the time thus dearly bought must be conscientiously used. This inevitably fostered an atmosphere of intensity, a fever of preparation which continued long after the direct making of it had ceased, and which the later girls accepted, as they did the campus and the buildings, without knowing that it could have been otherwise.

(3) There was, moreover, always present in the school a larger or smaller group of girls who consciously accepted this heritage and persistently endeavored to fulfill its obligation. We worked in those

---

in lieu of—in place of

to afford—to provide

humdrum—ordinary

Mount Holyoke—a women's college in Massachusetts

had been thrown about—had been attributed to

privations—lack of comforts

thus dearly bought—obtained with much difficulty

early years as if we really believed the portentous statement from Aristotle . . . "There is the same difference between the learned and the unlearned as there is between the living and the dead."

(4) As I attempt to reconstruct the spirit of my contemporary group by looking over many documents, I find nothing more amusing than a plaint registered against life's indistinctness, which I imagine more or less reflected the sentiments of all of us. At any rate here it is for the entertainment of the reader if not for his edification: "So much of our time is spent in preparation, so much in routine, and so much in sleep, we find it difficult to have any experience at all."

(5) That this group of ardent girls, who discussed everything under the sun with unabated interest, did not take it all out in talk may be demonstrated by the fact that one of the class who married a missionary founded a very successful school in Japan for the children of the English and Americans living there; another of the class became a medical missionary to Korea, and because of her successful treatment of the Queen, was made court physician at a time when the opening was considered of importance in the diplomatic as well as in the missionary world; still another became an unusually skilled teacher of the blind; and one of them a pioneer librarian in that early effort to bring "books to the people."

(6) Perhaps this early companionship showed me how essentially similar are the various forms of social effort, and curiously enough, the actual activities of a missionary school are not unlike many that are carried on in a Settlement situated in a foreign quarter.

(7) It is hard to tell just when the very simple plan which afterward developed into the Settlement began to form itself in my mind I

portentous—very significant

Aristotle—Greek philosopher

plaint—complaint

sentiments—feelings

edification—improvement, education

ardent—enthusiastic, intense

unabated—enthusiastic

Settlement—a welfare establishment, located in a poor area and providing assistance to the people there

foreign quarter—neighborhood of foreign immigrants

gradually became convinced that it would be a good thing to rent a house in a part of the city where many primitive and actual needs are found, in which young women who had been given over too exclusively to study, might restore a balance of activity along traditional lines and learn of life from life itself; where they might try out some of the things they had been taught and put truth to "the ultimate test of the conduct it dictates or inspires." I do not remember to have mentioned this plan to anyone until . . . April, 1888.

(8) I had made up my mind that next day, whatever happened, I would begin to carry out the plan, if only by talking about it. I can well recall the stumbling and uncertainty with which I finally set it forth to Miss Starr, my old-time school friend . . . . I even dared to hope that she might join in carrying out the plan, but nevertheless I told it in the fear of that disheartening experience which is so apt to afflict our most cherished plans when they are at last divulged, when we suddenly feel that there is nothing there to talk about, and as the golden dream slips through our fingers we are left to wonder at our own fatuous belief. But gradually the comfort of Miss Starr's companionship, the vigor and enthusiasm which she brought to bear upon it, told both in the growth of the plan and upon the sense of its validity, so that [soon], the scheme had become convincing and tangible although still most hazy in detail.

(9) The next January found Miss Starr and myself in Chicago, searching for a neighborhood in which we might put our plans into execution. In our eagerness to win friends for the new undertaking, we utilized every opportunity to set forth the meaning of the Settlement . . . . [We believed] that the mere foothold of a house, easily accessible,

so apt to afflict—so likely to trouble or upset
divulged—expressed, revealed

fatuous—silly, foolish

foothold—the first secure step, the basis of further action

ample in space, hospitable and tolerant in spirit, situated in the midst of the large foreign colonies which so easily isolate themselves in American cities, would be in itself a serviceable thing for Chicago.

(10) I was surprised and overjoyed on the very first day of our search for quarters to come upon the hospitable old house . . . . The house had passed through many changes since it had been built in 1856 for the homestead of one of Chicago's pioneer citizens, Mr. Charles J. Hull, and although battered by its vicissitudes, was essentially sound . . . . The fine old house responded kindly to repairs, its wide hall and open fireplaces always insuring it a gracious aspect . . . . On the 18th of September, 1889, Miss Starr and I moved into it . . . . In our enthusiasm over "settling," the first night we forgot not only to lock but to close a side door opening on Polk Street, and were much pleased in the morning to find that we possessed a fine illustration of the honesty and kindliness of our new neighbors.

(11) In the very first weeks of our residence Miss Starr started a reading party in George Eliot's "Romola," which was attended by a group of young women who followed the wonderful tale with unflagging interest. The weekly reading was held in our little upstairs dining room, and two members of the club came to dinner each week, not only that they might be received as guests, but that they might help us wash the dishes afterwards and so make the table ready for the stacks of Florentine photographs.

(12) Volunteers to the new undertaking came quickly; a charming young girl conducted a kindergarten in the drawing room, coming regularly every morning from her home in a distant part of the North Side of the city . . . . Her daily presence for the first two years made it

foreign colonies— neighborhoods of foreign immigrants

vicissitudes—changes (in life)
sound—solid, reliable

George Eliot's "Romola"— an 1863 novel that takes place in Florence, Italy
unflagging—strong, determined, not weak or tired

Florentine photographs— photographs of Florence

quite impossible for us to become too solemn and self-conscious in our strenuous routine, for her mirth and buoyancy were irresistible and her eager desire to share the life of the neighborhood never failed, although it was often put to a severe test. One day at luncheon she gaily recited her futile attempt to impress temperance principles upon the mind of an Italian mother, to whom she had returned a small daughter of five sent to the kindergarten "in quite a horrid state of intoxication" from the wine-soaked bread upon which she had breakfasted. The mother, with the gentle courtesy of a South Italian, listened politely to her graphic portrayal of the untimely end awaiting so immature a wine bibber; but long before the lecture was finished, quite unconscious of the incongruity, she hospitably set forth her best wines, and when her baffled guest refused one after the other, she disappeared, only to quickly return with a small dark glass of whisky, saying reassuringly, "See, I have brought you the true American drink." The recital ended in seriocomic despair, with the rueful statement that "the impression I probably made upon her darkened mind was, that it was the American custom to breakfast children on bread soaked in whisky instead of light Italian wine."

(13) The dozens of younger children who from the first came to Hull-House were organized into groups which were not quite classes and not quite clubs. The value of these groups consisted almost entirely in arousing a higher imagination and in giving the children the opportunity which they could not have in the crowded schools, for initiative and for independent social relationships. The public schools then contained little hand work of any sort, so that naturally any instruction which we provided for the children took the direction of this sup-

mirth—gaiety, merriment
buoyancy—cheerfulness

temperance principles—principles against alcohol

untimely end—early end or death
bibber—drinker

recital—story, account
seriocomic—partly serious, partly comical
rueful—pitiable, deplorable
darkened—ignorant, without the light of intelligence

hand work—work done with the hands to make small useful items

plementary work. But it required a constant effort that the pressure of poverty itself should not defeat the educational aim. The Italian girls in the sewing classes would count that day lost when they could not carry home a garment, and the insistence that it should be neatly made seemed a super-refinement to those in dire need of clothing.

(14) We were also early impressed with the curious isolation of many of the immigrants; an Italian woman once expressed her pleasure in the red roses that she saw at one of our receptions in surprise that they had been "brought so fresh all the way from Italy." She would not believe for an instant that they had been grown in America. She said that she had lived in Chicago for six years and had never seen any roses, whereas in Italy she had seen them every summer in great profusion. During all that time, of course, the woman had lived within ten blocks of a florist's window; she had not been more than a five-cent car ride away from the public parks; but she had never dreamed of faring forth for herself, and no one had taken her. Her conception of America had been the untidy street in which she lived and had made her long struggle to adapt herself to American ways.

(15) But in spite of some untoward experiences, we were constantly impressed with the uniform kindness and courtesy we received. Perhaps these first days laid the simple human foundations which are certainly essential for continuous living among the poor; first, genuine preference for residence in an industrial quarter to any other part of the city, because it is interesting and makes the human appeal; and second, the conviction . . . that the things that make men alike are finer and better than the things that keep them apart, and that these basic likenesses, if they are properly accentuated, easily

super-refinement—unnecessary concern
in dire need—in great need

faring forth—going out

untoward—unfavorable, unfortunate

accentuated—emphasized

transcend the less essential differences of race, language, creed, and tradition.

creed—religious belief

(16) Perhaps even in those first days we made a beginning toward that object which was afterwards stated in our charter: "To provide a center for a higher civic and social life; to institute and maintain educational and philanthropic enterprises, and to investigate and improve the conditions in the industrial districts of Chicago."

charter—a formal document to explain the purpose of an organization

PART 2: PUBLIC ACTIVITIES AND LEGISLATION
(Paragraphs 17–40)

After a few months, Addams and her friends became aware that their neighbors had problems that could not be solved with clubs and classes alone.

(17) We early found ourselves spending many hours in efforts to secure support for deserted women, insurance for bewildered widows, damages for injured operators, furniture from the clutches of the installment store. The Settlement is valuable as an information and interpretation bureau. It constantly acts between the various institutions of the city and the people for whose benefit these institutions were erected. The hospitals, the county agencies, and State asylums are often but vague rumors to the people who need them most. Another function of the Settlement to its neighborhood resembles that of the big brother whose mere presence on the playground protects the little one from bullies.

(18) We early learned to know the children of hard-driven mothers who went out to work all day, sometimes leaving the little things in the casual care of a neighbor, but often locking them into their tenement rooms. The first three crippled children we encountered in the neighborhood had all been injured while their mothers were at work: one had fallen out of a third-story window, another had been burned, and the third had a curved spine due to the fact that for three years he had been tied all day long to the leg of the kitchen table, only released at noon by his older brother who hastily ran in from a neighboring factory to share his lunch with him. When the hot weather came the restless children could not brook the confinement of the stuffy rooms, and, as it was not considered safe to leave the doors open because of sneak thieves, many of the children were locked out. During our first summer an increasing number of these poor little mites would wander into the cool hallway of Hull-House. We kept them there and fed them at noon, in return for which we were sometimes offered a hot penny which had been held in a tight little fist "ever since mother left this morning, to buy something to eat with." Out of kindergarten hours our little guests noisily enjoyed the hospitality of our bedrooms under the so-called care of any resident who volunteered to keep an eye on them, but later they were moved into a neighboring apartment under more systematic supervision.

(19) Hull-House was thus committed to a day nursery which we sustained for sixteen years first in a little cottage on a side street and then in a building designed for its use called the Children's House. It is now carried on by the United Charities of Chicago in a finely equipped building on our block, where the immigrant mothers are

hard-driven—forced to work hard

brook—to tolerate or put up with

mites—little things, children

cared for as well as the children, and where they are taught the things which will make life in America more possible.

(20) Our very first Christmas at Hull-House, when we as yet knew nothing of child labor, a number of little girls refused the candy which was offered them as part of the Christmas good cheer, saying simply that they "worked in a candy factory and could not bear the sight of it." We discovered that for six weeks they had worked from seven in the morning until nine at night, and they were exhausted as well as satiated. The sharp consciousness of stern economic conditions was thus thrust upon us in the midst of the season of good will.

(21) During the same winter three boys from a Hull-House club were injured at one machine in a neighboring factory for lack of a guard which would have cost but a few dollars. When the injury of one of these boys resulted in his death, we felt quite sure that the owners of the factory would share our horror and remorse, and that they would do everything possible to prevent the recurrence of such a tragedy. To our surprise they did nothing whatever, and I made my first acquaintance then with those pathetic documents signed by the parents of working children, that they will make no claim for damages resulting from "carelessness."

(22) The visits we made in the neighborhood constantly discovered women sewing upon sweatshop work, and often they were assisted by incredibly small children. I remember a little girl of four who pulled out basting threads hour after hour, sitting on a stool at the feet of her Bohemian mother, a little bunch of human misery. But even for that there was no legal redress, for the only child-labor law in Illinois, with

sweatshop work—sewing clothes at home rather than in a factory

any provision for enforcement, had been secured by the coal miners' unions, and was confined to children employed in mines.

(23) We learned to know many families in which the working children contributed to the support of their parents, not only because they spoke English better than the older immigrants and were willing to take lower wages, but because their parents gradually found it easy to live upon their earnings. A South Italian peasant who has picked olives and packed oranges from his toddling babyhood cannot see at once the difference between the outdoor healthy work which he has performed in the varying seasons, and the long hours of monotonous factory life which his child encounters when he goes to work in Chicago. An Italian father came to us in great grief over the death of his eldest child, a little girl of twelve, who had brought the largest wages into the family fund. In the midst of his genuine sorrow he said: "She was the oldest kid I had. Now I shall have to go back to work again until the next one is able to take care of me." The man was only thirty-three and had hoped to retire from work at least

during the winters. No foreman cared to have him in a factory, untrained and unintelligent as he was. It was much easier for his bright, English-speaking little girl to get a chance to paste labels on a box than for him to secure an opportunity to carry pig iron. The effect on the child was what no one concerned thought about, in the abnormal effort she made thus prematurely to bear the weight of life.

(24) While we found many pathetic cases of child labor and hard-driven victims of the sweating system who could not possibly earn enough in the short busy season to support themselves during the rest of the year, it became evident that we must add carefully collected information to our general impression of neighborhood conditions if we would make it of any genuine value.

sweating system—system of employing workers to work at home for low wages

(25) There was at that time no statistical information on Chicago industrial conditions, and Mrs. Florence Kelley, an early resident of Hull-House, suggested to the Illinois State Bureau of Labor that they investigate the sweating system in Chicago with its attendant child labor. The head of the Bureau adopted this suggestion and engaged Mrs. Kelley to make the investigation. When the report was presented to the Illinois Legislature, a special committee was appointed to look into the Chicago conditions. I well recall that on the Sunday the members of this commission came to dine at Hull-House, our hopes ran high, and we believed that at last some of the worst ills under which our neighbors were suffering would be brought to an end.

attendant—accompanying, resulting

ills—problems

(26) As a result of its investigations, this committee recommended to the Legislature the provisions which afterward became those of the first factory law of Illinois, regulating the sanitary conditions of the

sweatshop and fixing fourteen as the age at which a child might be employed.

(27) . . . [T]he sense that the passage of the child labor law would in many cases work hardship, was never absent from my mind during the earliest years of its operation. I addressed as many mothers' meetings and clubs among working women as I could, in order to make clear the object of the law and the ultimate benefit to themselves as well as to their children. I am happy to remember that I never met with lack of understanding among the hard-working widows, in whose behalf many prosperous people were so eloquent. These widowed mothers would say, "Why, of course, that is what I am working for—to give the children a chance. I want them to have more education than I had"; or another, "That is why we came to America, and I don't want to spoil his start, even although his father is dead"; or "It's different in America. A boy gets left if he isn't educated." There was always a willingness, even among the poorest women, to keep on with the hard night scrubbing or the long days of washing for the children's sake.

(28) There are many examples of touching fidelity to immigrant parents on the part of their grown children; a young man, who day after day, attends ceremonies which no longer express his religious convictions and who makes his vain effort to interest his Russian Jewish father in social problems; a daughter who might earn much more money as a stenographer could she work from Monday morning till Saturday night, but who quietly and docilely makes neckties for low wages because she can thus abstain from work Saturdays to please her father; these young people . . . through many painful experiences

fidelity—loyalty

have reached the conclusion that pity, memory, and faithfulness are natural ties with paramount claims.

paramount claims—greatest importance

(29) This faithfulness, however, is sometimes ruthlessly imposed upon by immigrant parents who, eager for money and accustomed to the patriarchal authority of peasant households, hold their children in a stern bondage which requires a surrender of all their wages and concedes no time or money for pleasures.

stern bondage—harsh servitude, almost like slavery

(30) There are many convincing illustrations that this parental harshness often results in juvenile delinquency. A Polish boy of seventeen came to Hull-House one day to ask a contribution of fifty cents "towards a flower piece for the funeral of an old Hull-House club boy." A few questions made it clear that the object was fictitious, whereupon the boy broke down and half-defiantly stated that he wanted to buy two twenty-five cent tickets, one for his girl and one for himself, to a dance of the Benevolent Social Twos; that he hadn't a penny of his own although he had worked in a brass foundry for three years and had been advanced twice, because he always had to give his pay envelope unopened to his father; "just look at the clothes he buys me" was his concluding remark.

(31) Perhaps the girls are held even more rigidly. In a recent investigation of two hundred working girls it was found that only five per cent had the use of their own money and that sixty-two per cent turned in all they earned, literally every penny, to their mothers. It was through this little investigation that we first knew Marcella, a pretty young German girl who helped her widowed mother year after year to care for a large family of younger children. She was content for the most

part although her mother's old-country notions of dress gave her but an infinitesimal amount of her own wages to spend on her clothes, and she was quite sophisticated as to proper dressing because she sold silk in a neighborhood department store. Her mother approved of the young man who was showing her various attentions and agreed that Marcella should accept his invitation to a ball, but would allow her not a penny towards a new gown to replace one impossibly plain and shabby. Marcella spent a sleepless night and wept bitterly, although she well knew that the doctor's bill for the children's scarlet fever was not yet paid. The next day as she was cutting off three yards of shining pink silk, the thought came to her that it would make her a fine new waist to wear to the ball. She wistfully saw it wrapped in paper and carelessly stuffed into the muff of the purchaser, when suddenly the parcel fell upon the floor. No one was looking and quick as a flash the girl picked it up and pushed it into her blouse. The theft was discovered by the relentless department store detective who, for "the sake of the example," insisted upon taking the case into court. The poor mother wept bitter tears over this downfall of her "frommes Madchen" and no one had the heart to tell her of her own blindness.

waist—a blouse

muff—a roll of fabric or fur to keep the hands warm

"frommes Madchen"—pious girl in the German language

(32) Most of these premature law breakers are in search of Americanized clothing and others are only looking for playthings. They are all distracted by the profusion and variety of the display, and their moral sense is confused by the general air of openhandedness.

(33) Many of these children have come to grief through their premature fling into city life, having thrown off parental control as they have impatiently discarded foreign ways. Boys of ten and twelve will refuse to sleep at home, preferring the freedom of an old brewery vault or an

fling—short period of fun

brewery vault—underground storeroom of a brewery

empty warehouse to the obedience required by their parents, and for days these boys will live on the milk and bread which they steal from the back porches after the early morning delivery. Such children complain that there is "no fun" at home . . . . Certainly the bewildered parents, unable to speak English and ignorant of the city, whose children have disappeared for days or weeks, have often come to Hull-House, evincing that agony which fairly separates the marrow from the bone, as if they had discovered a new type of suffering, devoid of the healing in familiar sorrows. It is as if they did not know how to search for the children without the assistance of the children themselves. Perhaps the most pathetic aspect of such cases is their revelation of the premature dependence of the older and wiser upon the young and foolish, which is in itself often responsible for the situation because it has given the children an undue sense of their own importance and a false security that they can take care of themselves.

(34) On the other hand, an Italian girl who has had lessons in cooking at the public school, will help her mother to connect the entire family with American food and household habits. That the mother has never baked bread in Italy—only mixed it in her own house and then taken it out to the village oven—makes all the more valuable her daughter's understanding of the complicated cooking stove. The same thing is true of the girl who learns to sew in the public school, and more than anything else, perhaps, of the girl who receives the first simple instruction in the care of little children,—that skillful care which every tenement-house baby requires if he is to be pulled through his second summer. As a result of this teaching I recall a young girl who carefully explained to her Italian mother that the rea-

---

evincing that agony—showing extreme suffering

fairly separates the marrow from the bone—takes the strength away

undue—unreasonable

to be pulled through—to be kept alive through

son the babies in Italy were so healthy and the babies in Chicago were so sickly, was not, as her mother had firmly insisted, because her babies in Italy had goat's milk and her babies in America had cow's milk, but because the milk in Italy was clean and the milk in Chicago was dirty. She said that when you milked your own goat before the door, you knew that the milk was clean, but when you bought milk from the grocery store after it had been carried for many miles in the country, you couldn't tell whether it was fit for the baby to drink until the men from the City Hall who had watched it all the way, said that it was all right.

(35) One of the striking features of our neighborhood twenty years ago, and one to which we never became reconciled, was the presence of huge wooden garbage boxes fastened to the street pavement in which the undisturbed refuse accumulated day by day. The system of garbage collecting was inadequate throughout the city but it became the greatest menace in a ward such as ours, where the normal amount of waste was much increased by the decayed fruit and vegetables discarded by the Italian and Greek fruit peddlers, and by the residuum left over from the piles of filthy rags which were fished out of the city dumps and brought to the homes of the rag pickers for further sorting and washing.

refuse—garbage

ward—district of a city

residuum—residue, remainder
fished out of—searched for in

(36) It is easy for even the most conscientious citizen of Chicago to forget the foul smells of the stockyards and the garbage dumps, when he is living so far from them that he is only occasionally made conscious of their existence but the residents of a Settlement are perforce constantly surrounded by them. During our first three years on Halsted Street, we had established a small incinerator at Hull-House and

perforce—of necessity

we had many times reported the untoward conditions of the ward to the city hall. We had also arranged many talks for the immigrants, pointing out that although a woman may sweep her own doorway in her native village and allow the refuse to innocently decay in the open air and sunshine, in a crowded city quarter, if the garbage is not properly collected and destroyed, a tenement-house mother may see her children sicken and die, and that the immigrants must therefore, not only keep their own houses clean, but must also help the authorities to keep the city clean.

untoward—unfavorable, unfortunate

(37) Possibly our efforts slightly modified the worst conditions but they still remained intolerable . . . . [W]e began a systematic investigation of the city system of garbage collection, both as to its efficiency in other wards and its possible connection with the death rate in the various wards of the city.

(38) The Hull-House Woman's Club had been organized the year before . . . . The new members came together, however, in quite a new way that summer when we discussed with them the high death rate so persistent in our ward. After several club meetings devoted to the subject, despite the fact that the death rate rose highest in the congested foreign colonies and not in the streets in which most of the Irish American club women lived, twelve of their number undertook in connection with the residents, to carefully investigate the conditions of the alleys. During August and September the substantiated reports of violations of the law sent in from Hull-House to the health department were one thousand and thirty-seven. For the club woman who had finished a long day's work of washing or ironing followed by the cooking of a hot supper, it would have been much easier to sit on her

doorstep during a summer evening than to go up and down ill-kept alleys and get into trouble with her neighbors over the condition of their garbage boxes. It required both civic enterprise and moral conviction to be willing to do this three evenings a week during the hottest and most uncomfortable months of the year. Nevertheless, a certain number of women persisted . . . .

ill-kept—not kept well, not taken care of

(39) Many of the foreign-born women of the ward were much shocked by this abrupt departure into the ways of men, and it took a great deal of explanation to convey the idea even remotely that if it were a womanly task to go about in tenement houses in order to nurse the sick, it might be quite as womanly to go through the same district in order to prevent the breeding of so-called "filth diseases." . . . The careful inspection combined with other causes, brought about a great improvement in the cleanliness and comfort of the neighborhood and one happy day, when the death rate of our ward was found to have dropped from third to seventh in the list of city wards and was so reported to our Woman's Club, the applause which followed recorded the genuine sense of participation in the result, and a public spirit which had "made good."

abrupt departure—quick change from usual behavior

(40) We have been much impressed during our twenty years, by the ready adaptation of city young people to the prosperity arising from their own increased wages or from the commercial success of their families. This quick adaptability is the great gift of the city child, his one reward for the hurried changing life which he has always led. The working girl has a distinct advantage in the task of transforming her whole family into the ways and connections of the prosperous when she works down town and becomes conversant with the manners and

conversant—familiar with

conditions of a cosmopolitan community. Therefore having lived in a Settlement twenty years, I see scores of young people who have successfully established themselves in life, and in my travels in the city and outside, I am constantly cheered by greetings from the rising young lawyer, the scholarly rabbi, the successful teacher, the prosperous young matron buying clothes for her blooming children. "Don't you remember me? I used to belong to a Hull-House club." I once asked one of these young people, a man who held a good position on a Chicago daily, what special thing Hull-House had meant to him, and he promptly replied, "It was the first house I had ever been in where books and magazines just lay around as if there were plenty of them in the world. Don't you remember how much I used to read at that little round table at the back of the library? To have people regard reading as a reasonable occupation changed the whole aspect of life to me and I began to have confidence in what I could do."

❖ EXERCISES ❖

Comprehension Questions

Answer these question in paragraph form, using complete sentences in Modern English. Do not copy your answers directly from the reading passages. (See pages 218–21 in the Yellow Pages for a review of paragraph form.)

REFORMERS: JANE ADDAMS

Part 1: "The Beginnings of Hull-House" (Paragraphs 1–16)

1. What did the girls learn at Rockford Seminary? What kinds of work did their education lead to?

2. What benefits did the settlement house have for the young women who worked there?

3. What opportunities did the settlement house provide for the neighborhood families?

Part 2: "Public Activities and Legislation" (Paragraphs 17–40)

1. How did Addams and her friends become aware of the problems of their immigrant neighbors? Why hadn't they been aware of these problems before?

2. What problems were addressed by these Hull-House projects?
   a. the day nursery
   b. the child labor laws
   c. classes in cooking and childcare
   d. garbage collection

Vocabulary Development

Part 1: "The Beginning of Hull-House" (Paragraphs 1–16)

1. A person of strong feelings, Jane Addams often uses words that indicate her emotions. Study the list of words below, and write a sentence for each word that explains the reason for Addams' feeling. You can change the part of speech of the word if you like. The first one has been done as an example.

   a. *impressed* (1): <u>Jane Addams was impressed by her sister's experiences in Europe.</u>

   b. *disappointed* (1): _____

   c. *absorbed* (1): _____

READING AND RESEARCHING AMERICA

d. *intensity* (2): _____

e. *endeavored* (3): _____

f. *convinced* (7): _____

g. *disheartening* (8): _____

h. *enthusiasm* (8): _____

i. *eagerness* (9): _____

j. *pleased* (10): _____

k. *baffled* (12): _____

l. *conviction* (15): _____

Part 2: "Public Activities and Legislation" (Paragraphs 17–40)

1. In paragraphs 17 and 18, Addams writes about *deserted women, bewildered widows, injured operators,* and *crippled children.* Explain in your own words what happened to these people.

2. Here are more useful vocabulary words to study and learn:

tangible (8)	*eloquent* (27)	*concede* (29)
bullies (17)	*vain* (28)	*profusion* (32)
hospitality (18)	*docilely* (28)	*menace* (35)
remorse (21)	*abstain* (28)	*congested* (38)
pathetic (21)	*ruthlessly* (29)	*convey* (39)

Quotations and Paraphrases

Write the quotation with an introductory explanation of the source and the content, paying close attention to punctuation. Then paraphrase it in your own words. (See pages 246–52 in the Yellow Pages for help with quotations and paraphrases.)

Part 1: "The Beginnings of Hull-House" (Paragraphs 1–16)

1. (paragraph 4) "So much of our time is spent in preparation, so much in routine, and so much in sleep, we find it difficult to have any experience at all."

2. (paragraph 15) "... the things that make men alike are finer and better than the things that keep them apart, and ... these basic likenesses ... easily transcend the less essential differences of race, language, creed, and tradition."

3. Choose your own quotation and follow the same directions.

READING AND RESEARCHING AMERICA

Part 2: "Public Activities and Legislation" (Paragraphs 17–40)

1. (paragraph 23) "We learned to know many families in which the working children contributed to the support of their parents, not only because they spoke English better than the older immigrants and were willing to take lower wages, but because their parents gradually found it easy to live upon their earnings."

   _____
   _____
   _____
   _____

2. (paragraph 39) "... if it were a womanly task to go about in tenement houses in order to nurse the sick, it might be quite as womanly to go through the same district in order to prevent the breeding of so-called 'filth diseases.'"

   _____
   _____
   _____
   _____

3. Choose your own quotation and follow the same directions.

   _____
   _____
   _____
   _____

Writing Summaries

Write a one-paragraph summary in Modern English without plagiarism. (See pages 253–55 in the Yellow Pages for help in writing a summary.)

1. Summarize the aspects of Jane Addam's background that led her to establish Hull-House. (paragraphs 2–5)

2. Summarize the ways in which Addams and her friends acted as go-betweens for the people of the neighborhood and the governments of the city of Chicago and the state of Illinois. (paragraphs 17, 25–26, 37–39)

3. Summarize Addams' discoveries about the relationships between the immigrant parents and their American children. (paragraphs 27–34)

4. Summarize the differences between the immigrants' lives in their home countries and their lives in Chicago. (paragraphs 23, 34, 36)

Questions for Discussion and Writing

Discuss your answers to these questions with your classmates. These questions may also be used as essay topics. (See pages 221–24 in the Yellow Pages for a review of essay form.)

1. In the late 1800s, there were not many opportunities for young women to use their education and skills. What opportunities were available? Is the situation different for young women today?

2. According to Addams, immigrant families faced many problems in Chicago in the 1880s.
   a. Which of these problems do you think were the responsibility of the city and which were the responsibility of the people themselves?
   b. Do you think immigrant families face similar problems today?

3. Read the goals of Hull-House in the charter in paragraph 16. To what extent did the activities provided by Hull-House fulfill these goals? What kinds of organizations provide these services today?

4. In paragraphs 23–34, Addams describes the relationships between immigrant parents and their children. Explain the relationships. Do immigrant parents and children have similar relationships today?

5. A popular slogan in the women's labor movement of the early 1900s was, "We fight for bread, and roses too." To what extent did Hull-House supply both bread and roses for the poor people of Chicago?

6. Carnegie and Addams give different views of child labor. What are their views, and which one do you think is more accurate? How do you account for the differences?

Scanning for Specific Information

Scanning means looking over a page quickly to find a specific detail rather than beginning at the top of the page and reading every word. Working alone or with one or two other students, use a reference book to find the information to complete the sentences. Try to work quickly to find just the information you need to fill in to complete the exercise. You will probably have to consult more than one source. Make sure that your answers fit the structure of the sentence.

Reference book(s) used _____

_____

MUCKRAKERS, TRADE UNIONISTS, AND SOCIALISTS

The rapid change in the late 1800s from a society of small farmers and tradesmen to an urban industrialized society brought a variety of problems to American and immigrant workers trying to achieve the dream of individual economic opportunity. Living and working conditions in the big cities were deplorable, and the government was either too unresponsive or too corrupt to deal with the problems. Several groups of people recognized the problems and tried to find solutions.

Like Jane Addams, the muckrakers were educated, middle-class reformers working as _____ to bring public attention to the problems of exploitation and corruption. In 1904, Ida Tarbell completed a history of _____, exposing its abusive business practices. Upton Sinclair wrote about corruption in the _____ industry in his 1906 novel _____, leading to passage of the nation's first meat inspection bill.

Trade unionists gathered workers together to fight for improved working conditions such as a _____-day work week of _____-hour days. They demanded cleaner work sites to prevent chronic illnesses such as _____ and safer machinery to prevent injuries and deaths. The confrontations between labor and management tended to be violent: The late 1800s saw two of the nation's most violent labor strikes, one in the year _____ at the Carnegie Steel Company plant in the city of _____, and the second in the year _____ at the Pullman Palace Car Company in Chicago, a company that later bought the Woodruff Sleeping-Car Company that Carnegie had invested in.

The third approach to solving the economic and political problems called for a revolutionary change in government. Following the theories of Karl Marx as described in his books _____ written in 1848 and _____ written in 1867, socialists and communists predicted that workers would unite and seize ownership of the means of production such as _____; the working class would own and manage all means of production and profits would be shared equally. Eugene V.

213

Debs, both a socialist and a union leader in the _____ Strike, ran for president five times between 1900 and 1920.

Trade unionists and socialists sometimes worked together and at other times in competition to organize the workers to improve their lives. Their efforts, along with those of the muckrakers like Jane Addams, led to the extensive legislation that Americans have today for the protection of workers and consumers.

Research Topics

Choose one of these topics or another topic that interests you to do one of the research exercises in the Yellow Pages. Share the results of your research with your classmates as you become experts in your own research areas.

Jane Addams	women's education	reform movement
Chicago	settlement houses	Hull-House
urbanization	immigration	labor movement
garment industry	sweat shops	meat-packing industry
muckrakers	Homestead Strike	Pullman Strike

Expansion Activities

1. Read this description that Addams wrote about Halsted Street (the street on which Hull House was located) and the people who lived in the neighborhood. Draw a map of the neighborhood showing where the different ethnic groups of people lived. Does the city that you live in also have ethnic neighborhoods? If it does, find or draw a map of your city showing the different neighborhoods.

    Halsted Street has grown so familiar during twenty years of residence, that it is difficult to recall its gradual changes,—the withdrawal of the more prosperous Irish and Germans, and the slow substitution of Russian Jews, Italians, and Greeks. A description of the street such as I gave in those early addresses still stands in my mind as sympathetic and correct.

Halsted Street is thirty-two miles long, and one of the great thoroughfares of Chicago; Polk Street crosses it midway between the stockyards to the south and the ship-building yards on the north branch of the Chicago River. For the six miles between these two industries the street is lined with shops of butchers and grocers, with dingy and gorgeous saloons, and pretentious establishments for the sale of ready-made clothing. Polk Street, running west from Halsted Street, grows rapidly more prosperous; running a mile east to State Street, it grows steadily worse, and crosses a network of vice on the corners of Clark Street and Fifth Avenue. Hull-House once stood in the suburbs, but the city has steadily grown up around it and its site now has corners on three or four foreign colonies. Between Halsted Street and the river live about ten thousand Italians—Neapolitans, Sicilians, and Calabrians, with an occasional Lombard or Venetian. To the south on Twelfth Street are many Germans, and side streets are given over almost entirely to Polish and Russian Jews. Still farther south, these Jewish colonies merge into a huge Bohemian colony, so vast that Chicago ranks as the third Bohemian city in the world. To the northwest are many Canadian-French, clannish in spite of their long residence in America, and to the north are Irish and first-generation Americans. On the streets directly west and farther north are well-to-do English-speaking families, many of whom own their houses and have lived in the neighborhood for years; one man is still living in his old farmhouse.

2. Look up Hull-House on the Internet to find out about its activities today. Does the organization still seem to fulfill the charter that Addams wrote about in paragraph 16? Find out about any similar organizations in your city.

3. To learn more about the lives of turn-of-the-century European immigrants, check out the websites for these real-life locations in New York City. The Ellis Island Immigration Museum features the millions of immigrants who entered the United States at this island in New York Harbor, and the Lower East Side Tenement Museum shows typical living quarters for immigrant families.

THE YELLOW PAGES
★ ★ ★

THE BASICS OF RESEARCH AND WRITING

Conducting research and writing about the results are an integral part of American college courses. In addition to learning from textbooks and lectures, students are expected to make connections between the course content and information gathered from other sources, such as from their own lives or from the library and the Internet, and then to write about it in the form of essays, reports, and research papers.

The Random House Dictionary defines research as the "diligent and systematic inquiry or investigation into a subject in order to discover . . . facts, theories, applications, etc." These words are worth a closer look: the "subject" of the inquiry is a **topic** that you would like to learn more about, and the purpose of the research is to discover something new and interesting about the topic. The words "diligent and systematic" indicate that information is gathered in a careful, thoughtful way.

In some fields of study, research data are gathered from experiments and surveys, while in English classes, the information for your inquiry or investigation can be gathered from both personal and impersonal **sources.** For some assignments, you can use yourself as the source of information—your own experiences, perceptions, feelings, thoughts, and opinions. For example, you are the only source of information for a personal essay, the kind of essay that teachers assign in order to engage your interest in a topic and to encourage you to think more deeply about its connection to your own life. In this textbook, each chapter begins with **Pre-Reading Questions** that can be used as topics for a personal essay for exactly these purposes.

The Basics of Research and Writing

Most college writing assignments, however, require you to go beyond the circle of your own experience to larger circles of sources, including sources that are easily available to you—your textbook and the class lectures, your classmates, friends, and family—and sources that require a library and Internet search. The **Questions for Discussion and Writing** at the end of each chapter require you to do some research beyond your immediate experience, and the **Suggested Topics for Research and Writing** involve the larger circles of library and Internet research.

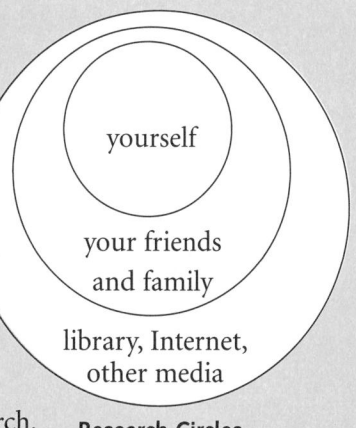

Research Circles

The Research Process

Regardless of the sources you use, the process of research follows similar steps: First is the systematic search for information on a topic followed by the discovery of an idea about this information. This question from Chapter 1 can be used as an example:

> Comprehension Question 1: What kinds of books did young Franklin read?

The *topic* of this question is the kinds of books that young Franklin read, and the *source* of our information is the reading passage. The first step of our investigation is to gather information about the books from the reading passage and to make a list:

> Bunyan's works
> R. Burton's historical collections
> books about polemic divinity
> Plutarch's *Lives*
> *Essay on Projects* by Daniel Defoe
> *Essays to do Good* by Dr. Cotton Mather
> books borrowed from a printer and a bookseller
> poetry
> his father's books of dispute about religion
> the *Spectator*

Using this information, a student might answer the question in the following way:

> Young Franklin read books by Bunyan, Burton's historical collections, books about polemic divinity, Plutarch's *Lives*, *Essay on Projects* by Daniel Defoe, and *Essays to do Good* by

Dr. Cotton Mather. Later he borrowed books from a
printer and a bookseller and also read the *Spectator*.

But this answer is simply a list of books: There is no discovery of the point or purpose of the list, and no answer to the question about the *kinds* of books. In order to discover an idea of interest about the list, we can add the information that Franklin includes about the books:

Bunyan's works—Franklin's first acquisition
R. Burton's historical collections—about history
books about polemic divinity—Franklin regretted reading these books
Plutarch's *Lives*—"time spent to great advantage"
Essay on Projects by Daniel Defoe and *Essays to do Good* by
   Dr. Mather—"had an influence on some of the principal future events
   of my life"
books borrowed from a printer and a bookseller—"better books"
poetry—wrote some poetry himself
his father's books of dispute about religion—made Franklin too
   argumentative
the *Spectator*—helped Franklin improve his writing

Now we are ready to make a discovery about these books, a **generalization** that states an idea about them. For example, we may notice that Franklin read books about serious topics, such as history and religion, and that he used these books to educate himself. With this information, we can write a sentence to state the generalization that we have discovered:

> Young Benjamin Franklin read the kinds of books that he
> could learn from.
>
> Or
>
> When he was young, Franklin read nonfiction books that
> improved his character.

With a generalization, our answer is now more than just a list of books. When we add it to the list of books, the answer becomes a **paragraph,** a piece of writing on a single topic that states an idea of interest about that topic. The generalization informs the reader not only of the topic, the books that Franklin read, but also of the discovery of something new and significant, the purpose of writing. In a paragraph, the sentence that states the generalization is called the **topic sentence** and is most often placed at the beginning of the paragraph. The information we've gathered about the books provides the **supporting details,** the examples that illustrate or support the generalization.

The Basics of Research and Writing

> [**topic sentence**] Young Benjamin Franklin read the kinds of books that he could learn from. [**supporting details**] For example, from Burton's historical collections and Plutarch's *Lives*, he learned history, and from poetry and the essays in the *Spectator*, he learned to be a better writer. His father's books about polemic divinity taught him to be argumentative. The essays by Daniel Defoe and Dr. Mather also had a big influence on his later life.

Good writing includes both a thoughtful generalization and relevant supporting details. Before you begin to write, it is a good idea to spend some time thinking about your topic to find a generalization that can be supported by the details you have gathered. The details that you choose to include in your paper must be relevant to the topic as it is expressed in your generalization.

★ EXERCISES:

1. Relevant or irrelevant? *Relevant* details are details that are about the topic and can support the generalization; *irrelevant* details are not about the topic or do not help to support the generalization.

    In the following paragraph, two sentences are not relevant to the topic. Find these sentences and cross them out.

    > When Benjamin Franklin was just a boy, he read the kinds of books that he could learn from. He had only a little money, but he spent it all on books. He learned history from Burton's historical collections and Plutarch's *Lives,* and he learned to write well from poetry and the essays in the *Spectator*. His father's books about polemic divinity taught him to be argumentative. When he borrowed books, he was always careful to return them promptly. The essays by Daniel Defoe and Dr. Mather also had a big influence on his later life.

2. Practice your generalization skills by writing a paragraph of several sentences, beginning with a sentence that states your generalization. Then make a copy of your paragraph without the generalization on another piece of paper or on the board. Can your classmates write a generalization for your paragraph? Do their sentences make the same discovery that you did? Or do their sentences make a different discovery that is supported equally well by the details?

Using the Generalization to Organize Your Writing

The paragraph in Exercise 1 is a satisfactory answer for Comprehension Question 1 on page 217, but in fact, we can investigate the list of books more closely to notice that some of the books that Franklin read had a good influence on him while others had a bad influence and tended to make him argumentative. We can group the books into two **categories** according to their influence, using the words *good* and *bad* to distinguish between the two groups:

Books that Franklin read

Books with a Good Influence	Books with a Bad Influence
R. Burton's historical collections	books about polemic divinity
Plutarch's *Lives*	his father's books of dispute about religion
essays by Defoe and Mather	
poetry	
the *Spectator*	

With this grouping of the books into two different categories, we can add another idea to our generalization:

> Young Benjamin Franklin read the kinds of books that he could learn from, some that had a good influence on him and some that had a bad influence.

With this topic sentence, the details can be organized in a logical way into two groups rather than simply a list. In the following example, the books are listed in the two groups, signaled by the use of the contrast word *but:*

> [**topic sentence**] Young Benjamin Franklin read books that he could learn from, some that had a good influence on him and some that had a bad influence. [**supporting details—good influence**] He learned history from R. Burton's historical collections and Plutarch's *Lives,* was influenced greatly by the essays of Defoe and Mather, and used essays from the *Spectator* to improve his writing. [**supporting details—bad influence**] But he felt that some of the books about religion, such as the books about polemic divinity from his father's library, made him too argumentative.

An **outline** using Roman numerals illustrates the organization of the paragraph:

<u>Topic sentence</u>: Young Benjamin Franklin read books that he could learn from, some that had a good influence on him and some that had a bad influence.

    I. books that had a good influence

        examples: R. Burton's historical collections
                   Plutarch's *Lives*
                   essays by Defoe and Mather
                   the *Spectator*

    II. books that had a bad influence

        examples: books about polemic divinity
                   disputes about religion

In a longer piece of writing, such as an **essay** or **research paper,** the use of the generalization to suggest a method of organization becomes especially important to control the content of the paper. In these longer forms of writing, the generalization is called the **thesis statement,** and it is expected to suggest the organization of the paper by mentioning several groups or categories. The paragraphs in the body of the paper develop the categories in the same order given in the thesis statement. Like the topic sentence of a paragraph, the thesis statement comes at the beginning of the paper and is followed by supporting details, explanations, examples, statistics, and any other kind of information that supports and explains the generalization, arranged in paragraphs in a logical order.

While a paragraph has several sentences of support, an essay may have many paragraphs of support. If we gathered more information about Benjamin Franklin's youthful reading habits, for example from the library or the Internet, we could expand our paragraph to an essay of several paragraphs, following the outline below. In the outline, the Roman numerals I and II may represent paragraphs, or if we can gather a lot of information about these books, each capital letter could represent a separate paragraph.

<u>Thesis statement</u>: Young Benjamin Franklin read books that he could learn from, some that had a good influence on him and some that had a bad influence.

    I. books that had a good influence

        A. R. Burton's historical collections

        B. Plutarch's *Lives*

        C. essays by Defoe and Mather

        D. the *Spectator*

II. books that had a bad influence
- A. books about polemic divinity
- B. disputes about religion

A paragraph and an essay are organized in a similar way, beginning with the generalization followed by the supporting details, but they differ in length and in the amount of detail:

A Paragraph

> Topic Sentence
> Supporting Details
> Concluding Sentence

An Essay

> Introductory Paragraph with Thesis Statement

> Body Paragraph 1, with a Topic Sentence and Supporting Details

> Body Paragraph 2, with a Topic Sentence and Supporting Details

> Body Paragraph 3 (or beyond)— as needed to support the Thesis Statement

> Concluding Paragraph

★ **EXERCISE:** In an article in *U.S. News & World Report,* writer Jay Tolson wrote that Benjamin Franklin was the most important of the Founding Fathers and used the following thesis statement in his article. How many parts or categories would you expect to find in the body of the paper? What are they, and in what order would you expect to find them? Write an outline for this article.

" . . . Largely because of his great practical genius, his commitment to public service, his considerable PR skills, and his international fame, he [Franklin] was the essential figure in the founding enterprise [of the United States of America]."

The Basics of Research and Writing

The generalization of a piece of writing not only helps you as a writer to focus on your topic and decide what supporting details to include and how to organize them, but it also helps readers: It tells readers the topic and the point of the writing and prepares them for the ideas that will follow. For example, if a generalization makes three points about a topic, the reader can expect to find three points in the paper, in the same order as in the generalization.

★ EXERCISES:

1. What are the categories in the following generalization? Which books from our list would you include in each of these categories?

    > When he was a boy, Benjamin Franklin read books about history and religion.

2. What are the categories in the following generalization? Which details from this list would you choose to support these categories?

    > Benjamin Franklin is an American hero because he had an independent and democratic spirit.

    a. Franklin came from an ordinary family of poor working people.

    b. Franklin arrived in Philadelphia with no money or connections but soon began a successful printing business.

    c. Franklin had strong opinions and enjoyed arguing with his friends.

    d. Franklin enjoyed attending fancy dinners and balls in Paris and London.

    e. Franklin educated himself by reading books about history and religion.

    f. In Philadelphia, Franklin began several institutions to help the common people of the city, such as a library, a hospital, and a fire department.

    g. Franklin avoided luxury goods and never wore a wig or fancy clothing.

    h. Franklin wrote articles for his brother's newspaper criticizing the colonial government.

    i. Franklin had many wealthy friends, both in the colonies and in Europe.

    j. Franklin didn't agree with his father's ideas about religion.

More Requirements for the Topic Sentence and the Thesis Statement

In addition to these functions, the generalization must also meet other requirements of grammar, style, and content:

a. It is a complete sentence, a statement rather than a question or phrase.

b. It does not refer to the writer, the reader, or the writing directly with words that announce the writer's purpose, such as "I am going to explain . . ." or "The following paragraphs will show you . . . ."

c. It does not state a fact, such as the fact that Franklin was born in Boston and died in Philadelphia, because then there would be no need to give supporting details.

d. It does not state matters of personal feelings, such as that Franklin is your favorite of the Founding Fathers, because there is no reason to try to influence a reader's personal feelings.

e. It must be on a topic that you can find information about, from your own experiences or from sources in the library or on the Internet.

★ EXERCISE: According to the criteria above, why would the following sentences not make good general statements for a paragraph or essay about the kinds of books that Franklin read? What changes can you make to improve them?

a. The books that Benjamin Franklin read and how they influenced him.

b. When Franklin borrowed books, he always returned them promptly.

c. Benjamin Franklin read a lot of books.

d. What kinds of books did Franklin read?

e. Benjamin Franklin read a lot of popular novels.

f. The books that Franklin read are my favorites too.

g. Benjamin Franklin was a good reader.

h. In this essay, I will explain what kinds of books Franklin read.

Final Remarks

Much college writing in English follows the pattern described here of a generalization followed by specific supporting information; there are few digressions, and every detail is relevant to the point. The conventional writing patterns in other languages, however, may not follow the general-specific pattern that English does. In some languages, a good writer puts a generalization at the end of a piece of writing, while in other languages, a writer may use only details or only generalizations and may expect the reader to fill in the missing parts. In some languages, it is acceptable to write digressions that seem "off the topic" in English. In fact, English can be called a "writer-responsible" language, in that it is the writer's responsibility to be clear about his or her purpose for writing and to organize his or her material in a logical way. If the reader has to work hard to understand the meaning of a piece of writing, then it is not considered to be well-written.

In our examples, the details come from a single source, just a few paragraphs of Franklin's autobiography. If we expand the scope of our research to include library books and Internet sources, it's possible to gather much more information about Franklin's early reading, enough information to write a long essay or research paper. But no matter what the length of a piece of writing is, the basic research process is still the same: The writer gathers information on the topic and then discovers a general statement that makes a point about the information. As the amount of information increases, the demands on the writer are greater to investigate and choose information carefully and to make a discovery that is supported by the information. The following sections of the Yellow Pages will introduce you to the most common sources of information used in college classes and to the writing skills used to present the results of your research in written form.

★ **REVIEW EXERCISE:** Using the skills you have learned in this chapter, study these passages from Franklin's account of his early life, when he was 12–17 years old. What discovery or generalization can you make about his character or personality? Write a well-organized paragraph of 200–300 words, using your generalization as the topic sentence and these passages for the supporting details.

1. "... my father was impatient to have me bound to my brother. I stood out some time, but at last was persuaded and signed the indenture, when I was yet but twelve years old." (paragraph 2)

2. "This might be one occasion of the differences we began to have about this time. Though a brother, he considered himself my master and me as his apprentice, and accordingly expected the same services from me as he would from another; while I thought he degraded me too much in some he required of me, who from a brother expected more indulgence." (paragraph 7)

3. "... I had the management of the paper, and I made bold to give our rulers some rubs in it, which my brother took very kindly, while others began to consider me in an unfavourable light as a young genius that had a turn for libeling and satire." (paragraph 8)

4. "It was not fair in me to take this advantage, and this I therefore reckon one of the first errata of my life . . . . Perhaps I was too saucy and provoking." (paragraph 8)

5. "... I was the rather inclined to leave Boston when I reflected that I had already made myself a little obnoxious to the governing party; and from the arbitrary proceedings of the Assembly in my brother's case, it was likely [that] I might if I stayed soon bring myself into scrapes, and further that my indiscreet disputations about religion began to make me pointed at with horror by good people as an infidel or atheist." (paragraph 9)

THE BASICS OF RESEARCH AND WRITING

★ Glossary ★

topic—the subject or area of inquiry

source—a book, article, person, or website that supplies information. A source can take many forms, such as print, oral, multimedia, or electronic.

generalization—a statement expressing an idea of interest

paragraph—the smallest unit of writing, made up of several sentences on one topic, usually expressing a point about that topic

topic sentence—the sentence that expresses the main idea or generalization of a paragraph

supporting details—any kind of specific information that illustrates or explains the generalization, such as statistics, examples, description, etc.

categories—divisions into groups based on similarities and differences

outline—a graphic representation of the generalization and categories of a piece of writing

essay—a piece of writing made up of several paragraphs on one topic and including a generalization

research paper—a long essay using information gathered from library and Internet sources

thesis statement—the generalization of an essay or research paper

1. RESEARCH SOURCES: DIFFERENT SOURCES FOR DIFFERENT PURPOSES

When we do research, we can gather information in a variety of ways. For example, in the sciences, researchers do carefully controlled lab experiments, and in the social sciences, researchers take surveys of large numbers of people. In the humanities, research means the gathering of ideas from sources such as yourself and people you know; TV programs and movies you've seen; and most important, the written texts of books, magazines, newspapers, and Internet sites. Because written texts are the foundation of most college research assignments, this introduction will concentrate on these sources.

The written sources can be divided for convenience into four categories—**reference materials, books, periodicals,** and the **Internet**—each with advantages and disadvantages for the research process. Students often prefer to use the Internet, but, in fact, they should learn to use each kind of source appropriately, starting with reference materials for a factual overview, books for detailed information, periodicals for current information, and the Internet only when they have a good understanding of the topic.

All of these materials are available at college and city libraries, and some can be accessed from your home computer. Modern libraries have **online catalogs** to help you find all these kinds of sources, as well as **electronic databases** of specialized materials such as periodicals and government documents. The time you spend learning to use the library now will save you time and effort later and result in higher grades in all of your college classes. To learn the basics, take a library tour with your class or go to the orientation sessions offered by your library. Practice your skills, and then go on to the more advanced sessions on database and Internet searches. If your college offers a class on library research methods, take it early in your college career. Keep in mind that library technology is advancing rapidly and that you'll need to update your skills regularly to make effective use of new information management systems.

When you use information from sources in your own writing, it is necessary to give your readers information about the sources so that they can find them too, to do their own research or to check that you used your sources accurately. This information is called **documentation,** and the particular form it takes is called a **citation,** or citing a source. Scholars in English and the humanities tend to use the format in the *MLA Handbook for Writers of Research Papers* from the Modern Languages Association (MLA). In the social sciences, writers tend to use the format in the *Publication Manual* from the American Psychological Association (APA). Basic information about both styles is illustrated in this textbook. There is a variety of styles for writers in the fields of mathematics and science. You can find complete information about documentation in English handbooks and in inexpensive guides to documentation available in college bookstores.

RESEARCH SOURCES

The different kinds of sources are described in this chapter, in order of reliability and recommended use. Read about each kind, and do the exercises using topics of your choice from the Reading Passages in Chapters 1–6.

A. Reference Materials: Only the Facts

Reference materials include encyclopedias, dictionaries, almanacs, and atlases with factual information on almost any topic you can think of. Most fields of study, such as the social sciences, technology, and business, have their own specialized reference books. Written and edited by teams of scholars and updated regularly, reference books are the most reliable of sources: They provide an overview of all aspects of a topic from an unbiased point of view, give accurate and balanced information that experts agree on, and explain any areas of controversy that you should be aware of.

Libraries place their reference materials together in a special reference room or section of the library, available to users at all times. Reference materials can also be found on CD-ROM and on online databases that you can access from the library computers or your home computer.

Encyclopedias are especially useful when you begin a research project and want to get an overview of your topic. They are easy to find, quick to use, and provide guidance for further research. The basic information that these sources provide is considered to be background information or common knowledge, so it is usually not necessary to provide bibliographic information for encyclopedias unless you use exact numbers such as statistics; if you aren't sure, check with your teacher. Sometimes college teachers tell students not to use encyclopedias for their papers; in fact, they mean not to include them in a bibliography, but students should still use them as a first step in research to get a basic understanding of the topic and to guide them to worthwhile sources.

★ EXERCISES:

1. **Finding Encyclopedias.** Located in the reference section of the library, the print encyclopedias are easy to find and use. They do not circulate; that is, they cannot be taken out of the library, so they will be on the shelves where they belong or on tables nearby if someone has just used them. When new editions of encyclopedias are published, libraries usually keep the older editions because they are still useful for most topics; these older volumes may be shelved with the general collection and can be taken out of the library.

Some encyclopedias and reference sources such as *Encyclopædia Britannica* are available in electronic form in special databases that your library may subscribe to. Your library's online catalog will include information about the electronic databases available to you. These databases sometimes include both reference and periodical sources as well as Internet sites; be careful to distinguish between these kinds of sources, as they can look similar in electronic form.

These are some general-purpose encyclopedias:

Academic American Encyclopedia
Colliers Encyclopedia
Encarta
Encyclopedia Americana
Encyclopædia Britannica
Grolier Microsoft
World Book

2. **Evaluating Encyclopedias.** Choose a topic from one of the Reading Passages that you would like to learn more about. Look it up in two or three different encyclopedias and answer these questions (you might want to try one print and one electronic encyclopedia for comparison).

   a. Is the article a convenient length, long enough to contain complete information but short enough to read comfortably?

   b. Are there pictures, maps, or diagrams to help you understand the topic?

   c. Does the article have the name of the author or a bibliography or list of references that can be useful for further research?

   d. Does the article have a list of related topics or electronic links to guide you to more information on this topic?

   e. Is there anything else in the article that might help you find more information?

3. **Using Encyclopedias.** Use an encyclopedia article to do a scanning exercise from one of the chapters, or a quotation, paraphrase, or summary exercise from the Yellow Pages, pages 250, 252, or 255.

4. **Documenting an Encyclopedia Article.** You will need this information for an MLA citation:

>   Author's name if there is one, last name first
>   Title of the article, in quotation marks
>   Title of the encyclopedia, underlined or in italics
>   Edition year
>
>   <u>For an APA citation, you will also need:</u> Volume and page numbers
>   City and publishing company

>   <u>MLA:</u> "Benjamin Franklin." *World Book.* 2003 ed.

>   <u>APA:</u> Benjamin Franklin. (2003). In *World book* (Vol. F-7, pp. 486–492). Chicago: World Book International.

For an article from an electronic or CD-ROM encyclopedia, MLA requires the same information plus the name of the database, the name and location of the library <u>if</u> the library has a subscription, the date accessed, and the electronic or URL address. For APA, only the date accessed and the title of the database are required.

>   <u>MLA:</u>
>
>   "Benjamin Franklin." *Encyclopædia Britannica Online.* 2003. Encyclopædia Britannica. Shatford Library, Pasadena, CA. 10 Oct. 2004 <http://search.eb.com/eb/article>.
>
>   <u>APA:</u>
>
>   Benjamin Franklin. (2003). In *Encyclopædia Britannica.* Retrieved October 10, 2004, from Encyclopædia Britannica Online.

B. Books: For Details

Like reference materials, books are very reliable sources of information, but instead of being written from a neutral point of view by a committee of experts, they are written by individual authors in order to express their own personal point of view. In fact, the purpose of writing and publishing a book is to present a new interpretation or perspective on a topic, so a book that simply repeats the commonly accepted information isn't likely to get published.

THE YELLOW PAGES

The editors and publishers check the facts in a book for fairness and accuracy, but different authors can draw different interpretations from the same facts. If the ideas you find in a book are very different from the ideas you have found in reference books, check with a librarian or teacher about the reliability of the book as a source. The books purchased by college libraries are selected because they are reliable for academic use. City libraries have these books as well as many books of more general interest.

Unlike encyclopedia articles, which are essentially summaries of information, books contain a lot of very detailed information, sometimes an overwhelming amount of detail. It is not necessary to read the whole book: Instead, you should scan the table of contents and the index to locate just the information you need. If you find that it's necessary to read many pages of a book to get only a little information, then that book isn't a suitable source for a research project and you should look for another book that covers the topic in a more accessible way.

★ **EXERCISES:**

1. **Finding Books.** Books are listed in the library's card catalog or online catalog in different ways—by author, by title, and by subject, and in online catalogs, by key words. In order to do an author or title search, you must already know the name of an author or the title of a book: You can find recommendations in the bibliography or list of references of an encyclopedia article or your textbooks.

    A subject search and a key word search enable you to find books that you don't already know about. A subject search makes use of specific subject headings such as those determined by the Library of Congress (LC); for example, the LC system uses the subject term *United States–History–Revolution*. If you look up *American Revolution* or *Revolutionary War* in a catalog that uses LC subject headings, the catalog will refer you to the standard heading with the instruction *USE United States–History–Revolution*. If you don't know what subject headings to use to find the materials you need, check with a librarian or consult the large red LC subject-heading books that should be available to you at the reference desk.

    A key word search on an online catalog works differently: Rather than looking for standard subject headings, the computer searches for any appearance of the key words (your search terms) in the title, the citation, or in some cases, the entire text. You can use any subjects you want, such as *American Revolution* and *Revolutionary War,* for key word searches, and both will get results, but the results may be different. You may need to experiment with different names and subjects to get the results you want; again, if you need help finding key words that work successfully, ask your teacher or a librarian for help.

The computer screen for a basic search looks like this:

> BASIC SEARCH   Find this: TYPE YOUR SEARCH TERM HERE
> ○—Title Search
> ○—Author Search
> ○—Subject Search
> ○—Call Number Search
> ○—Key Word Search

Key word searches have a couple of advantages over subject searches. One is that you can use wildcard endings: For example, rather than looking up the words *slave*, *slaves*, and *slavery* separately, you can use an asterisk as an ending—*slave**— for all three words. Another advantage is that you can do an advanced search combining search terms such as *AND* to join terms (*Franklin AND lightning*), *OR* for choices (*Benjamin Franklin OR Ben Franklin*), and *NOT* to exclude something (*Benjamin Franklin NOT book review*).

The computer screen for an advanced search looks like this:

> ADVANCED SEARCH   Find this: TYPE ONE SEARCH TERM HERE
> ○—AND   ○—OR   ○—NOT   TYPE THE OTHER TERM HERE

When you find some books in the catalog that look useful, note the call numbers so that you can locate the books on the shelves or stacks. American libraries use two different systems of call numbers: Local city libraries and some small college libraries use the Dewey Decimal system, based on the numbers 100–999, while larger colleges and universities use the LC system based on the alphabet and numbers. The two systems are compared on page 234 for books on American history:

THE YELLOW PAGES

Dewey Decimal Call Numbers	Library of Congress Call Numbers
973 United States History	E American History
973.1 Early History to 1607	E11–143 America
973.2 Colonial Period, 1607–1775	E151–889 United States
973.3 Period of Revolution and Confederation, 1775–1789	E186–199 Colonial History
	E201–298 Revolution, 1775–1783
973.4 Constitutional Period, 1789–1809	E300–453 Revolution to Civil War
	E337–400 Early Nineteenth Century
973.5 1809–1845	E441–453 Slavery
973.6 1845–1861	E456–655 Civil War
973.7 Civil War 1861–1865	E660–738 Late Nineteenth Century
973.8 Reconstruction Period, 1865–1901	E740–837 Twentieth Century
973.9 Twentieth Century	E895–904 Twenty-first century

Use the call numbers to locate the books on the library shelves, called the stacks. Look around on the shelves nearby for other books on the same topic or do a call number search to see what other books are available on the topic. As you find suitable books, use their indexes and bibliographies to help you find more sources. When you begin to see the names of authors repeated in different sources, you'll know that they are experts in their field and worthwhile for your investigation.

2. **Evaluating Books.** Choose one book and answer these questions:

   a. Check the publication date: Is the book recent enough to have current information?

   b. Check the author's professional background: Is he or she a scholar in the field who has published other books on similar topics? Information about the author can usually be found on the book's back cover or inside flap.

   c. Does the book have a table of contents and an index to help you find information in the book?

   d. Are there pictures, diagrams, or maps to help you understand the topic?

   e. Is there a bibliography or list of additional readings to help you find more books on the topic?

   f. Is there anything else that might help you find more information?

RESEARCH SOURCES

3. **Using Books.** Use a few pages from a book to do a quotation, paraphrase, or summary exercise from the Yellow Pages, pages 250, 252 or 255.

4. **Documenting a Book.** You will need this information:

>   Author's name, last name first
>   Title of the book, underlined or in italics
>   City of publication
>   Publishing company
>   Year of publication

>   <u>MLA:</u>

>   Isaacson, Walter. *Benjamin Franklin: An American Life.* New York: Simon & Schuster, 2003.

>   <u>APA:</u>

>   Isaacson, W. (2003). *Benjamin Franklin: An American life.* New York: Simon & Schuster.

C. Periodicals: *Magazines, Journals, and Newspapers*

Periodicals are published at regular intervals, every day like **newspapers,** every week like many popular **magazines,** or every month like some magazines and most academic **journals,** also known as scholarly or peer-reviewed journals. They are the best sources for current information. The editors of periodicals do as careful of a job as possible within their time limits to be sure that the information they publish is accurate, but sometimes errors in factual information occur. It is important to evaluate your periodical sources using the information you have already gathered from encyclopedias and books and to avoid sources that are inaccurate or do not present a balanced point of view.

Some popular magazines may not be appropriate sources for academic topics, although it is difficult to generalize; a magazine like *Reader's Digest* could have a useful feature on a historical figure such as Benjamin Franklin or Frederick Douglass. Like books, the magazines, newspapers, and journals found in college libraries are chosen for purchase because they are reliable and useful for academic work. City libraries have some of these sources as well as many magazines of general interest. As always, if you have questions about a source, ask your teacher or a librarian.

Libraries keep current newspapers, magazines, and journals on open shelves for several days or weeks, then store older editions in bound volumes or on microfilm or microfiche. Another convenient way to access periodical articles is to use an electronic database such as Infotrac or ProQuest; these databases may provide only an **abstract** or summary of an article, or they may provide the entire **text** of the article that you can print, download onto a disk, or e-mail to your home computer. Some databases, such as the *Biography Resource Center* and the *Discovery Collection,* include reference materials as well as periodical articles, so as you use them, be careful to note these different kinds of sources.

★ EXERCISES:

1. **Finding Periodicals.** Use a periodicals database to locate an article, using a subject or key word search. The subject search uses subject headings similar to those used by the LC for books, while a key word search looks for the occurrence of these words in the title, abstract, or complete text of an article. It's a good idea to try both subject and key word searches, as the results are usually different.

2. **Evaluating Periodical Articles.** Find an article, photocopy or print it, and answer these questions:

   a. Check the publication date: Is the article recent enough to have current information?

   b. Does the article include the name of the author? Is there any information about his or her professional background? Does the author or periodical have a particular point of view?

   c. Does the article have an appropriate balance of general information and specific details for you to understand the topic?

   d. Are there pictures, diagrams, or maps to help you understand the topic?

   e. Is there anything else that might help you find more information?

3. **Using Periodical Articles.** Use a periodical article to do a quotation, paraphrase, or summary exercise from the Yellow Pages, pages 250, 252, or 255.

4. **Documenting a Periodical Article.** You will need this information for the print version of an article:

   > Author's name if there is one, last name first
   > Title of the article, in quotation marks
   > Title of the periodical, underlined or in italics
   > Volume number and issue number for a scholarly journal
   > Date of publication
   > Page numbers

> MLA:
>
> Tolson, Jay. "The Many Faces of Benjamin Franklin." *U.S. News & World Report* 23 June 2003: 35–38.
>
> APA:
>
> Tolson, J. (2003, June 23). The many faces of Benjamin Franklin. *U.S. News & World Report,* 90, pp. 35–38.
>
> For a periodical article from an electronic database, MLA requires the same information plus the name of the database, the library and its location if it has a subscription, the date accessed, and the electronic or URL address. For APA, you need only the date accessed and the name of the database.
>
> MLA:
>
> Tolson, Jay. "The Many Faces of Benjamin Franklin." *U.S. News & World Report* 23 June 2003. ProQuest Direct. Shatford Library, Pasadena, CA. 10 Oct. 2004 <http://proquest.umi.com/pdqweb>.
>
> APA:
>
> Tolson, J. (2003, June 23). The many faces of Benjamin Franklin. *U.S. News & World Report.* Retrieved October 10, 2004, from ProQuest database.

D. The Internet: Users Beware!

The Internet may be the newest, most exciting research tool, but it is also the most difficult to use to find reliable information. Anyone can put information on the Internet: There is no editor or publishing company to determine if the information is accurate, and no librarian to decide if it is worthwhile to make it available to the public. This free dissemination of information is both an advantage and a disadvantage: Students must be knowledgeable enough to evaluate the information themselves, so it is best to start your research project with print sources and use the Internet only when you have a good understanding of your topic.

A second difficulty is that there is so much information on the Internet that a search may turn up hundreds or even thousands of sites. The sites can vary widely in quality and in relevance; for example, a search using the name "Benjamin Franklin" turns up as many as 100,000 sites, including commercial sites, for example, sites advertising books, posters, and all kinds of memorabilia related to Franklin. A related problem is that the topic may be covered unevenly, with very detailed information about some aspects and none at all about others. So if you rely only on Internet sources for your research, your paper can be unbalanced in its treatment of the topic.

A third disadvantage is that it is extremely easy to plagiarize from the Internet by downloading information onto your own computer. Remember, plagiarism from the Internet is just as illegal as plagiarism from print sources, so be careful to paraphrase and summarize all the source materials you use.

Keeping in mind all these warnings, do use the Internet to supplement your research from conventional sources.

> ★ EXERCISES:
> 1. **Finding Information on the Internet.** Using a search engine such as Yahoo!, AltaVista, or Google, enter a search term for your topic and take a look at some of the results. Some search engines use the search term as a conventional subject heading, but most use it as a key word or phrase located in the title or in the entire text of the article. Experiment with your search terms and, as always, check with a librarian if you don't get useful results. Most search engines allow you to do an advanced search with the words *ALL* or *AND* to join terms, *ANY* or *OR* for either term, and *EXCLUDING* or *NOT* to leave out certain kinds of sites or topics. Search engines also allow you to do a phrase search, putting two or more words together in quotation marks—for example, *"Poor Richard's Almanac"*—so that you don't get a list of sites with the word *Poor*, other sites with the word *Richard's*, and still other sites with the word *Almanac*.
> 2. **Evaluating Internet Sources.** It is extremely important to evaluate an Internet source thoroughly, as anyone can post any kind of information on the Internet. There are two approaches to making an evaluation. One way is to consider the reliability of the person or organization that put the information on the Internet. This name should appear somewhere in the site, often at the end, and in abbreviated form in the URL address. The URL address also includes an abbreviation that identifies the kind of organization it is: .edu for an educational institution, .gov for a government office, .org for a non-profit group or public service organization, and .com for a commercial business. The use of a tilda (~) indicates a personal webpage. If you cannot determine who or what organization put the information on the Internet, it probably is not reliable. When you find a site that looks useful, answer these questions:
>   a. Does the site include information about your topic? What kind of information does it include?
>   b. Is the person or group that is responsible for this site easy to identify? Who or what group put this information on the Internet?

c. Does the presentation seem balanced and fair? Does the site promote a particular point of view?

d. Are there links to other useful sources of information on this topic?

The second way to evaluate Internet sources is to compare the information you get from the Internet to the information that you have already gathered from the more reliable print sources. For example, students who have already done some research on Franklin will probably recognize the name of J. A. Leo Lemay as the author of a biography or an encyclopedia article about Franklin.

Internet information might be more current or detailed, but it should be similar in attitude or point of view to print sources. The treatment should be balanced, and the conclusions should be thoroughly supported by evidence. The use of English should be correct and clear. If you are in doubt about the reliability of an Internet source, check with a librarian or teacher before using it.

e. Study this page of websites and decide which ones look like reliable sources of information about Benjamin Franklin.

Benjamin Franklin: Glimpses of the Man
Describes his roles as a scientist, inventor, statesman, printer, philosopher, musician, and economist. From the Franklin Institute Science Museum in Philadelphia. *http://sln.fi.edu/franklin/*

Sophisticated Shirts
Order a lovely Ben Franklin t-shirt. T-shirts with quotes, inventions, drawings, witty sayings, history—printed front/back. Genius t-shirts. Hundreds more—artists, writers, music, women, wisdom, philosophy. *www.historyshirt.com*

Benjamin Franklin: An Extraordinary Life. An Electric Mind.
Companion site to the PBS series chronicling Franklin's life as a player in the Age of Scientific Discovery, the American Revolution, and the early Republic. *www.pbs.org/benfranklin/*

Benjamin Franklin: A Documentary History—J. A. Leo Lemay
Offers an in-depth look at the many phases of Franklin's life. *www.english.udel.edu/lemay/franklin/*

Amazon.com. Books: Benjamin Franklin
Music customers interested in Benjamin Franklin may also be interested in Sponsored Links Feedback. *www.amazon.com/*

3. **Using Internet Sources.** Use a website to do a quotation, paraphrase, or summary exercise from the Yellow Pages, pages 250, 252, or 255.

4. **Documenting an Internet Source.** Because the Internet is a relatively new phenomenon, there is not yet complete agreement about the kind of bibliographic information to include in a citation or the form to put it in. The most important pieces of information to include are the URL address and the date of access, both of which are easy to determine and should appear at the bottom of the pages you print out. Include as much of the information listed below too, if it is available, starting with the author and title in the usual way. On a reliable website, this information should be easy to find; if not, you should question the reliability of the source and check with your teacher or a librarian.

> Author
> Title in quotation marks
> Any publication information that is given
> Title of the website, underlined or in italics
> Any version, volume, or issue numbers
> Date of electronic publication or last update
> Name of the subscription service and the library, if used
> Name of the institution or organization sponsoring the website
> The date that you accessed this website
> The URL or electronic address of the website
>
> MLA:
>
> Lemay, J. A. Leo. "Benjamin Franklin: A Documentary History." 1997. Dept. of English, University of Delaware. 10 Oct. 2004 <http://www.english.udel.edu/lemay/franklin/>.
>
> APA:
>
> Lemay, J. A. L. (1997). *Benjamin Franklin: A documentary history.* Retrieved October 10, 2004, from Dept. of English, University of Delaware Web site: http://www.english.udel.edu/lemay/franklin

RESEARCH SOURCES

Summary Chart for Research Sources: Different Sources for Different Purposes

What kind of information can you find with each type of source? What are the advantages and disadvantages of each type of source? Complete this chart with your ideas.

Reference books are best for this kind of information:

Advantages:

Disadvantages:

Books are best for this kind of information:

Advantages:

Disadvantages:

Periodical articles are best for this kind of information:

Advantages:

Disadvantages:

The Internet is best for this kind of information:

Advantages:

Disadvantages:

★ Glossary ★

reference material—a publication with facts, statistics, and background information

periodical—magazine, journal, or newspaper published at regular intervals

magazine—periodical written for general readers with articles on popular topics

journal—periodical written for professional readers with articles on scholarly topics

newspaper—periodical published daily about events as they happen

Internet—a network of computers connected worldwide by phone lines

online catalog—a catalog of all of a library's materials, accessible by computer

electronic database—a selected set of sources chosen by topic (for example, the arts or medicine) or by format (for example, reference sources or periodicals), and stored in electronic form

abstract—a summary of an article

text—an entire article

citation—a list of information that can be used to evaluate or locate a source, including the author, title, and publishing information

documentation—the formal system of citations to indicate the use and location of a source. Some common systems are MLA (Modern Languages Association), APA (American Psychological Association), and the *Chicago Manual of Style*. The system used in this book is the MLA, but examples of APA are also provided.

2. RESEARCH WRITING SKILLS: DOCUMENTATION, QUOTATIONS, PARAPHRASES, SUMMARIES, AND THE RESEARCH PAPER

Most college writing assignments involve writing from sources, in other words, using the ideas of other people in your own writing. Not only do these assignments require careful reading of the sources, but also the analysis and synthesis of ideas and the skills to write about these ideas clearly, honestly, and in the proper format. Some assignments may involve reading one source, while other assignments such as research papers require the integration of information from several sources. The most common sources used for these assignments are those discussed in the first section of the Yellow Pages, but radio and TV shows, movies, lectures, and interviews can also be used as sources of information.

When you write from sources, you must be careful to differentiate clearly between the ideas of different authors and not to represent their ideas or their words as your own. In American law, the ideas and words of a person belong to him or her, just as a car or other property belongs to him or her, and is not available for you to use without his or her permission. The illegal use of another writer's ideas or words is called **plagiarism** and can lead to a failing grade for an assignment or even a course.

When you use an author's ideas and words, you must **cite** the source, in other words, give credit to the source and provide information so that readers can find it themselves if they want to, to get more information or to check to see that you have used the source accurately. This book includes examples of both MLA and APA **documentation**. On page ii of this text, for example, you can see the list of permissions for the use of the reading passages in Chapters 1–6.

This section introduces the basic skills of research writing—documenting sources; using quotations, paraphrases, and summaries; and writing a research paper.

A. Documentation

Whenever you use material from a source, either words or ideas, it's necessary to use documentation to give the reader information about where the material comes from and how to find it. Writers used to use footnotes to provide this information, while today's systems use in-text parenthetical citations and a Works Cited page; the citations are sometimes called "footnotes" for convenience although they are no longer placed at the foot of the page.

When you use sources to write your papers, you'll have to document any ideas that are not your own ideas and are not common knowledge. **Common knowledge** means ideas and facts that are generally known to an educated audience, but in practice it can be difficult to know what the average person might already know. Ideas that might be familiar to a person from one country or field of study may not be familiar to someone from another country or field of study. One helpful guideline is to consider the source of the material: Any information found in an encyclopedia can be considered to be common knowledge, and you don't need to document it. Information that appears only in certain books, periodicals, and websites probably needs to be documented, as well as any exact numbers and statistics. For example, many people might know that Benjamin Franklin had little formal education, but few people would know the exact numbers (one year in school and one year with a private tutor), so we might decide to document these details. If you are in doubt about what to document, ask a teacher or librarian.

When you document a source—book, periodical, or website—you'll need to provide enough bibliographic information about the source that readers can find the source for themselves in order to get more information or to check that you've used the source accurately. The information you'll need includes the author's name; title of the source; publishing details such as date, company, and city; and for online sources, the URL address and the date of access. It's a good idea to write down or print this information as soon as you begin to use a source so that you won't forget it later.

The documentation used in academic papers takes two forms: One kind, the in-text parenthetical citation, is used to document sources as they are used in the text of a paper, and the other, called the bibliography page, comes at the end of the paper and lists all the sources used to write it. In the MLA system, this page is called the Works Cited page, while in APA it is called the References page.

The format of the citation on the bibliography page includes the complete bibliographic information, while the in-text parenthetical citation includes just enough information so that the reader can locate the source on the bibliography page, usually only the author's last name, or the first words of the title if there is no author, as well as the page number for print sources if you are using an exact quote. Examples of both kinds of documentation used by a student quoting from an article by Jay Tolson about Benjamin Franklin follow. The first example shows the quotation as it is written in the text of the paper followed by an in-text parenthetical citation:

> MLA:
>
> Franklin was unique among the other Founding Fathers. According to Jay Tolson, a writer for *U.S. News & World Report*, "If there were a Founding Fathers theme park, Franklin would have to be the leading attraction" (35).

APA:

Franklin was unique among the other Founding Fathers. According to Jay Tolson, a writer for *U.S. News & World Report* (2003), "If there were a Founding Fathers theme park, Franklin would have to be the leading attraction" (p. 35).

Because the author's name is mentioned in the introductory phrase, it is omitted from the parenthetical citation. The next example shows the complete bibliographic citation for the same source as it would appear on the bibliography page:

MLA:

Tolson, Jay. "The Many Faces of Benjamin Franklin." *U.S. News & World Report* 23 June 2003: 35–38.

APA:

Tolson, J. (2003, June 23). The many faces of Benjamin Franklin. *U.S. News & World Report*, pp. 35–38.

Using the two forms of documentation together, a reader can understand that the words in quotation marks are from Tolson's article, not the writer's own words, and also can find the detailed information about the article on the bibliography page listed under Tolson's name. If the article has no author, both forms of citation begin with the title.

The basic MLA and APA formats for common sources are included in Part 1 of the Yellow Pages. For more information about MLA format, consult the *MLA Handbook for Writers of Research Papers, Sixth Edition,* and for APA, consult the *Publication Manual of the American Psychological Association.* The MLA does not publish its guidelines on its website, but the APA has a website with a link to the basic formats for citing electronic media: www.apastyle.org. More specific documentation information and examples can also be found in English handbooks and style manuals.

B. Quotations, Paraphrases, and Summaries

Quotations, paraphrases, and **summaries** are all ways to use sources without plagiarism. A quotation uses the exact words from a source, while in a paraphrase and summary, the ideas from a source are rewritten in your own words. In both cases, it's necessary to use an in-text parenthetical citation to cite the source.

Using a quotation with the author's exact words is certainly easier than writing your own paraphrase or summary. However, teachers want to know that you understand the ideas well enough to write them in your own words, so you can not rely very much on quotations in your papers. A common guideline in college classes is that quotations should make up no more than 10–15 percent of an essay or research paper, and they are generally not used at all in summaries and informal assignments.

This limit on quotations means that, most of the time, you must use paraphrases and summaries, rewriting the ideas in your own words in a style that is understandable and natural to you. At the same time, you must be careful not to change the author's meaning and attitude or to add any of your own ideas. When your rewritten passage is about the same length as the original passage, it is called a paraphrase, while if it is much shorter and highlights only the main ideas, it is called a summary.

Some students don't like to write paraphrases and summaries because they might make mistakes in grammar or vocabulary. However, it is better to make a few mistakes than to fail an assignment because of plagiarism. Teachers who work with students learning English will appreciate an honest effort to avoid plagiarism and won't mind a few small mistakes.

B.1. Quotations

Putting an author's words in quotation marks and citing the source is the only legal way that you can use an author's exact words in your own writing. Because quotations can be used only rarely in your assignments, choose them carefully: Look for phrases and sentences that are unique in content or expression. Don't use a quotation for words that you can paraphrase easily or for an idea you don't really understand.

To illustrate the choice of sentences for quotations, we can compare these two quotations from Tolson's article: "If there were a Founding Fathers theme park, Franklin would have to be the leading attraction," and "Franklin was probably the most indispensable of the Founding Fathers." The sentences make a similar point about Franklin, but the theme park sentence is unusual in its image and vocabulary and therefore a better choice for a quotation.

When you use a quotation in your paper, you must integrate it carefully into your organization and sentence structure. A good approach is to write an introductory phrase with the author's name or the title of the source and a few words to indicate its purpose in your paper, as the student did with the quotations on pages 244 and 245 from Tolson's article. There are a variety of introductory phrases used to introduce quotations, such as:

> According to Tolson, a writer for *U.S. News & World Report*, Franklin was . . . .
>
> Or

> Newswriter Jay Tolson writes (states, claims, etc.) that Franklin was . . . .
>
> Or
>
> In a recent article in *U.S. News & World Report,* Franklin was described as . . . .

When a quotation is short, three lines or less, you can incorporate it directly into your text using an introductory phrase and quotation marks. The first letter of a sentence and the final mark of punctuation can be changed to fit your sentence structure. Here is a short quotation from a biography of Franklin by Walter Isaacson, with an introductory explanation and in-text citation (use quotation marks and put the period after the citation):

> MLA:
>
> In his biography of Benjamin Franklin, Walter Isaacson writes that Franklin's most important invention was "an American national identity based on the virtues and values of its middle class" (3).
>
> APA:
>
> In his biography of Benjamin Franklin, Walter Isaacson (2003) writes that Franklin's most important invention was "an American national identity based on the virtues and values of its middle class" (p. 3).

When the quotation is four lines or more (MLA) or more than 40 words (APA), you must indent the quotation as shown below. Quotation marks are not used with indented quotations.

> MLA:
>
> In his biography of Benjamin Franklin, Walter Isaacson writes,
>> Franklin has a particular resonance in twenty-first century America. A successful publisher and consummate networker with an inventive curiosity, he would have felt right at home in the information revolution, and his unabashed striving to be part of an upwardly mobile meritocracy make him, in social critic David Brooks's phrase, "our first Yuppie." (3)

APA:

In his biography of Benjamin Franklin, Walter Isaacson (2003) writes,

> Franklin has a particular resonance in twenty-first century America. A successful publisher and consummate networker with an inventive curiosity, he would have felt right at home in the information revolution, and his unabashed striving to be part of an upwardly mobile meritocracy make him, in social critic David Brooks's phrase, "our first Yuppie." p. 3

Here the quotation marks around "our first Yuppie" indicate that these words are in quotations marks in Isaacson's text. If these words appear in a shorter quotation for which quotation marks are necessary, the internal set of quotation marks would be single quotation marks, while the external marks would be the usual double quotation marks:

> In his description of Franklin, Isaacson refers to social critic David Brooks's idea that Franklin was "'our first Yuppie.'"

When you choose a quotation, be careful to choose words that represent the author's point of view accurately. For example, the following quotation taken from Jay Tolson's article would be confusing to a reader because most of Tolson's comments about Franklin are favorable:

> Reporter Jay Tolson writes about Franklin,
>> Writers as diverse as Ralph Waldo Emerson, Henry David Thoreau, Herman Melville, Mark Twain, and F. Scott Fitzgerald saw him as the patron saint of the money-grubbing, soulless American bourgeois, the very cliché-spouting glad-hander that Sinclair Lewis would satirize in his novel *Babbitt*.

This quotation needs an introduction to explain why Tolson wrote this negative description of Franklin. In fact, Tolson's words represent other people's opinions of Franklin, not his own opinions; the following introduction makes this difference clear:

Jay Tolson admires Franklin greatly but admits that not everyone does:

> Writers as diverse as Ralph Waldo Emerson, Henry David Thoreau, Herman Melville, Mark Twain, and F. Scott Fitzgerald saw him as the patron saint of the money-grubbing, soulless American bourgeois, the very cliché-spouting glad-hander that Sinclair Lewis would satirize in his novel *Babbitt*.

The quotation has other problems too: The long list of authors is not necessary and the novel *Babbitt* may not be familiar to readers. Although a quotation uses the exact words of an author, it is possible to make small changes if you indicate them clearly: To leave out some words, according to the MLA system, you must replace them with three dots (called ellipses) in brackets—[...]. Using the APA system, replace the words with just three dots—...—and no brackets. You do not need to add ellipses at the beginning or end of any quotation unless you need to emphasize that the quotation begins or ends in midsentence. If you want to add some words to make the idea clear, put them in brackets—[added words]—for both MLA and APA. Here is Tolson's quotation with some changes:

MLA:

Jay Tolson admires Franklin greatly but admits that not everyone does: " . . . [some] writers [. . .] saw him as the patron saint of the money-grubbing, soulless American bourgeois [. . .]" (35).

APA:

Jay Tolson (2003) admires Franklin greatly but admits that not everyone does: "[some] writers . . . saw him as the patron saint of the money-grubbing, soulless American bourgeois" (p. 35).

Now the quotation is shorter, with only the important point that some writers are critical of Franklin for his interest in making money. The quotation still includes Tolson's unusual phrases to describe Franklin, an example of the unique style of language that we want to keep in quotations.

> ★ **EXERCISE: Using a Quotation**
>
> a. From one of the Reading Passages or from one of your sources, choose a sentence or part of a sentence that seems special to you—an interesting idea, expressed in a striking way. Photocopy or print out a hard copy of the source.
>
> b. On another sheet of paper, write an introductory explanation for your quotation: Include the author's name and/or the title of the source and a few words to indicate the significance of the quotation. Then write the quotation in quotation marks.
>
> c. Make sure that the quotation fits your sentence structure. If you make, add, or leave out words, indicate these changes clearly.
>
> d. Include a parenthetical citation and the complete bibliographic citation.
>
> e. Hand in the quotation with the hard copy of the source.

B.2. Paraphrases

A paraphrase is a rewriting of an author's ideas in your own words so that you can use the ideas in your paper without using quotation marks. Paraphrasing is not a hard skill to learn, but it does require a good knowledge of English vocabulary and grammar as well as some creativity.

To paraphrase well, it is necessary first to read the passage carefully and understand it. Then, being careful not to change the meaning, you can begin to make changes in the vocabulary and sentence structure. It is not necessary to change every word; in fact, that would be impossible, but you must make enough changes that the words in your paper are not easy to recognize as the words from your source. Some English handbooks recommend that no more than three consecutive words be taken from a source without making changes.

If not enough changes are made, the result is plagiarism, the unauthorized use of someone else's words. Here is an example of plagiarism of the quotation from Isaacson's book (see page 248). In this example, the writer mentions neither the author nor the article, but the words can easily be recognized as Isaacson's words by anyone who has read the article:

> Franklin has a particular resonance in America today. He was a successful publisher and consummate networker with an inventive curiosity, so he would have felt right at home in the information revolution, and his unabashed striving to be part of an upwardly mobile meritocracy make him, in social critic David Brooks's phrase, "our first Yuppie."

Although a couple of words have been changed, this version is too close to the original source in vocabulary and sentence structure, close enough to be called plagiarism. The expressions *consummate networker* and *upwardly mobile meritocracy* in particular are unusual expressions that many student writers would not know, and the quotation from David Brooks comes from another source; both are clear indications to a teacher that the student has plagiarized the passage. This dishonest use of Isaacson's words can lead to a failing grade in the assignment or in the course.

To write an acceptable paraphrase, start by making some changes in vocabulary: Some words, proper nouns like *America* and common words like *successful,* are hard to change, so look for words that have close synonyms, such as *appeal* instead of *resonance* and *was comfortable with* instead of *felt right at home in.* You can also make changes in the parts of speech, for example, changing the adjective *successful* to the noun *success* or the verb *succeed.* For unusual expressions like *meritocracy,* you can substitute the literal meaning, *a system that values individual abilities.*

After making some changes in vocabulary, you can also make changes in sentence structure. An active sentence can be changed to passive and passive to active, or phrases and clauses can be moved around in the sentences.

Remember that it's not necessary to change everything: A few changes can quickly transform the passage into your own voice. In the following example, some changes (shown in italics above the passage) have been made in vocabulary:

                 an appeal   *to modern Americans*
Franklin has <u>a particular resonance in twenty-first century</u>

      success in publishing   *networking*
<u>America.</u> A <u>successful publisher</u> and consummate <u>networker</u>

                                 been comfortable with
with an inventive curiosity, he would have <u>felt right at home in</u>

     the information age
the <u>information revolution</u>, and his unabashed striving to be

     a system that values individual abilities
part of <u>an upwardly mobile meritocracy</u> make him, in social

critic David Brooks's phrase, "our first Yuppie."

Now the student writer can make some changes in the sentence structure and the order of the ideas. The phrase "our first Yuppie" can be left out of the paraphrase or can be quoted as a unique use of language. As with a quotation, it is still a good idea to add an introductory explanation and still necessary to mention your source in order to give the author credit for the idea. The use of Isaacson's name at the beginning of the paraphrase and the parenthetical citation at the end indicate that the two sentences in between are paraphrases.

MLA:

Isaacson writes that Franklin has an appeal to modern Americans because of his curiosity and his success in publishing and networking. He also would have been comfortable with the information age and with our system that values individual abilities (3).

APA:

Isaacson (2003) writes that Franklin has an appeal to modern Americans because of his curiosity and his success in publishing and networking. He also would have been comfortable with the information age and with our system that values individual abilities.

★ **EXERCISE: Writing a Paraphrase**

a. From one of the Reading Passages or from one of your sources, choose a sentence or two to paraphrase. Photocopy or print out a hard copy of the source.

b. Read the sentence carefully until you understand it.

c. Make changes in the vocabulary and then in the sentence structure. Be careful not to change the ideas or to add any of your own ideas.

d. Begin your paraphrase with an introductory explanation that includes the author's name.

e. Include a parenthetical citation and the complete bibliographic citation.

f. Hand in your paraphrase with the copy of the source.

B.3. Summaries

Writing summaries is a good test of both reading and writing skills, so teachers often assign them for reports and tests. Summaries are also often a part of longer assignments that ask you to summarize an article and give your reactions.

A summary is similar to a paraphrase in that the ideas from a source are rewritten in your own words, but while a paraphrase is about the same length as the original source, a summary is always shorter, sometimes much shorter. Teachers usually ask for summaries of a specific length, for example a one-paragraph summary of a short article or a one-page summary of a longer article or chapter.

A summary always has as its source a single article or passage (when you use multiple sources, your paper becomes a research paper). Because a summary is shorter than the original passage, it contains only the main ideas and few details. It usually follows the same order as the original passage. A summary does not contain any of your own ideas, any ideas of other authors, or even any ideas of the author that are not found in the particular passage you are working with.

To write a summary, choose a passage that deals with a single topic, such as a short article or part of a longer article or chapter. This passage is your original source or text. Read the passage over carefully several times to understand it well and take notes of the main ideas. Paraphrase these main ideas by making changes in both vocabulary and sentence structure. Summarize the less important ideas, again changing to your own words.

A formal summary begins with some information about the source, such as the author's name, the title of the source, and the main idea of the passage. The remainder of the summary is organized in paragraph form like an essay and may end with a concluding sentence. Quotations are not generally used in a summary. The complete bibliographic information for the source can be written at the top or bottom of the page.

An informal summary that is part of a longer essay or paper includes only the main ideas and perhaps the author's name, as well as a clear explanation of why this information is important to the paper.

Here is an example of a formal summary of Tolson's article about Benjamin Franklin. Notice that the first sentence mentions the author, the title of the magazine, and the main idea of the article. The following sentences cover Tolson's main points, and the final sentence summarizes Tolson's concluding ideas. The critical comments made by other authors about Franklin are omitted because they are not among Tolson's main points.

In an article in *U.S. News & World Report*, Jay Tolson writes that Benjamin Franklin is the most important of the Founding Fathers because of his practical genius, his contributions to civic service, his public relations skills, and his international fame. Tolson points out that although most of us think we already know Franklin well, recent scholarship has added to our knowledge of Franklin as a complete human being. Many people know that he developed devices such as bifocals and the lightening rod that helped common people, but they might not know that he decided not to patent these devices so that everyone could benefit from them without paying fees. With the help of friends, he improved the civic life of Philadelphia by establishing a library, a fire insurance company, schools, and a hospital. He had a good understanding of public opinion and worked to create the image of him that we all recognize. In *Poor Richard's Almanac,* he included tips for success that management consultants and psychologists still recommend today. Finally, Franklin was admired in London and France as a rustic American philosopher who represented the common man, practical and democratic. Two recent biographers of Franklin emphasize that he valued ordinary people above the elite people and believed that the new government of the United States should be a government of the common man. According to Tolson, Franklin believed that the common people were ready to do the right thing.

MLA:

Tolson, Jay. "The Many Faces of Benjamin Franklin." *U.S. News & World Report* 23 June 2003: 35–38.

APA:

Tolson, J. (2003, June 23). The many faces of Benjamin Franklin. *U.S. News & World Report,* pp. 35–38.

★ **EXERCISE: Writing a One-Page Formal Summary**

a. From one of the Reading Passages or from one of your sources, choose several pages to summarize. Photocopy the pages or print them out.

b. Read the pages carefully and identify the main ideas.

c. Make changes in the vocabulary and sentence structure.

d. Begin your summary with a main idea sentence mentioning the author's name, the title, and the main idea of the original passage.

e. Write the summary in paragraph form following the order of the original source.

f. Make sure that the summary contains only the ideas in the original text, no ideas from other sources, and none of your own ideas or opinions.

g. Write the complete bibliographic citation.

h. Hand in your summary with the hard copy of the source.

C. The Research Paper

For most students, writing a research paper is their first step into original scholarship, their first opportunity to choose a topic, research it, and write about it from their own point of view. All of the material in a research paper comes from sources in the form of quotations, paraphrases, and summaries. However, the interpretation of the material and organization of the paper are the writer's, so even if students use similar source materials, their research papers will be different. Writing a research paper is hard work, but it should be enjoyable too, as you learn about and become an expert in your own chosen topic.

A research paper is organized like a long essay on a single topic, using ideas gathered from several sources to make a point about the topic. The writer's task consists of **analysis** and **synthesis:** The writer must read several sources, analyzing each one in order to understand the main points and the point of view of the author. Then the writer synthesizes or combines together all of the different ideas into a unified paper with a single thesis.

As in an essay, the thesis is the general statement of the paper, the sentence that states the point or reason for writing. It may be an informational thesis, a fact or an idea that most people would agree with, for example that Benjamin Franklin made many contributions to American independence. Or it may be an argumentative thesis, an idea that is controversial like Tolson's, that Franklin was the most important of the Founding Fathers, or Isaacson's, that Franklin invented the stereotypical American character. College teachers often require that you choose an argumentative thesis, one that reasonable people can disagree about, and that you reach a conclusion supported by your sources.

C.1. Choosing a Topic

The topic is the general area of research, stated in a few words. When teachers assign a research paper, they usually suggest some topics for investigation, but in most college classes, it is up to the student writer to limit the topic to something that fits the time schedule and the availability of sources and to decide on a workable thesis.

Start by looking up some of the teacher's suggestions in an encyclopedia to get an overview of the topic. Then, when you find a topic that interests you, go to the books and articles recommended in the encyclopedia for further reading. As you do this preliminary reading, think of some questions that might be interesting to answer in your paper.

For example, you might begin your research with this general topic in mind:

Topic: Benjamin Franklin and American Independence

This topic helps to guide your reading to Franklin's activities leading up to and during the Revolutionary War. You would not want to spend your time reading about Franklin's childhood, or his civic projects in Philadelphia, or his many inventions. But as it is still a very broad topic, you'll look for ways to narrow it further. As you gather ideas, you might discover that Franklin participated in writing three important documents—the Declaration of Independence; the Treaty of Paris, which ended the Revolutionary War; and the Constitution. You might ask yourself how he participated and how important his influence was for each document. The topic and these questions will continue to control your reading as you look for information that answers the questions.

C.2. Doing the Research and Writing a Working Thesis Statement

Gathering information can seem like a daunting task, with so many books, articles, and websites all with different points of view. Because the quality of your paper depends greatly on the quality of your sources, you'll want to find good ones: Don't waste time on sources that don't answer your questions, and don't collect a lot of sources with very little useful information. Use your search and evaluation skills to find a small number of high-quality sources. Use information from one good source to find another: Tolson, for example, mentions Isaacson's biography in his article.

You'll also want to look for sources that include different points of view. For example, your sources should not present all positive information or all negative information about your topic. To write a balanced and fair paper, you will need to explore both sides, or all sides, of your topic. Tolson provides an example of a balanced treatment in his analysis of

Benjamin Franklin when he includes the critical judgments of several authors and then presents his own opinion.

As you continue gathering ideas, your job as a researcher is to analyze the information you find, determining the essential relevant parts and separating them from information that doesn't help to answer your questions. When you discover that Franklin played a very influential role in all three documents, you can begin to write your thesis (it's called a working thesis because you might make changes in it later):

> <u>Working Thesis:</u> Benjamin Franklin was the most important of the Founding Fathers because of his influence in writing three important documents—the Declaration of Independence, the Treaty of Paris, and the Constitution.

This thesis makes a promise to the reader that you will write about Franklin's participation in all three documents and that you will show how important his influence was. Students often think that a broad, vague thesis is best because it gives them a lot to write about, but in fact a more specific thesis is better because it limits the research to a manageable size, indicating exactly what kind of information you'll need to support the thesis and develop the paper. On the other hand, if your thesis is too narrow and you are unable to find the information you need to support it, you'll need to broaden it.

Remember to make a record of the complete bibliographic information for each source as you use it. There are several methods for recording information, including taking notes on 3″ × 5″ or 4″ × 6″ index cards, photocopying material, or downloading and printing it from the Internet or database. In all cases, indicate carefully to yourself whether you have recorded an author's exact words or have paraphrased or summarized them.

C.3. Writing the Paper

As a writer, your job is now to synthesize or gather together all the information you plan to use into a logical and coherent paper. Keep in mind that even as you write your paper, it may be necessary to find more sources and do some more reading and even to make changes in your thesis. Be sure to leave yourself plenty of time for this process.

The organization of a research paper is similar to an essay, with an introduction, body, and conclusion, but of course each part is longer: The introduction and conclusion may be several paragraphs long (each 10–15 percent of the total length of the paper), and the body can be several pages long (70–80 percent).

The introduction includes general background information that your reader needs in order to understand the paper. The answers to the *wh-* questions—*who? what? when? where?*—can guide you to provide adequate background information. This information is usually common knowledge found in reference sources and doesn't need documentation. You may need to write more than one paragraph of background information in order to explain the circumstances thoroughly.

The thesis statement follows the background information and states the main point of the paper. It may be at the end of the introductory paragraph, or it may be in a separate short paragraph. Sometimes, if the background is especially complicated to explain, the paper begins with a short general introduction that includes the thesis statement, followed by paragraphs with more detailed background information.

As in an essay, the thesis provides a plan for writing the body. Use this plan to write a simple outline, using Roman numerals for the major divisions of the paper. As you gather information, you can use capital letters for further divisions. Some teachers may require that you turn in an outline as you are writing your paper or when you hand in the finished paper. Consider your first outline to be a working outline; if it doesn't make sense to you as you write, try out different ways until you find one that seems logical and appropriate. Here is a short outline for the thesis statement on page 257:

> <u>Thesis:</u> Benjamin Franklin was the most important of the Founding Fathers because of his influence in writing three important documents—the Declaration of Independence, the Treaty of Paris, and the Constitution.
>
> I. the Declaration of Independence
> II. the Treaty of Paris
> III. the Constitution

Because the body paragraphs include many specific supporting details, it's necessary to include in-text parenthetical citations in this part of the paper (but remember that you don't need to document common knowledge). As you organize the details, try to put the details from one source together so that it's not necessary to use documentation after every sentence. To indicate clearly that several sentences include details from a single source, use a "sandwich" approach: Start with an introductory phrase with the author's name, then after two or three sentences of details, end with a parenthetical citation. The reader will understand that all of the information between the introductory phrase and the citation comes from that source, as in this example from Tolson's article.

MLA:

Tolson writes that Franklin recognized the importance of public opinion and often worked to shape it. Most of the time he used it in a positive way, but sometimes he manipulated it for political advantage (36).

APA:

Tolson (2003) writes that Franklin recognized the importance of public opinion and often worked to shape it. Most of the time he used it in a positive way, but sometimes he manipulated it for political advantage.

As you work on the body of your paper, you may find that you need more information on a topic or even need to change the thesis statement or outline. This is normal: The writing process should be seen as circular, with many drafts between the first and the final draft. The more times you can revise the paper, the better it will be in the end.

The conclusion of your paper may be one or more paragraphs and can include a summary of the paper, not repeated exactly but in different words. The conclusion can also include effects, results, predictions, and recommendations. Another option is a quotation that illustrates an important point of the paper. Most important, you can give your own opinion or interpretation in the conclusion; if you've chosen an argumentative thesis, it is expected that you will end the paper with a clear statement of your own opinion supported by the details in the body. Whatever choices you decide on, remember that the conclusion includes general comments, not specific details, so documentation is not usually needed in the conclusion unless you choose to end with a quotation.

C.4. Documenting the Sources

Your accuracy and honesty in the use of sources is an important factor in the grade of your research paper. In addition to quotations, all information that is paraphrased and summarized needs to be documented with in-text parenthetical citations, unless it is common knowledge. If you are in doubt about whether to document something, ask your teacher or a librarian. All of the sources you use must be listed on the bibliography page.

C.5. Typing the Paper

A research paper is typed or printed in 10- or 12-point font, double-spaced, on standard white typing paper. The first page is the title page, with the title of your paper, your name, the class, and the date. The text of the paper follows, with margins of about an inch on each side. The last page is the bibliography page listing all of the sources you used for your paper, in alphabetical order and in the correct format. This page is titled Works Cited in MLA and References in APA.

Some teachers will allow you to use your word-processing skills to be creative with colors, fonts, and illustrations, while other teachers prefer a more conservative format. Check with your teacher before doing anything unusual with the format of your paper.

A sample student research paper, shown in both MLA and APA formats, can be found at the end of the Yellow Pages, pages 266–283.

Time Line/Check List for a Research Paper

Writing a research paper takes a lot of time. Often your first ideas don't work out, and you'll want to change your topic and look for new sources. Start working on your paper well ahead of the due date to make sure you have all the sources you need and ample time to change your plans if necessary. Check off each step as you complete it.

When the teacher first assigns a research paper:

_____1. Start thinking about a topic that interests you, and look it up in a reference book or your textbook to get an overview of the topic. If these books have bibliographies or references to related topics, take note of the authors, titles, and topic headings and use them as aids in your research.

4–6 weeks before the paper is due:

_____2. When you have decided on a topic, continue your research in books, periodicals, and online sources. If you have trouble finding information, ask a librarian or your teacher for help. Read selectively: Use the table of contents, chapter titles and subtitles, and the index to find the information you want. Make sure that your sources represent different points of view.

_____3. As you read, think about a possible thesis that your material can support. Take careful notes from your sources, and be sure to get all the bibliographic information. Indicate quotations clearly so that you don't plagiarize inadvertently when you write your paper.

_____4. After reading from several sources, decide on a working thesis and make a working outline and bibliography.

2–4 weeks before the paper is due:

_____5. Continue reading, making changes to your thesis, outline, and bibliography as needed. Check that your presentation of the topic is balanced and thorough. If it is not, look for more sources.

2 weeks before the paper is due:

_____6. Using your outline as a guide, write the rough draft of the paper. Use a word processor if possible since it will make revising much easier. You still might need to make changes in your thesis, outline, and bibliography, or even go back to the library for more information.

_____7. Have someone look over your paper, checking it against the outline and making sure that you have done what your thesis says you will do. Make changes as necessary.

Last week before the paper is due:

_____8. Type the final draft of your paper. Follow your teacher's format carefully, including title page and bibliography page.

_____9. Proofread your paper carefully. Make sure that there is no plagiarism and that quotations and ideas are documented properly. Check for mistakes in grammar, spelling, punctuation, and typing; it is acceptable to make a few small neat corrections with a black pen on your typed paper.

On the due date:

_____10. Hand your paper in and look forward to a good grade!

The Yellow Pages

A Comparison of the MLA and APA Documentation Systems	
MLA	**APA**
Author, last name first	Author, last name first
Title of article, in quotation marks	Date in parentheses
Title of book or periodical, underlined or in italics	Title of article (no quotation marks)
Volume (if a scholarly journal), page numbers	Title of book or periodical, underlined or in italics
	Volume, page numbers
City of publication	City of publication
Publishing company	Publishing company
Date	
For electronic sources, add this information:	
Database	
Library and city (if part of a subscription)	
Date retrieved	"Retrieved" date
URL	"from" database or URL

Pages 263 and 264 show the bibliography page for this chapter in both MLA and APA styles. A sample research paper, adapted from a student paper, in both MLA and APA styles begins on page 266.

Works Cited (MLA)

"Benjamin Franklin." *Encyclopædia Britannica Online.* 2003. Encyclopædia Britannica. Shatford Library, Pasadena, CA. 10 Oct. 2004 <http://search.eb.com/eb/article>.

"Benjamin Franklin." *World Book.* 2003 ed.

Isaacson, Walter. *Benjamin Franklin: An American Life.* New York: Simon & Schuster, 2003.

Lemay, J. A. Leo. "Benjamin Franklin: A Documentary History." 1997. Dept. of English, University of Delaware. 10 Oct. 2004 <http://www.english.udel.edu/lemay/franklin/>.

Tolson, Jay. "The Many Faces of Benjamin Franklin." *U.S. News & World Report* 23 June 2003: 35–38.

Tolson, Jay. "The Many Faces of Benjamin Franklin." *U.S. News & World Report* 23 June 2003. ProQuest Direct. Shatford Library, Pasadena, CA. 10 Oct. 2004 <http://proquest.umi.com/pdqweb>.

References (APA)

Benjamin Franklin. (2003). In *World book* (Vol. F-7, pp. 486–492). Chicago: World Book International.

Benjamin Franklin. (2003). In *Encyclopædia Britannica.* Retrieved October 10, 2004, from Encyclopædia Britannica Online.

Isaacson, W. (2003). *Benjamin Franklin: An American life.* New York: Simon & Schuster.

Lemay, J. A. L. (1997). *Benjamin Franklin: A documentary history.* Retrieved October 10, 2004, from Dept. of English, University of Delaware Web site: http://www.english.udel.edu/lemay/franklin

Tolson, J. (2003, June 23). The many faces of Benjamin Franklin. *U.S. News & World Report, 90,* pp. 35–38.

Tolson, J. (2003, June 23). The many faces of Benjamin Franklin. *U.S. News & World Report.* Retrieved October 10, 2004, from ProQuest database.

★ Glossary ★

plagiarism—the representation of the language or ideas of another author as one's own language or ideas

cite—to provide information about a source and its availability

documentation—formal system of citations to indicate the use and location of a source

common knowledge—basic facts about a topic, such as those found in reference books

quotation—the use of an author's exact words in quotation marks and clearly credited to the author

paraphrase—a restatement of an author's ideas in different words

summary—a short version of a longer text; a restatement of the main points of the text, written in different words

research paper—a long essay that investigates a single topic using information from several sources and following a certain format

analysis—a critical examination to separate the essential parts or ideas

synthesis—the combination of separate parts or ideas into a new whole

3. SAMPLE STUDENT RESEARCH PAPER

This paper is adapted from a paper written by a student at Pasadena City College (Pasadena, CA) using MLA format. The 16-page, edited paper, reformatted in APA style, is on pages 275–283.

MLA Format
Title page

Child Labor ← Centered: title

Mei Kwan ← Student's name

ESL 33B ← Class

May 25, 2004 ← Date

(The title page may be bold and in 12- to 14-point font.)

Outline (optional)

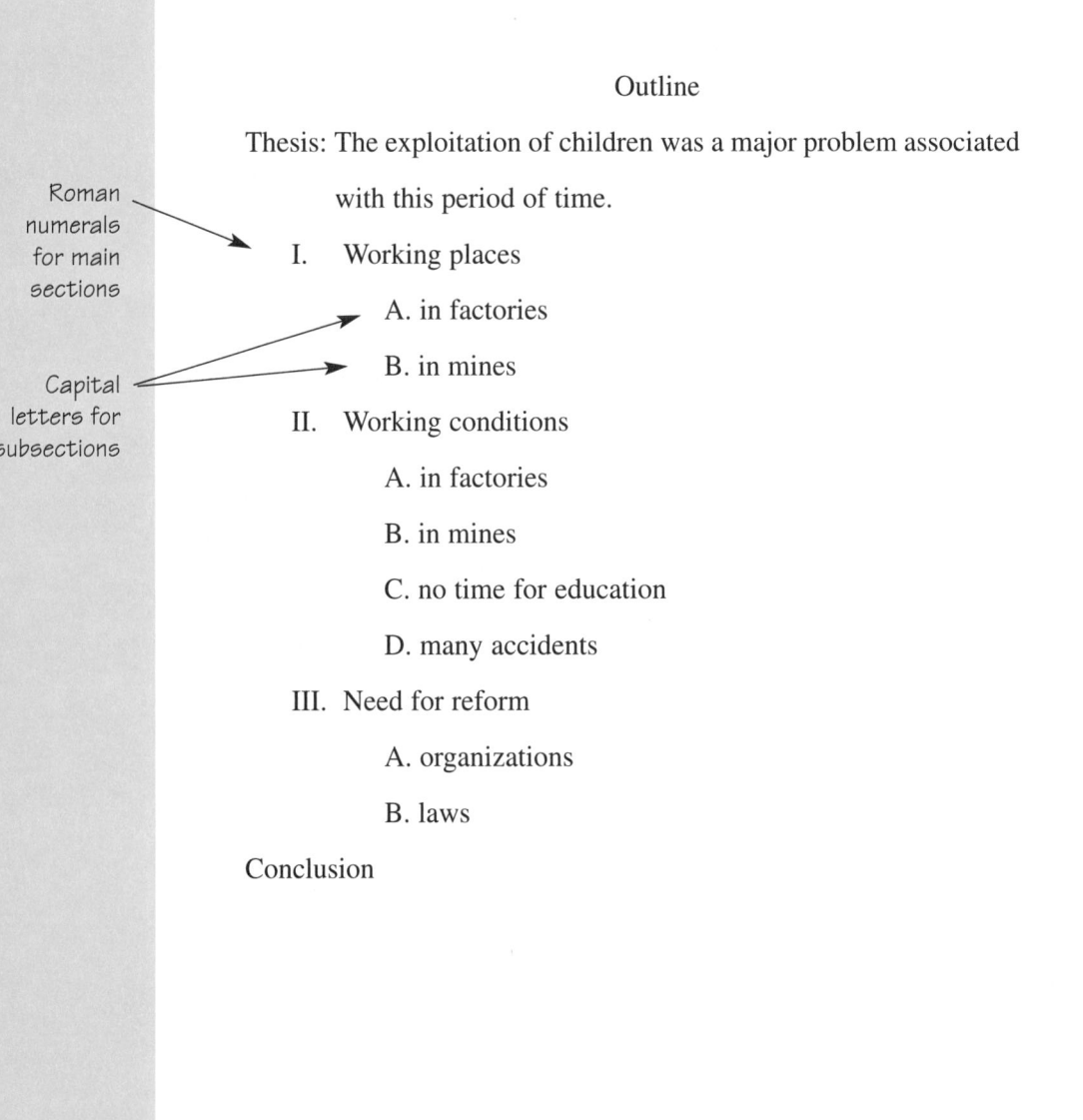

Outline

Thesis: The exploitation of children was a major problem associated with this period of time.

I. Working places

    A. in factories

    B. in mines

II. Working conditions

    A. in factories

    B. in mines

    C. no time for education

    D. many accidents

III. Need for reform

    A. organizations

    B. laws

Conclusion

Roman numerals for main sections

Capital letters for subsections

The late 1800's were exciting years for Americans. The nation's economy was on the rise and there were many good things to be bought and enjoyed. The growing cities became the centers of entertainment where people could find stores, restaurants, theaters, dance halls, and sporting events. In addition, many people had the money to enjoy these pleasures. However, this was not true for all Americans. Many people, particularly the millions of immigrants who came to the nation from all over the world at that time, had little money. Many of them were so desperate that they were forced to send their children to work at very early ages. The exploitation of children was a major problem associated with this period of time.

According to the census for 1900, there were about two million children under the age of 16 who were working. Children were hired because they were faster and more agile than adults and they worked for less money. Some people believed that work was good for children because it kept them out of trouble (Levine 18–23).

It was common at this time to find children working in the factories, the farms, the mines, or in other places. According to Cahn and Cahn, one of the places that children worked in was the textile factories. This type of factory made cloth using huge looms. Children worked as bobbin boys to watch the thread unwind from huge spools called bobbins. These spools supplied the looms with thread to make cloth. When a thread broke, the bobbin boy had to tie the broken ends together quickly. When there was no more thread on a spool, the child had to replace it with a full one. It was a dangerous job, because they needed to work barefoot to climb into the machines. When they made a careless move, they might fall to the ground or into the moving parts of the machines (Cahn and Cahn 11).

The second most common working place for children was the mines. This was a place where the miners dug out natural resources such as coal, iron ore, copper, and other minerals that lie under the ground. Coal, for example, was an important resource to produce heat and power in the 1800's. Therefore, many children were forced to work in the mines by their families. Working conditions were terribly dangerous. Children had to carry coal in packs on their backs and climb up long ladders from underground to the surface. Some others worked as breaker boys, who sat on benches and picked out pieces of slate from the coal (Sandler 24).

The factories and mines were not pleasant places to work in. The rooms where children worked in the factories were terrible. The light was dim. The air was full of tiny particles of lint. The rooms were steaming hot in the summer and freezing cold in the winter. The working places were often overcrowded and it was dangerous to work around the machines in such a condition (Sandler 62). When the children got to work late or did not work quickly enough, the supervisor would whip them (Cahn and Cahn 22). The working conditions in the mines were more awful. The children worked long hours in the damp and dark. They had a high possibility to have accidents or serious injuries due to the lack of safety equipment and protections (Sandler 21–23). These children often worked for twelve or more hours a day under dangerous conditions and received meager wages.

The children who went to work had little time for education or for play. Many of the child workers never had a chance to go to school. In 1879, only seven states had a law to require children under twelve to go to school (Levine 26). Some of the parents did not want to remove their children from work to send them to school because they were afraid that if they took a child away from work, the entire family might lose their jobs. Some of the kindhearted factory owners had their own schools in the factories and they arranged for the children to go to class during the working hours. However, these schools were not very good and often the children could attend class only once or twice a week. Moreover, sometimes boys and girls went to night school after work. It was hard for them to remain awake; they often fell asleep during the lecture (Cahn and Cahn 25–26).

As the years went on, the accident rate increased. Many children died because of accidents and explosions. The long hours of work increased the possibility of injury. Many workers became ill from breathing the dusty air every day, or from working with dangerous chemicals. The newspapers often published the accidents involving children (Cahn and Cahn 40–42).

III.
A.
In the late 1800's the public began to realize that children should grow up under healthy conditions. People began to form organizations to fight against child labor abuses. Those who opposed child labor were known as reformers. The reformers tried to improve working conditions. They wanted to abolish poverty because it was the major cause of child labor. They argued that even children who were from poor families should have the opportunity to play and go to school. A writer wrote a poem to call attention to the problem of child labor:

> The golf links lie so near the mill
>
> That almost every day
>
> The laboring children can look out
>
> And see the men at play.
>
> (Cahn and Cahn 46)

B.
One of the most famous organizations opposing child labor was the National Child Labor Committee. It began in 1904 and was led by Mrs. Florence Kelley. Their job was to study the children's working conditions. They often sent inspectors to factories and mines to see how

the working children were being treated (Cahn and Cahn 45–49). The National Child Labor Committee realized that a law was needed to oppose child labor. In 1836, Massachusetts had been the first state to pass a law to oppose child labor. This law stated that a factory owner could not hire any child under the age of 15. Other states also passed laws to oppose child labor, but the laws were weak and didn't have much enforcement. A national law was needed to oppose child labor. The first national law against child labor was finally passed by Congress in 1916, and it was signed by President Woodrow Wilson. However, two years later, the U. S. Supreme Court ruled that the law was unconstitutional. They argued that the law violated the rights of states because only states had the right to control business or trade (Cahn and Cahn 50–52).

After the failure of the first national child labor law, Congress passed a new law in 1919. It taxed the profits of any employer who broke it. However, this law was also ruled unconstitutional by the Supreme Court because Congress did not have the power to impose this tax. In 1924, the National Child Labor Committee had a new approach. They wanted to pass an amendment to the Constitution to protect children. It needed the approval of three-fourths of the states, but only 28 out of 48 states voted to approve it. The plan had failed (Cahn and Cahn 52). At last a law against child labor called the Fair Labor Standards Act passed in 1938 when Franklin D. Roosevelt was president (Levine 29). It stated that it was illegal for children who are under 16 years old to work at most jobs and children who are under 18 years old cannot work on dangerous jobs (Levine 36).

Today most American children can enjoy their childhoods and play and go to school. However, the exploitation of children is still common in agriculture in the United States because the Fair Labor Standards Act does not cover farm work. Many children of poor immigrants work on farms with their families (Cahn and Cahn 55). Child labor also remains a major problem in developing countries. According to a U. S. Department of Labor report, more than 200 million children in the world today have to work and half of them do not go to school. It is a goal of the United Nations to provide a free education for every child in the world by 2015 (U.S. Department of State 1–2). The world will be a better place if all children can grow up happy and safe.

Works Cited page: center title

Works Cited

Cahn, William, and Rhoda Cahn. *No Time for School, No Time for Play.* New York: Simon & Schuster, 1972.

Levine, Martin J. *Children for Hire: The Perils of Child Labor in the United States.* Westport: Praeger, 2003.

Sandler, Martin W. *The Way We Lived.* New York: Little, Brown, 1977.

U.S. Department of State (DOS). "Developing Countries' Struggle to Pay for Education Reported." *Washington File.* 5 Feb. 2004. SIRS Knowledge Source. Shatford Library, Pasadena, CA. 12 May 2004 <http://sks20.sirs.com/cgi-bin/hst-article-display>.

APA Format
Title page

Upper right-hand corner: start numbering with title page. Write the title and page number.

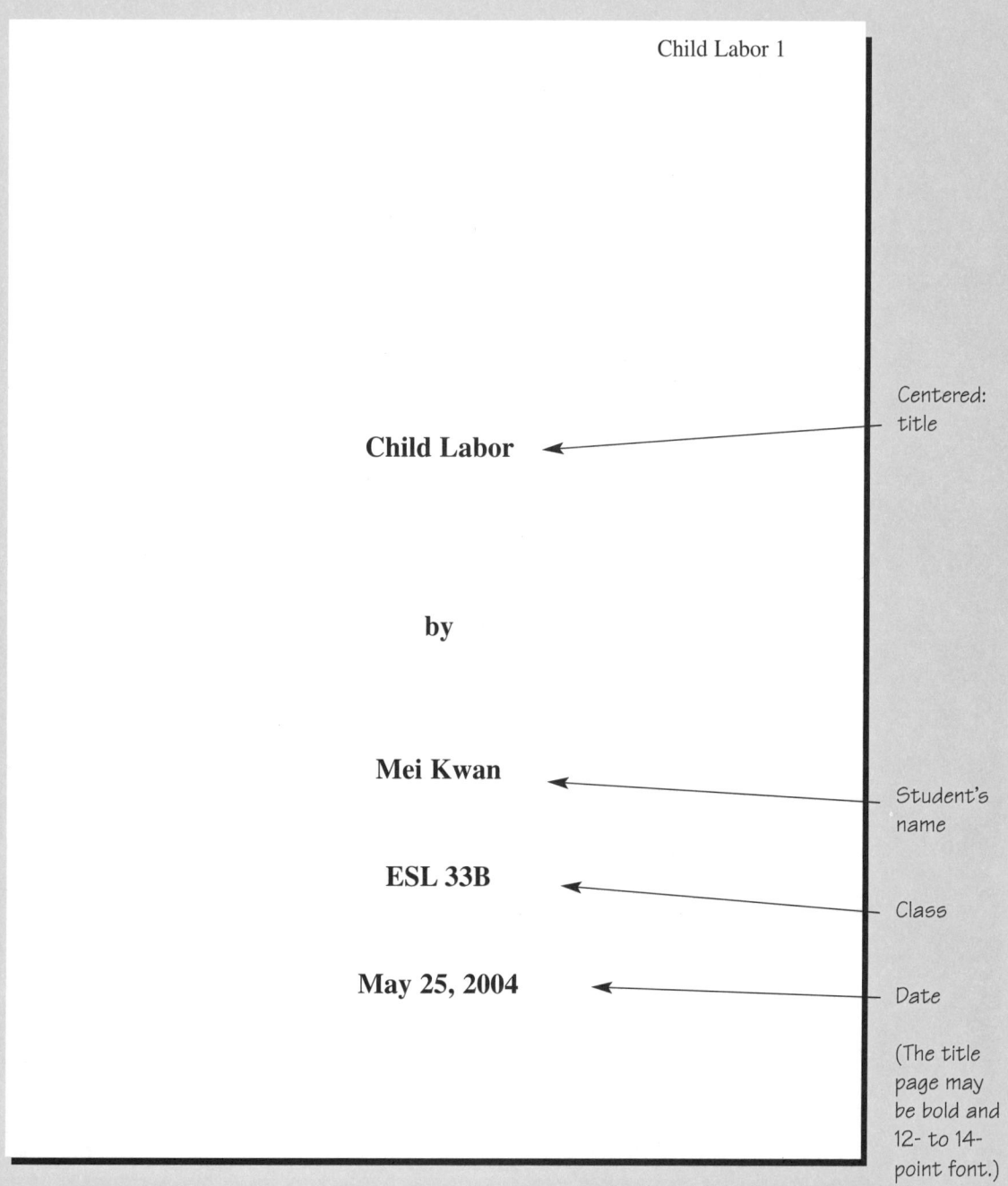

Child Labor 1

Child Labor ← Centered: title

by

Mei Kwan ← Student's name

ESL 33B ← Class

May 25, 2004 ← Date

(The title page may be bold and 12- to 14-point font.)

Outline (optional)

Roman numerals for main sections

Capital letters for subsections

Child Labor 2

Outline

Thesis: The exploitation of children was a major problem associated with this period of time.

I. Working places

A. in factories

B. in mines

II. Working conditions

A. in factories

B. in mines

C. no time for education

D. many accidents

III. Need for reform

A. organizations

B. laws

Conclusion

Child Labor 3

The late 1800's were exciting years for Americans. The nation's economy was on the rise and there were many good things to be bought and enjoyed. The growing cities became the centers of entertainment where people could find stores, restaurants, theaters, dance halls, and sporting events. In additions, many people had the money to enjoy these pleasures. However, this was not true for all Americans. Many people, particularly the millions of immigrants who came to the nation from all over the world at that time, had little money. Many of them were so desperate that they were forced to send their children to work at very early ages. The exploitation of children was a major problem associated with this period of time.

According to the census for 1900, there were about two million children under the age of 16 who were working. Children were hired because they were faster and more agile than adults and they worked for less money. Some people believed that work was good for children because it kept them out of trouble (Levine, 2003).

Working Places

It was common at this time to find children working in the factories, the farms, the mines, or in other places. According to Cahn and Cahn (1972), one of the places that children worked in was the textile factories. This type of factory made cloth using huge looms. Children worked as bobbin boys to watch the thread unwind from huge spools called bobbins. These spools supplied the looms with thread to make cloth. When a thread broke, the bobbin boy had to tie the broken ends together quickly. When there was no more thread on a spool, the child had to replace it with a full one. It was a dangerous job, because they needed to work barefoot to climb into the machines. When they made a careless move, they might fall to the ground or into the moving parts of the machines.

B. The second most common working place for children was the mines. This was a place where the miners dug out natural resources such as coal, iron ore, copper, and other minerals that lie under the ground. Coal, for example, was an important resource to produce heat and power in the 1800's. Therefore, many children were forced to work in the mines by their families. Working conditions were terribly dangerous. Children had to carry coal in packs on their backs and climb up long ladders from underground to the surface. Some others worked as breaker boys, who sat on benches and picked out pieces of slate from the coal (Sandler, 1977).

Working Conditions

II.
A. The factories and mines were not pleasant places to work in. The rooms where children worked in the factories were terrible. The light was dim. The air was full of tiny particles of lint. The rooms were steaming

hot in the summer and freezing cold in the winter. The working places were often overcrowded and it was dangerous to work around the machines in such a condition (Sandler, 1977). When the children got to work late or did not work quickly enough, the supervisor would whip them (Cahn & Cahn, 1972). The working conditions in the mines were more awful. The children worked long hours in the damp and dark. They had a high possibility to have accidents or serious injuries due to the lack of safety equipment and protections (Sandler, 1977). These children often worked for twelve or more hours a day under dangerous conditions and received meager wages.

The children who went to work had little time for education or for play. Many of the child workers never had a chance to go to school. In 1879, only seven states had a law to require children under twelve to go to school (Levine, 2003). Some of the parents did not want to remove their children from work to send them to school because they were afraid that if they took a child away from work, the entire family might lose their jobs. Some of the kindhearted factory owners had their own schools in the factories and they arranged for the children to go to class during the working hours. However, these schools were not very good and often the children could attend class only once or twice a week. Moreover, sometimes boys and girls went to night school after work. It was hard for them to remain awake; they often fell asleep during the lecture (Cahn & Cahn, 1972).

D. As the years went on, the accident rate increased. Many children died because of accidents and explosions. The long hours of work increased the possibility of injury. Many workers became ill from breathing the dusty air every day, or from working with dangerous chemicals. The newspapers often published the accidents involving children (Cahn & Cahn, 1972).

III.
A.

Need for Reform

In the late 1800's the public began to realize that children should grow up under healthy conditions. People began to form organizations to fight against child labor abuses. Those who opposed child labor were known as reformers. The reformers tried to improve working conditions. They wanted to abolish poverty because it was the major cause of child labor. They argued that even children who were from poor families should have the opportunity to play and go to school. A writer wrote a poem to call attention to the problem of child labor:

> The golf links lie so near the mill
> > That almost every day
> The laboring children can look out

And see the men at play.

(Cahn & Cahn, 1972, p. 46)

One of the most famous organizations opposing child labor was the National Child Labor Committee. It began in 1904 and was led by Mrs. Florence Kelley. Their job was to study the children's working conditions. They often sent inspectors to factories and mines to see how the working children were being treated (Cahn & Cahn, 1972). The National Child Labor Committee realized that a law was needed to oppose child labor. In 1836, Massachusetts had been the first state to pass a law to oppose child labor. This law stated that a factory owner could not hire any child under the age of 15. Other states also passed laws to oppose child labor, but the laws were weak and didn't have much enforcement. A national law was needed to oppose child labor. The first national law against child labor was finally passed by Congress in 1916, and it was signed by President Woodrow Wilson. However, two years later, the U. S. Supreme Court ruled that the law was unconstitutional. They argued that the law violated the rights of states because only states had the right to control business or trade (Cahn & Cahn, 1972).

After the failure of the first national child labor law, Congress passed a new law in 1919. It taxed the profits of any employer who broke it.

However, this law was also ruled unconstitutional by the Supreme Court because Congress did not have the power to impose this tax. In 1924, the National Child Labor Committee had a new approach. They wanted to pass an amendment to the Constitution to protect children. It needed the approval of three-fourths of the states, but only 28 out of 48 states voted to approve it. The plan had failed (Cahn & Cahn, 1972). At last a law against child labor called the Fair Labor Standards Act passed in 1938 when Franklin D. Roosevelt was president (Levine, 2003). It stated that it was illegal for children who are under 16 years old to work at most jobs and children who are under 18 years old can not work on dangerous jobs (Levine, 2003).

Today most American children can enjoy their childhoods and play and go to school. However, the exploitation of children is still common in agriculture in the United States because the Fair Labor Standards Act does not cover farm work. Many children of poor immigrants work on farms with their families (Cahn & Cahn, 1972). Child labor also remains a major problem in developing countries. According to a U. S. Department of Labor report, more than 200 million children in the world today have to work and half of them do not go to school. It is a goal of the United Nations to provide a free education for every child in the world by 2015 (U.S. Department of State, 2004). The world will be a better place if all children can grow up happy and safe.

References

Cahn, W., & Cahn, R. (1972). *No time for school, no time for play.* New York: Simon & Schuster.

Levine, M. J. (2003). *Children for hire: The perils of child labor in the United States.* Westport, CN.: Praeger.

Sandler, M. W. (1977). *The way we lived.* New York: Little, Brown.

U.S. Department of State (DOS). (2004, February 5). Developing countries' struggle to pay for education reported. *Washington File.* SIRS Knowledge Source. Retrieved May 12, 2004, from SIRS Publishing Web site: http://sks20.sirs.com/cgi-bin/hst-article-display

Answer Key

for Scanning for Specific Information

Chapter 1 REVOLUTION (pages 26–27, 15 answers)

During the early years of the American colonies, the British government allowed the colonists to make many of their own decisions in small local assemblies. Consequently, the American colonists were outraged when, in the mid-1700s, the British government began to assert more control over the colonies.

For the British, the maintenance of the North American colonies was becoming more expensive, as they had to support and protect the colonies from attacks from Native Americans and from other European countries that wanted to claim territory in North America. The French and Indian Wars in the years <u>1754–1763</u>, for example, cost Britain <u>14 million</u> pounds.

The colonies were expected to pay back these expenses by sending valuable raw materials such as <u>tobacco, furs, silk, cotton, rice, and/or indigo</u> back to England, but there were no direct taxes on the colonies until 1764, when the British parliament voted to impose a tax on molasses and sugar, called the <u>Sugar Act</u>. Another tax, called the <u>Stamp Act</u>, which passed in the year <u>1765</u>, required seals and stamps on legal documents, licenses, and newspapers. These taxes were passed by the members of Parliament in England, not by the local governments, so the colonists resolved to boycott English goods; their rallying cry was "No Taxation without Representation!" In 1773, Parliament passed the Tea Act, which enabled the British East India Company to sell tea at low prices. This act led to the Boston Tea Party, in which <u>men dressed as Native Americans</u> threw 10,000 pounds worth of tea into the water of <u>Boston Harbor</u>. In retaliation, the British government closed the harbor and began interfering with the local government. The American colonists were ready for a revolution.

In the year <u>1774</u>, representatives of 12 colonies met in the city of <u>Philadelphia</u> for the first Continental Congress and affirmed the independence of the colonies. The next year, 1775, the first shots of the Revolutionary War took place in the Massachusetts towns of <u>Lexington</u> and <u>Concord</u>, and in 1776, Thomas Paine wrote a pamphlet entitled <u>Common

ANSWER KEY

Sense calling for a complete break with Britain. During the Second Continental Congress, on the date July 4, 1776, the delegates from the colonies signed the Declaration of Independence, listing their complaints against Britain and declaring the colonies to be free and independent states, the United States of America.

Chapter 2 SLAVERY IN THE UNITED STATES (pages 64–65, 15 answers)

In the years before the Civil War, there were about 4 million slaves in the southern states. They worked on huge plantations, providing the cheap labor that was necessary to grow crops such as sugar, tobacco, rice, cotton. Living conditions for the slaves varied greatly, as Frederick Douglass described: Slaves who worked at skilled jobs, such as craftsmen, mechanics, cooks, seamstresses, were generally treated better than the field hands. However, whether slaves were treated well or cruelly, they had no control over their own lives, being unable to choose their work, their home, and sometimes even their spouse.

Actions to bring slavery to an end occurred on several different fronts in the years before the Civil War. In some cases, the slaves themselves revolted, such as the uprisings led by Denmark Vesey in the year 1822 and Nat Turner in the year 1831. The Abolitionist Movement began in the northern states at the time of the American Revolution when several states made slavery illegal and religious leaders began to speak out against slavery. In 1831, the abolitionist William Lloyd Garrison began to publish a newspaper, called the Liberator, and in 1833, he founded the American Anti-Slavery Society. Anti-slavery literature became popular, such as the book *Uncle Tom's Cabin* by the author Harriet Beecher Stowe. Northern abolitionists organized boycotts of southern goods and encouraged slaves to escape through networks of safe houses called the Underground Railroad.

On a national level, the states were at first equally divided between free and slave states, but as new states began to be formed in the West, it didn't seem possible to maintain this balance. The Missouri Compromise of 1820 and the Compromise of 1850 were attempts by Congress to maintain the balance as new states entered the union, but it soon became clear that the economies of the western states were not suited to slavery. In 1854, Congress passed the Kansas-Nebraska Act, which allowed new states to make their own decisions about slavery; in the same year, the Supreme Court wrote the Dred Scott Decision, declaring that Blacks were not citizens and that laws to limit slavery were illegal. These actions worsened already heated feelings and motivated abolitionists to form a new political party, the Republican Party, to fight slavery. The party's candidate in the presidential election of 1856 lost, but its candidate in 1860, Abraham Lincoln, won the election, leading to the secession of the southern states and to the beginning of the Civil War in 1861.

ANSWER KEY

Chapter 3 NATIVE AMERICANS (pages 99–100, 17 answers)

The Indians of the Americas came from Asia, crossing the Bering Strait between <u>Siberia and Alaska</u> over a land bridge that existed during the Ice Ages. They probably crossed in small bands, following animals they could hunt and extending farther into the American continent with each generation. No one knows the exact dates and numbers, but most migration is estimated to have taken place about <u>20,000 to 35,000</u> years ago, and in 1492, when Christopher Columbus landed in America, there may have been <u>40–75</u> million people living there. Believing that he had landed close to India, Columbus called the people Indians.

The great native civilizations of Central and South America, the Aztecs and Incas, drew the immediate attention of the European explorers because of their vast wealth in <u>gold and silver</u>. The Indians of North America, numbering <u>1–9</u> million, had little contact with Europeans until the 1700s and even 1800s, as Black Elk described. Their ways of life varied from the settled farmers of the Southwest who lived in adobe houses of several stories called <u>pueblos</u> to the small nomadic bands that lived in <u>tepees</u> and wandered the Plains in search of <u>buffalo or bison</u>. The Native Americans lived close to nature and believed that spirits lived in natural objects such as <u>animals, rocks, water, the sky, etc.</u> They did not own land but only used it for <u>their own needs/fishing, farming, hunting, gathering</u>. They did not have many material goods, but some tribes are known for their crafts; for example, the Northwest Indians are known for their <u>totem poles</u>, the Plains Indians for <u>beadwork</u>, the Desert Indians for <u>basketry</u>, the Pueblo Indians for <u>pottery</u>. The Native Americans introduced Europeans to several new crops and animals, such as <u>potatoes, corn, tomatoes, chile peppers, turkeys, rubber, tobacco</u>.

Today the Native American population of the United States is about <u>1.4</u> million. They were granted citizenship in <u>1924</u> and have the same rights that all other American citizens do. Those who live on reservations have additional rights of self-government and support themselves using the lands' natural resources, but most today live modern lives in urban areas.

Chapter 4 MANIFEST DESTINY (pages 145–146, 13 answers)

As the United States acquired lands beyond the Mississippi River, there was a shared belief among Americans that the country would eventually reach the Pacific Coast. A New York journalist, <u>John L. O'Sullivan</u>, gave this belief the name Manifest Destiny when he wrote in a magazine article in the year <u>1845</u> that Americans had the right to spread their democratic ideals and prosperous way of life westward across the continent.

The West, thought at first to be a wasteland of deserts and grasslands, was soon discovered to have a variety of rich natural resources. The first resource to be exploited was the furs of animals such as <u>otters and beavers</u>. Then, in the year <u>1849</u>, gold was discovered in

California, and a decade later, the Comstock Lode of silver was discovered in the state of Nevada. After the rush for these precious minerals, families began to settle in the rich agricultural lands of Texas, Oregon, and California, traveling together across the plains in covered wagons/wagon trains.

The lands of the West belonged to the government and were distributed to settlers at low prices. In the late 1700s, the government surveyed the land and passed the Northwest Ordinances of 1785 and 1787, allowing the purchase of sections of land of the size 640 acres or one square mile for about $640 a section. In the year 1862, Congress passed the Homestead Act, providing 160 acres of land free to any settler who lived on the land for five years and made certain improvements. The resources of the West could also be used for free by ranchers, miners, and loggers. Many poor people, including immigrants, found opportunities to become successful through hard work and luck. Still, the lives of the settlers were not easy, as Alderson describes.

Although historian Frederick Jackson Turner declared in 1893 that the frontier days were over, the West lives on today in the American ideals of self-reliance and egalitarianism that were characteristic of these pioneers.

Chapter 5 GREAT CAPITALISTS OR ROBBER BARONS?
(pages 181–183, 14 answers)

In the early 1900s, the GNP (Gross National Product) of the United States surpassed that of any other country, and Americans became the wealthiest people in the world. The nation had rich natural resources that contributed to this wealth, but equally important were the businessmen who invented or developed new technology and organized and managed growing industries.

Examples include Thomas Edison, the inventor of the telephone, motion picture camera, phonograph, incandescent light bulb. The Edison Company was the first to install a central system to generate and deliver electricity to a neighborhood in New York City. Gustavus Swift used assembly line techniques and refrigerated railroad cars to produce inexpensive meat products. Andrew Carnegie made cheap, high-quality steel using new technology such as the Bessemer and open-hearth processes and investing in sources of raw materials like iron ore, coal, oil.

J. P. Morgan, an investment banker and financier, reorganized industries by merging small competing companies into larger companies that could operate more efficiently. He began with railroads and later merged the Edison Company with other electric companies to form General Electric and the Carnegie Steel Company with other steel companies to form United States Steel Corporation, the world's largest corporation at the time.

These giant corporations, called trusts or monopolies, were run by small groups of men: The president of one company would sit on the board of directors of several other companies so that these men could work together to control prices and competition. This concentration of wealth and power in just a few individuals frequently led to corrupt business practices, but the government, following a capitalist policy called *laissez-faire*, which means <u>hands off, free,</u> did nothing to limit the power of the trusts.

With no <u>income, corporate</u> taxes, these powerful men became extremely wealthy while their workers lived in poverty. This inequality was justified by the theory of Charles Darwin, who wrote in his 1859 book, <u>The Origin of the Species</u>, that competition leads to the survival of the fittest; his biological principle was applied to human society to explain that the more intelligent and aggressive men should be more successful than the weaker. But some people were appalled by the cruel cutthroat methods of the capitalists and their lack of sympathy for the workers, hence the other common name for the Great Capitalists—the Robber Barons.

In the late 1800s, the government began to take action to control business practices and maintain competition. In the year <u>1887</u>, Congress established the first federal regulatory agency, the Interstate Commerce Commission, with powers to regulate <u>interstate railroads</u>. In the year <u>1890</u>, the Sherman Antitrust Act was passed, making it illegal for businesses to <u>work together to control rates and prices</u>. Since then, much legislation has been enacted in the United States to control the relationships between workers, business owners, and consumers.

Chapter 6 MUCKRAKERS, TRADE UNIONISTS, AND SOCIALISTS
(pages 212–214, 14 answers)

The rapid change in the late 1800s from a society of small farmers and tradesmen to an urban industrialized society brought a variety of problems to American and immigrant workers trying to achieve the dream of individual economic opportunity. Living and working conditions in the big cities were deplorable, and the government was either too unresponsive or too corrupt to deal with the problems. Several groups of people recognized the problems and tried to find solutions.

Like Jane Addams, the muckrakers were educated, middle-class reformers working as <u>writers, journalists, editors</u> to bring public attention to the problems of exploitation and corruption. In 1904, Ida Tarbell completed a history of <u>the Standard Oil Company</u>, exposing its abusive business practices. Upton Sinclair wrote about corruption in the <u>meat-packing</u> industry in his 1906 novel *The Jungle*, leading to passage of the nation's first meat inspection bill.

Trade unionists gathered workers together to fight for improved working conditions such as a <u>six</u>-day work week of <u>10–11</u>-hour days. They demanded cleaner worksites to prevent chronic illnesses such as <u>lung disease, cancer, tuberculosis</u> and safer machinery to prevent injuries and deaths. The confrontations between labor and management tended to be violent: The late 1800s saw two of the nation's most violent labor strikes, one in the year <u>1892</u> at the Carnegie Steel Company plant in the city of <u>Homestead, Pennsylvania</u>, and the second in the year <u>1894</u> at the Pullman Palace Car Company in Chicago, a company that later bought the Woodruff Sleeping-Car Company that Carnegie had invested in.

The third approach to solving the economic and political problems called for a revolutionary change in government. Following the theories of Karl Marx as described in his books <u>The Communist Manifesto</u> written in 1848 and <u>Das Kapital</u> written in 1867, socialists and communists predicted that workers would unite and seize ownership of the means of production such as <u>railroads, factories, farms</u>; the working class would own and manage all means of production and profits would be shared equally. Eugene V. Debs, both a socialist and a union leader in the <u>Pullman</u> Strike, ran for president five times between 1900 and 1920.

Trade unionists and socialists sometimes worked together and at other times in competition to organize the workers to improve their lives. Their efforts, along with those of the muckrakers like Jane Addams, led to the extensive legislation that Americans have today for the protection of workers and consumers.

ANSWER KEY FOR YELLOW PAGES

Exercises (page 219)
1. When Benjamin Franklin was just a boy, he read the kinds of books that he could learn from. ~~He had only a little money, but he spent it all on books.~~ He learned history from Burton's Historical Collections and Plutarch's *Lives*, and he learned to write well from poetry and the essays in the *Spectator*. His father's books about polemic divinity taught him to be argumentative. ~~When he borrowed books, he was always careful to return them promptly.~~ The essays by Daniel Defoe and Dr. Mather also had a big influence on his later life.

2. Answers will vary.

Exercise (page 222)
Four parts, in this order: great practical genius, commitment to public service, considerable PR skills, his international fame

Outline
Thesis: Largely because of his great practical genius, his commitment to public service, his considerable PR skills, and his international fame, he [Franklin] was the essential figure in the founding enterprise [of the United States of America].

ANSWER KEY

I. great practical genius
II. commitment to public service
III. considerable PR skills
IV. his international fame

Exercises (page 223)
1. The categories: history and religion
   The books: History: *R. Burton's historical collections*, Plutarch's *Lives*
              Religion: *books about polemic divinity, books of dispute about religion*
2. The categories: independent (spirit) and democratic spirit
   a. democratic
   b. independent
   c. independent
   d. not relevant (or contradictory to the thesis)
   e. independent
   f. democratic
   g. democratic
   h. independent
   i. not relevant (or contradictory to the thesis)
   j. independent

Exercise (page 224)
a. not a complete sentence
b. a fact
c. a fact
d. a question
e. no information about this topic
f. a personal feeling
g. no information about this topic
h. refers to the writer and the essay directly

Review Exercise (page 226)
Answers will vary.

Exercise (page 239)
first site: a reliable site (.edu, Franklin Institute Science Museum)
second site: a commercial site (.com)
third site: a reliable site (.org, PBS = Public Broadcasting System)
fourth site: a reliable site (.edu, Lemay, udel = University of Delaware)
fifth site: a commercial site (.com, Amazon = company that sells books)

Exercise: Using a Quotation (page 250)
Answers will vary.

Exercise: Writing a Paraphrase (page 252)
Answers will vary.

Exercise: Writing a One-Page Formal Summary (page 255)
Answers will vary.

ADDITIONAL WRITING ASSIGNMENTS: CONNECTIONS

The Autobiographical Reading Passages in this textbook share a variety of themes that students may want to explore in discussion and writing. Students can select a theme and consider how it is developed or exemplified in one or more passages. Some possible themes include the following:

- the writer's portrayal of himself/herself
- any qualities that the writers share
- any opposing qualities between the writers
- the qualities of two or more writers as a hero or heroine
- the writer's relationship to his or her society
- the writer's "message" for the reader
- overcoming hardships
- support from family and/or friends
- travel to new places
- adapting to new circumstances
- the writer's relationship to the American Dream
- the writer's contribution to American life
- the importance of reading and/or writing
- other ideas? _____
  _____
  _____